Violent
Ignorance

Author biography

Hannah Jones writes, researches and teaches about racism, migration control, belonging and public sociology at the University of Warwick, where she is Associate Professor of Sociology. Hannah is the author of *Negotiating Cohesion, Inequality and Change: Uncomfortable Positions in Local Government* (2013), which won the British Sociological Association Philip Abrams Prize for best first and sole-authored monograph in UK sociology, and co-author of *Go Home?: The Politics of Immigration Controversies* (2017). On Twitter she is @uncomfy.

Violent
Ignorance
Confronting Racism
and Migration Control

Hannah Jones

ZED

LONDON • NEW YORK • OXFORD • NEW DELHI • SYDNEY

Zed Books
Bloomsbury Publishing Plc
50 Bedford Square, London, WC1B 3DP, UK
1385 Broadway, New York, NY 10018, USA
29 Earlsfort Terrace, Dublin 2, Ireland

BLOOMSBURY and Zed Books are trademarks of Bloomsbury Publishing Plc

First published in Great Britain 2021

This edition published in 2021
Reprinted 2021

ISBN: HB: 978-1-7869-9862-0
        PB: 978-1-7869-9863-7
      ePDF: 978-1-7869-9861-3
     eBook: 978-1-7869-9859-0

Typeset by Integra Software Services Pvt Ltd.

To find out more about our authors and books visit www.bloomsbury.com and
sign up for our newsletters.

Contents

Figure vi

Acknowledgements vii

Preface ix

1 More in common 1

2 Puncturing violent ignorance 33

3 Normal violence 61

4 Enduring crisis 83

5 Haunting families 109

6 Bystanders 139

7 Manifesto 165

Notes 185

Bibliography 219

Index 240

Figure

2.1 Alan Kurdi. Photograph by Nilüfer Demir, © AP Archive. 48

Acknowledgements

For reading and commenting on sections of the book in progress, thank you Claire Blencowe, Thom Davies, Katy Harsant, Emily Henderson, Judith Kahn, Alice Mah, Elsa Oommen, Michael Riley Jones and Khursheed Wadia – but especially Emily, for such detailed, nuanced and generous engagement with the drafts and for being a staunch cheerleader and advocate for the book (and for finishing it!) throughout. Thanks for the insightful comments of the anonymous peer reviewers, who helped to clarify and tighten the arguments of the book. Thank you Les Back for your belief in and enthusiasm about this project and Tom Dark for encouragement at the early stages.

For conversations over the last few years that, whether you know it or not, wound their way more or less directly into shaping what is in this book, thank you Safrina Ahmed, Cleo Forstater, Davinia Gregory, Corrin Harding, Yasemin Karsli, Rachel Lewis, Linda Nagy, Tana Nolethu Forrest and Eiri Ohtani.

For the supportive discipline of writing retreats for getting actual words on the actual page, thank you, Rowena Murray, and the other retreaters at Bowfield, Chapelgarth and Gartmore. For believing in and commissioning this book, and for your patience, thank you, Kim Walker and Melanie Scagliarini at Zed (and then Bloomsbury).

For excellent colleagueship and camaraderie supporting all the other aspects of academic life being juggled at the same time as trying to think up and squeeze out a book, thank you Darani Anand, Faye Brown, Špela Drnovšek Zorko Saba Hussain, Virinder Kalra, Cath Lambert, Goldie Osuri, Maria do Mar Pereira, Lynne Pettinger, Janet Smith, John Solomos, Sivamohan Valluvan, Khursheed Wadia and many others.

For your patience, and for the joy of working with you on other projects that sometimes took a back seat while working on the book, or which germinated my thinking towards the book, thank you Yasmin Gunaratnam, Ala Sirriyeh, Carly Hegenbarth, Helena Holgersson, Vanessa Hughes, Katie Klaassen, Meleisa Ono-George, Ida Persson, Gargi Bhattacharyya, Will Davies, Sukhwant Dhaliwal, Kirsten Forkert, Emma Jackson and Roiyah Saltus – and also, sorry, I will get on with that other bit of writing I promised now.

For unwavering insistence I take a break and look up from the serious side of life sometimes, thank you Jennifer Sheddan, Cath Lambert, Lisa Metherell, Anne Malcolm, Tara Mulqueen, Mairead Enright, Lucy Hubbard, Naaz Rashid, and Alex, TJ, Henry, Rebecca, Kuba and Iris.

For everything – good humour (mostly), support (of all kinds), encouragement, love and inspiration, thank you Judith Kahn, Rick Jones, Carla Jones and Bob Follen, Gwen Riley Jones and Michael Riley Jones, Hrishikesh Jones, and last but by no means least, Riley Riley-Jones.

And for all of the love, ideas, nourishment, laughs, mutual weeping, dancing, debating, proofreading, care and joy, and for being my partner in everything, and always, thank you Simone Helleren.

Preface

Who is responsible? Is it excusable? Was it inevitable?
Is there some state of affairs which we have accepted up to now that
ought to be challenged?

– SUSAN SONTAG, *REGARDING THE PAIN OF OTHERS*[1]

This book sets out a phenomenon I have named 'violent ignorance': what it looks like, how it works, its consequences and possible ways to resist it. Put simply, violent ignorance is a name for the action of turning away from painful knowledge and for the further violence this can bring. The choice to 'ignore' is not always a conscious or deliberate one, but it still matters. By ignoring violence, we become implicated in that violence continuing; often, the reason we find it painful to think about this violence is that we may realize we are implicated, even if in a roundabout way.

Throughout this book I often use the term 'we'. This is not to suggest that 'we are all in it together', in the sense governments use it, to imply there is no difference between the suffering of the powerful and that of the powerless. No – I mean to recognize that I am writing from a space inside the contradictions of violent ignorance and to follow cultural critic Susan Sontag's observation that when viewing violence against 'others', there is a need for a reflection on how our privileges are located on the same map as their suffering, and may – in ways we might prefer not to imagine – be linked to their suffering, as the wealth of some may imply the destitution of others.[2]

Most of the examples of violent ignorance in the book are concerned with the construction of national and transnational histories, belonging, racism and migration control. Sometimes people express surprise that migration control and racism should be discussed together. In many of the examples of violent ignorance I discuss, it becomes clear how they are linked because they operate in similar ways. Controlling who has access to a territory and the right to safety and dignity in a territory is a process of deciding who matters, based usually on where they were born, to whom they are related, or what material resources they have – or a combination of these. Racism comes in many forms, but it certainly includes enforcing differential access to dignity, safety and resources based on where a person comes from, to whom they are related and on what resources they can call. The failure to see the connections between racism, nationhood and border control – even when these connections have been explicitly inscribed in law in many cases – is itself a form of violent ignorance.

This book was written between 2018 and 2020, a period many have described as part of a 'post-truth' era,[3] one I would describe as a political crisis of violent ignorance. This violent ignorance has been refracted through resurgences of bordering, nationalism, racism and citizenship discrimination, both globally and, acutely, where I live in Britain.[4] This is not just a question of Brexit, but of longer histories of everyday restrictions on health, wealth and dignity for those deemed unworthy by received wisdom. This unfolding crisis must be read through histories of empire while still recognizing reconfigured and changing hierarchies of power and belonging. The concept of violent ignorance is a provocation to recognize those longer histories within the early twenty-first-century crisis by thinking in terms of ignorance and its violent effects. Furthermore, history itself is a process of forgetting as well as remembering.[5] What is remembered is a choice (passive or active), and forgetting some aspects of history can make it harder to see the reasons for continued injustice (or new forms of injustice) and hampers attempts to address those injustices.

The first draft of this manuscript was finished on 1 January 2020. On 11 March 2020, Covid-19 was declared a global pandemic by the World Health Organization, after the disease was first detected in December 2019 in Wuhan province, China, and spread rapidly across continents. In the continuing chaos as I write this preface in late April 2020, many parts of the world are experiencing increased death rates and massive pressure on health services and strains as a result of the global measures intended to prevent the spread of the virus. Schools have been closed, whole populations have been confined to their homes, food supplies have been disrupted and elections have been called off.

Writing this preface at the end of April 2020, it is not possible to know what the long-term effects will be of these massive changes to ways of life across much of the world. What is clear, however, is that the pandemic and response to it have intensified existing inequalities while shaking up some seeming certainties. The crisis has brought attention to injustices that were previously ignored, while reviving other instances of violent ignorance.

The pandemic has illustrated quite clearly how interdependent human society is, across borders and across class. It has made clear how vital healthcare is for human survival and how unevenly distributed access to healthcare is – both across the world and within territories. While in Britain concern was expressed about the health service's access to only 4,000 ventilators for treating the virus at the beginning of the pandemic and the need for many times that number, it was reported that ten African countries had no ventilators at all, weeks into its global spread. People in many parts of the world do not even have easy access to handwashing facilities, the key public health measure advised for slowing the spread of the virus.[6] In countries where people have been told to work from home unless their work is essential, the situation has highlighted that essential workers – home carers, delivery drivers, food producers, shop workers – are often some of the lowest paid, and lowest status, people in society. It has clarified that home is not always a safe place to be, as increases in domestic violence reports surge. And it has made more visible the stark differences in resources between those who can survive lockdown by arranging for delivery of food, entertainment and luxuries, and those whose ability to access any income or basic necessities is on a knife-edge.

None of these situations should be viewed as a revelation; they are not new discoveries that come with the novel coronavirus. Covid-19 has ripped a hole in the veil of violent ignorance that had helped most of the world to function as if these facts could be lived with as 'business as usual'. As I write, it remains to be seen whether this period will lead to a reimagining of the world or a resurgence of violent ignorance as the norm.[7]

Emerging reports about the UK government's preparedness for the global pandemic suggested that ministers were distracted from pandemic preparations by the politics of Brexit as late as February, even when the likely extent of the disease, deaths and related disruptions worldwide was becoming evident.[8] A government which had been apparently single-minded about closing borders and focusing inwards within an 'independent' and self-sufficient set of islands was apparently unable to recognize that not only do diseases not respect territorial borders, but the interconnectedness of all aspects of life in the early twenty-first century is an empirical fact, rather than an ideological choice to be accepted or rejected. Ignoring the nature of the social world, like ignoring the advice from medical advisers and other governments, does not make problems go away. It can, though, make them more acute and more deadly.

1

More in common

Breaking point

It is a warm June day. I'm hurrying, late as usual. I've a train to catch to London, an evening event to attend for work, the day disappeared quickly. I hustle through the underpass from the bus stop to the train station, barely acknowledging the figure hunched in a sleeping bag asking 'spareanychangeplease' as I shrug apologetically and navigate other passers-by passing by, while checking emails and what platform the train will leave from, on my phone. A text message pings onto the screen from a friend: 'Just heard abt the mp. Bleugh.'

When I search back through my text messages now, thinking about writing this, I see that I replied within a minute. But when I got her text, I had no idea what had happened. What MP? 'Just heard about the MP,' followed by an indication of resigned disgust, could mean anything, a week before the referendum on Britain's membership of the European Union. Someone had said or done something offensive, stupid? I opened a news browser. A pro-Remain MP had been murdered.

My response, within a minute? 'oh shit'.

I kept going and got on the train. The rest of the journey, I read more. The sign that morning, released by Nigel Farage MEP for the Leave campaign: 'BREAKING POINT', emblazoned across an image of a snaking line of men, apparently on their way into Europe. A promise to 'take back control', and the image only circulating widely because of the breathlessly outraged coverage of it in the press, Farage's grinning face, adoring the outrage, posed in front of the picture of hopeless, rejected people. Two polar opposite folk devils – the destitute migrants and the rabble-rousing Farage – the latter knowingly revelling in his notoriety and the ways it will help his message reverberate.

The details of the murder as they drip in – the words from that poster – seem too apt. A very bad joke. This, this is the breaking point. Not inevitable, but not unexpected. The point when the weight of things makes them crack.

An MP has been shot. Stabbed. Dead. Her attacker shouted, '[P]ut Britain first.' If this isn't a crisis, what is? What happens when politics becomes polarized like this? What happens next after democratic representatives are murdered?

At that moment, I don't want to know. Or rather, I don't want to start thinking it through because it feels like madness and fear. I keep working on the book we're writing that starts from another billboard on the side of an advertising van, when the home secretary – who then became prime minister – asked people, 'In the UK illegally? GO HOME OR FACE ARREST.'[2] 'Go home,' the echo of 1970s playground taunts we had thought confined to the past, but now splashed across government signage. I have said this last thing countless times now, each time feeling that stating this is redundant, but then, it must need restating, or else how could this have come to pass?

That Go Home van, from 2013, also worked like Farage's Breaking Point provocation, using media and social media outrage to circulate way beyond the audience that would have seen it had the van simply gone about its business on its designated route. In 2013, it seemed the language itself produced the outrage that pushed the image into every newspaper and hundreds of social media posts, which makes it resound three, four, five years later, every time an immigration scandal hits the government. Farage's face was not pictured grinning in front of the 'GO HOME' sign, but he and fear of his party were widely credited as the motivation for it. It signalled the beginning of the UK government's overt 'hostile environment' for migrants which would seep into every aspect of life, as this book details.

As I begin to write this book, it is two years on from that day. I keep going back to think about the murder of Jo Cox. I keep wondering how it can be that the slaughter of an MP which seemed like such a significant turning point that it might wake people up to how divided political discourse had become, how unthinkable the situation was, seems to have simply faded away. I have fixated on the ways she has been memorialized, picked over the pieces of her life as they are laid out in her widower's writing and campaigns for her remembrance, and the ways her friends and family have tried to preserve her 'message' in national campaigns for togetherness, like a 'Great Get Together' of a national picnic, and in supporting more women to become politicians. I have understood the urge to remember Cox for her life and not for the way she died. But I can't shake the feeling that as a society, we should be taking more time over understanding and facing up to the manner in which she died, how it could happen, and what it says about the world we are living in right now. Why haven't we?[3]

That question is part of what drives this book. The need to understand not just what happened to Jo Cox, and to a country when a political representative was assassinated for stark politically motivated reasons, but also to understand the widespread turning away from thinking about, let alone trying to come to terms with, such an event.

In the pages that follow, I set out to ask why we turn away from such difficult moments, what it would mean to confront them, and how we could go on if we did face up to knowledge about such painful and complicated events. This is an attempt to recognize how hard it is to live with the pain of discomfort and worry, but also a suggestion that by ignoring or turning a blind eye to painful questions, we do not avoid their consequences. Instead, we live with the difficulty in everyday, multiple, and sometimes equally painful ways.

In the rest of this chapter, I consider further the death of Jo Cox, which felt like a 'breaking point', and why it turned out not to be a breaking point at all, and how we might use the perspective of violent ignorance to consider what can happen when seeking comfort from disturbing events is prioritized over dealing with their origins. The reaction to Cox's death was deeply felt – but the feelings that were amplified were about an attack on a 'defenceless' wife and mother, rather than an attack on a democratically elected representative. The grief for the loss of Cox in her personal and domestic role channelled attention away from seeing this as an attack precisely on her (and others') moves *outside* of the domestic, an attack on a woman holding political power, and using that power to defend refugees and transnational links.

This refusal to see Cox as a politician in the context of her death turned her murder into a meaningless and sad event, rather than a too-meaningful part of a struggle over political questions of race, nation and gender. To understand why that happened, I think we have to consider what was ignored and why. We ignore things all the time, in order to function – for example, in the opening to this chapter, I describe manoeuvring around people who are living in destitution, without much thought, an everyday experience for many people. Indeed, there is an academic field that studies what we don't know and what we refuse to know – it's called 'ignorance studies' or sometimes 'agnotology'. What do (or don't) they think about in ignorance studies?

Ignorance, thoughtlessness, responsibility

The 'ignorance' in 'ignorance studies' is not about stupidity. Though it sounds like a paradox, ignorance can be knowing; it can mean the deliberate 'ignoring' of knowledge that could easily be acquired.[4] Ignorance can also mean the 'thoughtlessness' referred to in the epigraph to this chapter. Thoughtlessness might seem like the opposite of a deliberate act, but it is an act of omission to refuse to think. Very often, this is an act encouraged by structural and political powers. It is also a way to avoid unpleasant feelings of discomfort, guilt, fear or shame.

The epigraph for this chapter is taken from the analysis of the trial of a senior Nazi, Adolf Eichmann, by German Jewish social theorist Hannah Arendt.[5] This is the work in which Arendt coined the now famous phrase, 'the banality of evil', to show that considering Eichmann an out-of-the-ordinary monster missed the point. He was an ordinary – banal – man who made ordinary – banal – choices, within the extraordinary situation of Nazi Germany. To consider him an exception allows the rest of us to exempt ourselves, to imagine 'I would never act like that'. What Arendt demonstrated was that to understand, and hopefully to avoid, similar atrocities, one has to recognize that the evil seen to be embodied in Eichmann is something which stems from everyday and ordinary practices. To reject Eichmann as outside the norm, as non-human, is an easy way to reject a proper analysis of why the Holocaust happened and how it could happen.

Arendt's analysis of the Eichmann trial turns on questions of responsibility, but also on questions of 'thinking'. She uses the term 'thinking' to describe the ability to reflect – to have an ongoing 'dialogue between me and myself'.[6] Someone in this kind of dialogue would realize they have to literally live with themselves. In Arendt's view, most people given the choice would avoid living with a murderer or an instigator of terrible crimes. Most of the time, the decision about what is a terrible crime comes from society – if you are caught committing a crime, you will be punished by society's institutions. However, in the situation of Nazi Germany, society's institutions insisted that citizens enact atrocities. Therefore, those *without* the ability to 'think' – to reflect on an internal ethics – would, simply by obeying the law, become Nazis. Without a conscience – 'thinking' – they did not resist the requirements of the regime. As Eichmann claimed, many believed they were behaving morally by following the law of the land in sending millions of people to death camps. This is important when considering the various criticisms of how Arendt wrote of Eichmann.[7] Many centred on whether Eichmann should be considered a monster. Arendt's argument was not that Eichmann should be forgiven – she made it clear that she wished him to be hanged for his crimes – but that he was not an exceptional person.

This is where 'thoughtlessness' comes in. Arendt suggested it was not necessarily a conscious intention to commit evil that motivated Eichmann – indeed, in his testimony he expressed his horror at seeing some of the crimes he had ordered being carried out in Poland, where he saw naked Jews told to enter mobile gas vans where they were killed, followed by the most horrible sight I had thus far seen in my life … the corpses were thrown out, as though they were still alive … They were hurled into the ditch, and I can still see a civilian extracting the teeth with tooth pliers.[8]

As he makes these visits, he remarks to a local SS Commander:

Well, it is horrible what is being done around here … young people are being made into sadists. How can one do that? Simply bang away at women and children? That is impossible. Our people will go mad or become insane, our own people.[9]

Eichmann expresses this horror without recognizing his responsibility, as the head of the Nazi 'Department for Jewish Affairs'. The reason he can do so is, according to Arendt, his 'thoughtlessness', his lack of capacity for 'thinking'. Arendt makes clear she does not mean 'thinking' as something that requires particular intellectual capabilities or education (i.e. she is not saying 'stupid/uneducated people don't think and are irresponsible'). For Arendt, Eichmann simply did not have a conscience, an ability to reflect on what he had done.

However, I would suggest there can be an element of choosing not to 'think' in this manner. He knew these were his orders. He refused to contemplate the consequences. We can see this by stepping away from this extreme example, to more banal cases of the shock of being confronted with the violent consequences of one's own actions. Look, for instance, at Conservative MP, Heidi Allen, wiping away tears and unable to speak in Parliament on hearing of the destitution and desperation of fellow MP Frank Field's constituents living without food or hope.[10] Allen had voted consistently to reduce financial support for people in need, including for housing costs, and for disabled people.[11] That did not stop her heartfelt demonstration of empathy for Field's constituents – despite the fact that reflection on how their situation might have arisen could have led to an understanding that it was directly linked to her own (and others') political decisions.

The philosopher Charles W Mills writes of 'white ignorance' and how throughout the history of Western philosophy there has been a persistent emphasis on (wealthy) white men as the norm, particularly in conceptions of justice.[12] He gives the example of how classical philosophies of fundamental rights, such as those put forward by seventeenth-century thinker John Locke and eighteenth-century philosopher Immanuel Kant, have been used in political philosophy in a way that only applies to people designated as white, and not to others, creating 'a universe divided between persons and racial subpersons, *Untermenschen*, who may variously be black, red, brown, yellow – slaves, aborigines, colonial populations – but who are collectively appropriately known as "subject races"'.[13] In this, those in power not only reject the rights of 'others' to fundamental rights, but reject *knowledge* of what life is like on the other side of this 'universe'. To know the effects of white supremacy – colonial domination, occupation, extermination, exploitation and slavery – would be to question the very basis of the 'good life' lived by those benefitting from it. Ignorance here is powerful and important because to know and to 'think' on these terms would be a painful and potentially revolutionary experience.

Relatedly, feminist scholar Gloria Wekker describes 'White Innocence' as a position in which a national culture (in her case, writing in the context of the Netherlands) imagines itself as small, kind and in need of protection, while erasing memories of being an aggressor in historical forms of oppression; 'innocence, not knowing, being one of the few viable stances that presents itself when the loss of empire is not worked through, but simply forgotten'.[14] Like Mills's use of 'ignorance', Wekker does not intend her term to be a get-out clause for those who practise it. Rather, in the context of the Netherlands, a former colonial power but which now sees itself as a bastion of inclusion and equality, being forced to confront the knowledge of former and – especially – ongoing domination and oppression is painful because it cuts to the heart of a national belief in being a 'good' nation in terms of valuing equality. Rather than being outraged and angry when confronted with the reality of institutional racism in which they are implicated, Wekker argues, people and institutions in the Netherlands are more likely to be hurt and upset. 'Innocence' here has an additional power, because it sucks up confrontation and turns it on its head; the person who challenges the status quo becomes the problem, not because they disagree with the way society should be structured, but because they are suggesting that the people or structures they accuse don't care.[15] A sense of wounded innocence can be a powerful tool in resisting attempts to uncover historical and ongoing structural violence. I expect it will emerge in some responses to what I have to say in this book.

Early sociologist WEB Du Bois famously wrote of 'the veil' that marked 'the color line' which starkly divided the lives and experiences of black and white people in early twentieth-century United States, even while those lives were intimately entwined.[16] The metaphor of the Veil allowed Du Bois to point to the obscured way in which both black and white Americans saw their world, with some knowledge hidden – but in plain sight. The Veil obscures the humanity of the oppressed and hides the inhumanity of oppression, and in doing so it enables the separation of oppressor and oppressed, even when they live side by side. For Du Bois, it is in becoming aware of the Veil that people are able to identify what is on the other side of it, and hence the social forces at work in racial segregation, rather than seeing this as natural. He describes this realization in the harrowing story of John Jones, who, on leaving his segregated hometown in Georgia for an education in the Northern States, grew slowly to feel almost for the first time the Veil that lay between him and the white world; he first noticed now the oppression that had not seemed oppression before, differences that erstwhile seemed natural, restraints and slights that in his boyhood days had gone unnoticed or been greeted with a laugh.[17]

We might think of this recognition of the Veil as a recognition of the process of violent ignorance. Some of the power of ignorance is challenged when we acknowledge it exists. But confronting it also brings pain – as we see when John's sister Jennie asks him:

> 'does it make every one – unhappy when they study and learn lots of things?'
>
> He paused and smiled. 'I am afraid it does,' he said.
>
> 'And, John, are you glad you studied?'
>
> 'Yes,' came the answer, slowly but positively.[18]

Considering Du Bois's work in the context of violent ignorance is important because it reminds us that this crisis and its apparent contradictions – which are actually its foundations – are not new.

Ignorance studies and agnotology have tended to focus on fields other than race and racism. For example, sociologists Linsey McGoey and Matthias Gross have brought together an impressive collection of studies into how ignoring (or not knowing) matters, in fields spanning economic theory, risk management, literature and philosophy, journalism, neurology, criminology, environmental science and more.[19] In the United States, historian Robert Proctor has examined how the tobacco industry supported, withdrew from and influenced different forms of scientific research into cancer; in doing so, possible knowledge about the connections between cancer and tobacco use remains unexplored.[20] The emphasis of these and associated researchers has been on how science – in particular the 'hard' sciences which are more often seen at face value as accurate and 'objective' – is shaped by decisions about what to study and *what not to study*. This has been described as 'undone science'; decisions might seem nefariously made (what pharmaceutical firms are prepared to fund to make profit), or could be relatively arbitrary (no one was interested in the life cycle of that particular snail species in that particular lab), or might seem arbitrary but have direct socially destructive consequences (no one in the lab in the UK is interested in studying and finding a cure for a disease which predominantly affects South Asian women).[21] They could also be made as an ethical choice – to refuse to pursue scientific endeavour that could be used to produce weapons, for example. In any case, choices are made which are not solely driven by an all-encompassing drive for knowledge, and some areas for exploration remain unknown. Haitian historian Michel-Rolph Trouillot demonstrated a similar pattern in his landmark work *Silencing the Past*, in which he showed how certain areas of 'what happened' are systematically forgotten – or rather, might never be considered worthy of record in the first place.[22]

Social scientists and philosophers are fond of talking about 'epistemology', that is, theories of knowledge. Put more simply, 'epistemology' means reflections on how we know what we know and what counts as knowledge. Charles W Mills and others have argued for an 'epistemology of ignorance', which means the need to consider systematically what we do not know, or refuse to know, and why and how this happens.[23] Though I say 'we', this experience is not the same for everyone, and often what a person knows, does not know, or refuses to know, is linked to their position within society. Linked to his concept of the Veil, W E B Du Bois wrote of how African Americans experienced a 'double consciousness' because they both knew themselves as persons with all their individual facets and also knew how the majority of white people saw them with 'contempt', as 'a problem'.[24] This 'double consciousness', argued Du Bois, might be seen as a bind – and indeed, its cause was segregation, racism, slavery and its legacies – but the ability to 'know' from both within and without the self was also a resource. As Du Bois and others have shown, knowing that things are more complicated than one single version of 'the truth' is important to being able to imagine a different – perhaps more socially just – world.[25] Often such multiple 'knowledges' are more accessible to people who are excluded from the mainstream, because they have no choice but to engage with mainstream understandings, while also being aware that these understandings do not completely fit their everyday reality. On the other hand, people who have the most power and influence – for example, in the UK, white, wealthy, enabled, cisgender, heterosexual men – are often more able to make sense of the world using the forms of understanding that are 'common sense'. Not only do they have no need, often, to think about questions of racism or poverty, but by avoiding those questions, they also avoid confronting their own relative comfort and safety in society. As Hannah Arendt argued, no one wants to have to live reflecting on how their own actions put others into danger or hardship; by avoiding thinking about those challenging subjects, and avoiding political conflict or personal discomfort, it is much easier to live with oneself.

This raises the question then – why engage with what is or seems unbearable? And how to do that? A question to answer first, though, is who is asking these questions, and of whom?

Surviving: The focus on the present

For many, perhaps the majority of people, unbearable violence is borne every day. That this is a paradox is central to the idea of violent ignorance. The pain of the world is created, and unevenly spread, through unequal social relations and structures of power. That this seems inevitable means the only way to live is to survive this. People find ways to live with trauma, exclusion, deprivation and other forms of violence. One strategy for surviving in this context is a form of ignorance, which I will call (for now) the focus on the present. To continue to function in everyday ways can take away the ability, energy, resources, to struggle against the causes of violence against the person. But it does not always do so. This is not the same as a lack of class consciousness, the idea that people are waiting to discover that their difficulties are caused by the capitalist system, so that once this has been revealed the course of action is clear. It is rather a means of survival in the immediate moment. Many people are aware that their private troubles are the result of public issues but are unable to spend their energy contemplating or acting on this constantly because the pressure of everyday survival intervenes.

Of course, many people who are subject to acute and chronic violence such as poverty, racism and disability mount political struggles in large and small ways against the causes of their oppression and the everyday instances of it. Others in these extremes will have no interest in the cause of their troubles or will attribute the cause of their troubles to spurious but easily visible causes – such as undeserving competitors taking the resources they would otherwise have. But most often, people shift between these positions at different points in their life or their day. The structural violence against a person may be ever-present, and they may be ever-cognizant of it, but at the moment when they need to negotiate a welfare assessment in their local bureaucracy, focusing on proximate obstacles may be the most effective strategy to access necessary resources to meet immediate need.

But my criticism of violent ignorance in this book is not intended to address, in the first instance, those most cruelly served by current structural injustices of racial capitalism. Those who live in pain do know, by and large, that they live in pain and what they do to manage that is up to them. Those who live in the margins which are hidden (in plain sight) are well aware of the injustice they experience, whatever their political formulation about this. What I want to take aim at is the apparent 'bystander' who is in fact directly implicated in the multiple violences upon which the structures of our society depend. This does, of course, include myself. The kernel of this project is trying to work out the ethical stance to take from a position of privilege in a social system in which every attempt to challenge injustice can itself be re-incorporated as a reassertion of privilege and self-worth. At the same time, this project has a (perhaps misplaced) ethics of hope at its heart – a desire to (necessarily) fail again, but fail better.[26]

So the principal subject being asked to confront their violent ignorance and what it conceals is the person cast as a bystander or spectator to the underlying violence of our societies. Confronting this underlying violence is horrific, uncomfortable and threatening for someone so positioned. Why would anyone want to do this if they can avoid it? To do so in a proactive and ongoing, constant way requires a formidable political and ethical commitment to justice, which few people can muster all of the time. But sometimes confronting this violence is unavoidable. Is there something in those moments when such violence becomes impossible to ignore that might serve as a guide to what it takes to reveal violent ignorance and what might be achieved by unmasking it and confronting what it shields? That is the ultimate aim of this discussion, but to get there it is necessary to recognize how persistent, adaptive, tempting, resilient violent ignorance can be. These punctures to the shields of ignorance can quickly be patched over, leaving a mark but not a hole to see through, and still retaining the safety of not seeing. Can we learn from this too about the techniques of power entrenched in violent ignorance?

Memorialization of Jo Cox

Jo Cox MP was brutally murdered in the street by a man who targeted her as one of 'those white people whom he condemned in his writings as "the collaborators": the liberals, the left and the media', a campaigner to Remain in the EU, a supporter of Syrian refugees, and a woman.[27] The heartfelt response by those close to her was of course to mourn her as the person they lost, as wife, mother, friend, sister, daughter and colleague. The public response also memorialized her this way. The message from Cox's first speech in Parliament, that 'we have more in common than that which divides us,' referred to her ethnically and religiously diverse constituency of Batley and Spen in Yorkshire. After her death, this phrase became a rallying cry, summoning her work on the Remain campaign and Syrian refugee support, and a general feeling of togetherness. 'Love Like Jo' appeared on placards at rallies in her memory, after her husband Brendan told a memorial rally the week after her death:

> Jo was killed by hatred and if that happened to anyone else, Jo would not have been silent. She would've called it for what it was. I encourage you all to love the world like Jo did.[28]

But the hatred that killed her has not been addressed in the national reactions to her assassination. Instead, the call 'More in Common' became central to how she is remembered, in public tributes, the title of the biography written by her husband, and the name of one of the organizations dedicated to work in her memory. How we remember forms history; what we choose to remember (and what we choose to forget) informs political action. In this case, focusing on an ideal of having 'more in common' meant looking away from the political motivations of the murderer that resulted in this horrible death. It meant domesticating this brutality and violence, making it tame and manageable, so that rather than part of a pattern of political violence, it became a question of a family's loss; and rather than the murderer being a political actor who grew out of an environment where misogyny and white supremacy could thrive, he became treated as an aberration and exception.

I want to be clear – I am not suggesting that it was inappropriate for Jo Cox's family and friends to establish charities in her memory, working on the issues she was passionate about in life, such as bringing people of different backgrounds together. Nor am I questioning her loved ones' right to remember her as they do, as a warm, caring mother, sister, daughter and wife. What I do think is important to question is whether this should have been the sum of the national political response to the murder of a Member of Parliament by a far-right activist.[29]

Jo Cox's husband, Brendan, in his grief, demanded that Cox's death be recognized as a political assassination in which the murderer wished to 'silence her voice', as a voice that stood for inclusion (and remaining in the EU). Though it was clearly stated by both her husband and by the judge at her murderer's trial that Cox was murdered for her political beliefs and her murderer's hatred of how she used her democratic mandate, an engagement with that political conflict is almost absent from the response to her death. Even after the judge stated in his comments to the murderer that

> [t]here is no doubt that this murder was done for the purpose of advancing a political, racial and ideological cause, namely that

of violent white supremacism and exclusive nationalism most associated with Nazism and its modern forms[30]

and that

because she was a Member of Parliament, the reason you murdered her, your crime has an additional dimension which calls for particularly severe punishment[31]

the newspapers reporting the trial emphasized the judge's comments on the murderer's 'cowardice' and lack of patriotism, and Cox's love and family, without addressing this fundamental element of the crisis of her death directly. Several newspapers ran photographs of Cox in her wedding dress on the day of the trial verdict, emphasizing her role as wife and mother, over and above the national significance of the attack on a Member of Parliament. Perhaps this is because it is easier to mourn an apparently meaningless attack on an innocent woman than to confront the existence of such extreme hatred for what she was seen to represent.

The newspaper front pages both the day after her assassination and the day after her killer's sentencing, almost unanimously characterized Cox as a wife and mother first and foremost. For example, *The Sun* front page read:

MURDERED IN COLD BLOOD
Husband's moving tribute as MP shot 3 times and knifed 7 times by crazed loner
MY JO
The husband of MP Jo Cox wrote a poignant tribute to his wife less than an hour after she was murdered by a crazed loner yesterday. Heartbroken Brendan Cox also tweeted a photo of her by the River Thames, where the couple lived on a boat with their two young children. Jo, 41, was shot

three times and stabbed seven times in her West Yorks constituency yesterday afternoon.[32]

This was accompanied by images of Jo by their boat ('Home ... photo tweeted by husband Brendan showing Jo by Thames') and of the couple at their wedding ('HUSBAND Brendan & Jo on wedding day') and a photo of the murderer ('"KILLER" Loner Thomas Mair'). And in *The Daily Mail*:

> Devoted mother of two. Dedicated public servant. MP Jo Cox was a remarkable woman. Yesterday she was brutally murdered by a loner with a history of mental illness.
>
> WHAT A TRAGIC WASTE
>
> The husband of an MP allegedly murdered by a troubled loner last night called on Britain to unite and 'fight against the hatred that killed her' ... The rising Labour star and dedicated MP died from catastrophic injuries ... Witnesses saw the gunman shout 'put Britain first' as he kicked, stabbed and then shot the slightly-built 5ft mother-of-two.[33]

These front pages of the two highest circulation UK newspapers focused on Cox's relationship to her husband and children as the most pressing aspect of her murder, not her democratic role. Though the *Daily Mail* calls her a 'rising Labour star', *The Sun* does not even acknowledge which party Cox represented; the focus for both is the brutality of the attack, by a 'crazed' or 'troubled' 'loner', and on the consequences for Brendan Cox (and their children). The description of Cox's physique in the *Daily Mail* ('the slightly-built 5ft mother-of-two') is in line with Brendan's victim statement to the court regarding the murderer:

> [H]is only way of finding meaning was to attack a defenceless woman.[34]

Jo Cox, in these presentations, is a victim of random violence, rather than a political target. The focus on her family's grief as the key site of violence continued throughout reporting and memorialization of this political assassination.[35] What became of Brendan Cox's, and Justice Wilkie's, invocations of political assassination? Can a response of having 'more in common' ever be enough to address the crisis of a political assassination?

It is hard to find fault with the idea of having 'more in common', and this is no doubt one reason why it travelled so widely as a message of connection and, in the context of far-right violence, defiance. Amplifying the sentiment of 'more in common' in the immediate aftermath of Cox's assassination and in the days just before the referendum on the UK's membership of the EU was a way of turning grief and anger into hope. The demand that Cox be remembered and her words heard around the world seemed, at the time, an attempt to intervene in a political way to counter and engage with the politics of hate that had enabled this attack.

However, very little has been done either in the media or in public political statements or civic action to grapple with the implications of this anti-democratic murder by a far-right enthusiast. While the family expressed an understandable and legitimate concern for Cox to be remembered for the good things in her life, rather than for the way she was murdered, there is space for that to be respected in public arenas while also considering the wider implications of a political assassination of a national elected representative.

Activities that have emerged to maintain Jo Cox's legacy – the Great Get Together,[36] the Jo Cox Loneliness Commission,[37] the Jo Cox Women in Leadership Programme[38] and more – are all excellent ways to turn grieving into positive change and to remember someone loved by many. However, they need to be supplemented by a response that actively confronts the rage that led that man to murder her – not as an isolated incident of violence against a woman, but as part of a pattern of misogynistic and white supremacist attacks within society and in politics which challenge our ideas of a functioning democracy. Though this was an attack on a white woman, it was an attack by a white supremacist who saw her as a 'collaborator' and anti-racist and who had a particular hatred of women and researched 'matricide' in the days before the attack.[39] The way in which the political nature of this assassination has been minimized is itself particularly gendered, invoking pity and sadness at the death of a 'defenceless woman', over and above outrage at the death of a political representative.

When I talk of a pattern of this abuse and violence, I am thinking of a constellation of contemporary events which have targeted political women, particularly women of colour, Jewish and Muslim people, and anti-racist and feminist supporters, such as the following:

- The campaign of misogynist anti-Semitic abuse against Labour MP Luciana Berger on social media and in her private life, including 2,500 messages a day at some points from organized neo-Nazis, which led to a conviction in December 2016.[40]

- The increase in verbal and physical attacks on MPs documented after the 2017 election, with evidence that women and racially minoritized candidates face the worst abuse; 45 per cent of all 25,688 abusive tweets to female MPs during the 2017 UK election campaign were personally directed at Diane Abbott MP, the Shadow Home Secretary and the UK's first black woman MP.[41]

- The plot by members of banned white supremacist group National Action to assassinate Labour MP Rosie Cooper, for which one man pleaded guilty to preparing an act of terrorism by buying a machete for the purpose of the planned murder.[42]

- The planned attempt in June 2017 to assassinate Labour leader Jeremy Corbyn and Labour London Mayor Sadiq Khan by a man who instead drove his van into worshippers at Finsbury Park mosque and was later convicted of murder and attempted murder.[43]

- The attempt in January 2018 by a far-right group, the White Pendragons, to make a 'citizen's arrest' of Labour London Mayor, Sadiq Khan, for 'subverting our English constitution', apparently on the basis of his (Muslim) religion, as he made a speech on gender equality to the Fabian Society.[44] They also 'brought a homemade gallows with them to London'.[45]

What does it mean to consider Cox's assassination within this pattern of violence against elected officials who challenge – even in the mildest way – patriarchy and white supremacy, both in their political actions and their physical presence as elected officials? Might this increase the urgency of the need to ask what is at the root of this far-right political violence? And what does it mean that it has not been widely considered this way? Could it be that by turning away from directly knowing and addressing the causes of this murder and its implications for public life, we are simply storing up further violent consequences for the future? Could looking more closely at the connections between far-right political violence and longer histories of white supremacy embedded in our society raise too many uncomfortable questions? Might doing so provoke a crisis by questioning how 'inclusive' contemporary society is and pointing to some of the contradictions of the current political moment?

More in common than picnics

A year on from Cox's death, and her family and friends had established foundations in her name and her husband had published a biography of her. The most prominent intervention was the establishment of a

'Great Get Together', a national event in which people were called on to host picnics and street parties to share food with their neighbours on Cox's birthday, in her memory and in the spirit of having 'more in common than that which divides us'. Who can disagree with this sentiment?

In a video produced to promote the Great Get Together, and featuring many high-profile celebrities, this spirit of all-encompassing, cosy and unchallenging togetherness was emphasized. Oscar-winning actor Helen Mirren begins the video by asking 'So what does unite us as a country?' and is answered by a succession of musicians, sports players, actors and TV presenters (and one or two members of the public), most of whom emphasize quite uncontroversial things – mainly food:

> Ed Sheeran:[46] Fish and chips. Yeah.
>
> Andy Murray:[47] Everyone loves a bit of 007 don't they?
>
> Nadiya Hussain:[48] Cake. Correct me if I'm wrong!
>
> Andy Murray: Sean Connery's the best one for sure.
>
> Jamie Carragher:[49] Sport is what unites our great country.
>
> Stephen Fry:[50] Tea and biscuits.
>
> Minnie Driver:[51] Tea and hot cross buns.
>
> Bill Nighy:[52] Toast … Unless it's spread with Marmite.[53]

Amid the banal patriotism and acceptance that nationalism (expressed through love of elderly actors and jovial disagreement about sandwich spreads) is a common sense accepted by all – and has something to do with combatting hatred – the closest we get to dissent is actor Martin Sheen's claim that 'a sense of outrage at any injustice' is 'what unites us as a nation'. There is no hint of outrage from anyone about the assassination or any other injustice. How could a picnic continue with that discussion going on?

Of course, the More in Common response and others like it[54] are in part attempts to direct attention away from 'difference' in the sense it is often imagined – as a problematic difference *from* a norm of white (Anglican Christian) Britishness. The problem which 'more in common' is trying to dispel is that 'normal' Brits think that 'others' are too different from 'us' to assimilate. Then, sharing tea, cake and Marmite on toast is a way of showing that 'we' are all the same, all have to eat, and all enjoy sharing food, and once we get to know each other, these similarities are more important than different cooking styles, religions or employment rights.

But the difference that matters is actually a political difference. It is a difference in beliefs about ways of living together and who is entitled to live peacefully together in one place. Liking the same kinds of food, or all caring about looking after children, doesn't matter if it becomes overshadowed by a difference over who has the right to belong or to exist. It is not the people who are feared or hated as not fitting in or not having a right to exist that are the problem. It is rather the people who would go to any lengths to keep others out and the people who refuse to see this as a problem.

Put like this, surely it is clear that the message of having 'more in common' won't deal with the 'extremists'. But the term 'extremist' is another way of separating off a section of society as monsters so that the rest of us don't have to look at ourselves in the mirror – just as in Hannah Arendt's assessment of the problem of the Eichmann trial, discussed earlier.[55]

And what does having 'more in common than that which divides us' really mean? It is a focus on values, rather than on some of the real, material divisions in society. How does it sound when applied to the aftermath of the Grenfell Tower fire in London in 2017, for example, when 600 people lost their homes and seventy-two people died due to neglected and perhaps criminal standards in social housing – in one of the wealthiest neighbourhoods in the world? Many Grenfell survivors were left in temporary housing for months, some sleeping in cars and parks, while around them millionaire neighbours sent 'thoughts and prayers' and sometimes even water, milk, sanitary towels and money.[56] But did this really mark a unity to be celebrated, when those donating were celebrated, and able to return home (average house price in the area at the time of the fire: £1.4 million), while 1,399 millionaire-owned 'investment properties' which could have been homes sat empty and those made homeless stayed homeless?[57]

Two years on from Jo Cox's murder, and a year on from the anniversary of the appalling Grenfell Tower block fire, a Grenfell Great Get Together was held in North Kensington by local charity Nova New Opportunities. The pink gingham of the usual Great Get Together branding was turned green, the colour used to mark solidarity and mourning associated with the Grenfell tragedy. Nova tweeted that the event would show '[c]ommunity unity and solidarity … a human library, tech tea party & random acts of kindness.'[58] Are 'random acts of kindness' enough to take on the forces of deep inequality and indifference and/or malice that allow tragedies such as the Grenfell fire or the murder of Jo Cox? Or does the 'randomness' of this kindness really conceal a refusal to confront the inequality and political differences which need to be addressed?

The ignorance of the centre ground

I want to consider how and why the institutional response to Cox's assassination unfolded as it did. To begin with, it should be contextualized in the existing networks of charitable, lobbying and public policy organizations in the UK and internationally. This is a world in which both Jo Cox and her husband Brendan Cox were firmly embedded. Jo Cox had worked for Oxfam in a number of senior roles, been an adviser to MPs and MEPs, advised campaigner Sarah Brown (wife of former Prime Minister Gordon Brown) on pregnancy health campaigns and acted as an adviser to an anti-slavery charity. Brendan had worked for the UN, Save the Children, Oxfam and Crisis Action, and was a special adviser to Gordon Brown when he was prime minister. They were both firmly part of the world that sociologist Linsey McGoey describes as 'TED Heads' – a world of self-styled 'social entrepreneurs' and philanthropic billionaires who reinforce one another's beliefs in capitalism-friendly, technical fixes for problems of social injustice.[59] Indeed, the More in Common non-profit organization was established jointly by Brendan Cox and Tim Dixon, who is also a founder of Purpose, an international project for 'building movements that harness technology to engage large numbers of people and help make progress on major global problems', and both of them have been speakers and are members of the Skoll Foundation, one of the 'philanthrocapitalist' organizations McGoey pinpoints as part of the TED Head network, whose conferences on world poverty cost at least $1,300 (plus tax) to attend and are invitation-only.[60] If nothing else, these connections made it possible to organize the national rally on what would have been Jo Cox's forty-second birthday, the week after she was murdered and the day before the EU referendum, and to set up the high-profile organizations in her name, including More in Common,[61] the Jo Cox Foundation[62] and the Great Get Together.

It is worth noting that while More in Common's title did match a phrase in Cox's maiden speech in Parliament, the organization and its programme already existed some time before her tragic death; Dixon and Brendan Cox list the work on this project as beginning in 2015.[63] This isn't anything sinister; the phrase was clearly circulating among the circles in which the Coxes worked and the use of it in her speech and in the framing of an organization to which they had links makes sense. The boosting of the organization's profile and reach following her death can similarly be seen as using an existing vehicle to channel grief and anger into positive change. What this does go to show is that the Coxes were already working with key influencers to shape policy debate and that the shock of Jo's murder did not change their messaging, which avoids examining underlying, and more politically contentious, issues about inequality and power, to focus on reform and togetherness.

Indeed, the ideas circulating in think tank and policy circles around an emphasis on 'more in common than that which divides us' are linked to more comprehensive political philosophies and strategies, aimed at creating a grouping which appears to self-identify as the 'moderate middle'. In 2017, the first stirrings of public announcements about the possibility of a new UK political party of 'the centre ground' emerged, identifying this as a response to Brexit (with the party being a home for Remain MPs of both major parties dismayed with their respective leaderships' endorsement of the referendum result) and to Jeremy Corbyn's leadership of the Labour Party, seen by some MPs as too left wing to win votes.[64] This movement drew encouragement from the success of similarly styled 'centrist' parties and party leaders in France and Canada. One such initiative which aligned itself directly with Cox's legacy is 'More United', a crowdfunding campaign aimed at supporting MPs from any party who sign up to centrist 'more in common' values.[65] A short-lived attempt at such a centrist party materialized as 'Change UK – The Independent Group for Change', between February 2019 (when eleven MPs defected from Labour and the Conservatives) and December 2019 (when it failed to elect any representatives, having lost six MPs including its leader within three months of being established), suggesting such a project may not have the widespread popularity its architects anticipated.

What these projects have in common is an emphasis on moderation, or reformist politics, based on statements that a more just world can be built without fundamentally changing current political and economic systems. To some extent a legacy of New Labour years, there is a resonance with the idea from the early days of Tony Blair's premiership, borrowed from sociologist Anthony Giddens, of 'the Third Way'.[66] The Third Way was the idea that left/right class-based and state-led politics were no longer relevant and that reformist political parties should instead aim for consensus, value-driven centrism, rather than directly addressing power imbalances. In effect this was a statement that economic and social power now lay firmly with global, mobile capital, but still reasserting an intention to address inequality where possible. Both the basis of this philosophy and the execution of it have been widely criticized by social scientists, identifying how practices which may be useful in profit-based businesses do not meet the needs of public services, how introducing market ethics reduces standards and efficiency in many public services, and how the use of private capital in public services can effectively trade short-term access to funds for long-term public debt.[67] A broader critique of political 'centrism' that tries to find a compromise between right- and left-wing values has also been made by cultural theorist Stuart Hall: 'a project to transform and modernise society in a radical direction, which does not disturb any existing interests and has no enemies, is not a serious political enterprise'.[68]

These detailed and widespread criticisms of the Third Way project demonstrate that while it was pitched as a moderate, 'triangulating' project with which no one – left or right – would have reason to disagree, it produced an apparent centre ground which temporarily silenced critics from both left and right. From the British left, because of a belief in the value of a Labour government after eighteen years of Conservative government reduction in public services; from the right because many business and media lobbies remained highly influential even in this nominally 'left-leaning' administration.[69]

A source of particular power for the New Labour project was its belief in its own 'common sense', and this is a belief that appears to have persisted among those in Westminster circles who began their careers at the election of Tony Blair's first government in 1997. These are the forty-somethings who are now lobbying furiously for the 'centre ground' to regain control, pointing to policies which twenty-five years ago might have been considered uncontroversial – such as publicly owned railways, free university education, or caution about nuclear weaponry – as fanciful and/or far-left. Any form of 'common sense' which depicts itself as protected from challenge has had to exclude some perspectives, or sets of knowledge, from having value. The Great Get Together and More in Common are both ideas that seem like common sense, impossible to disagree with. So what uncomfortable questions are they ignoring in producing this common sense?

Confronting violent ignorance

In this chapter I have set out an argument that interventions like More in Common and the Great Get Together which appeal to togetherness and community are valuable ways to deal with grief and mourning of a much-loved person but that they do not address the crisis of a political assassination of a democratically elected representative. My position is that this violent anger cannot be addressed simply through appeals to having 'more in common', but that a political and contentious argument needs to be made. This is a direct contradiction of a dominant political movement of which 'more in common' forms part, of imagining a 'centre ground' of politics with which only 'extremists' could disagree. Do not mistake this argument; Jo Cox's murderer and others like him are in my view certainly extreme, and wrong, in their anger and actions. But in order to address their existence we also need to look at how their ideas and anger are made possible, and that means addressing the ways they have been incubated in wider society and in British and world history. We need to look at how the possibility of their existence is deeply embedded in our everyday lives.

This is not a pleasant thing to do. It is uncomfortable; it identifies situations from which most people will feel compelled to look away. This, I suggest, is one of the reasons for the public mourning of Jo Cox as a wife and mother and a dedicated fighter for social justice, but not as a politician and representative of democracy. The murder of a young woman can be seen as horrible, tragic, random and meaningless, whereas when put into a wider pattern of attacks it would take on a different meaning with implications for how society is structured. In a different situation, we can see such placing of seemingly isolated attacks into context by the work of the charities Women's Aid and nia to demonstrate the widespread and endemic nature of what they call femicide – the murder of women by men.[70] Cox's murder is part of that pattern, but it is also part of a wider assault on women, people of colour, Muslim and Jewish people, and their anti-racist and feminist supporters in public life. This is happening as the presence of these groups in public life and in power increases. We need to ask what is happening here and why. My suggestion is this happens through a process of ignorance, where people have turned away from confronting the risky and challenging questions raised by a fuller interrogation of the causes and consequences of this assassination. This ignorance is an ignorance of the causes and occurrence of violence, but it is also a violent ignorance because ignoring more troubling knowledge means that the wider threat continues to fester and white supremacist misogynist violence continues.

This book sets out to ask difficult questions. It does so by drawing attention to other moments of crisis and shifts in public attention which – sometimes only momentarily – have produced a focus on the fundamental contradictions and inequities in the distribution of power and comfort in contemporary society. In Chapter 2, this is considered through the reaction to the terrible Grenfell Tower fire of 2017, which has already been touched on. This incident which drew the attention and grief of a nation, the lead-up to it in which residents' warnings and fears were ignored, and the aftermath in which the lasting response is still uncertain, is an important lens for understanding what happens when uncomfortable realities are revealed and how they are addressed (or not). I suggest that there are parallels too with the (short-lived) eruption of feeling in response to the 'refugee crisis' at Europe's borders in 2015, which was seemingly triggered by a photo of toddler Alan Kurdi's body washed up on a Turkish beach. As with the response to Cox's death, many who were not touched directly by these tragedies felt real grief and trouble, which could have been transformed into political action to address the root causes of these events. To what extent were these feelings harnessed, and to what extent were they assuaged with more comforting actions of togetherness which papered over the cracks that these incidents had revealed?

Where Chapter 2 engages with moments of jarring desperation that are, at least momentarily, impossible to ignore, Chapter 3 considers how scenes of equal violence can become treated as unexceptional: ignored by moving them out of sight, or seen so close up that their meaning is impossible to take in, or treated as abstract concepts, too massive or too technical to engage with. Largely focusing again on the global border crisis and some of its longer histories, this chapter asks what might make the violence of borders harder to ignore. Drawing in particular on two art installations, *Barca Nostra* by Christopher Büchel and *10,148,451* by Tania Bruguera, I suggest that it is in connecting with *meaning* through *feeling*, rather than simply thought and argument, that a visceral connection with others' pain, and the impetus to reject violent ignorance, might be achieved.

Chapter 4 looks at the treatment of knowledge about the development of current national and global structures of power and structures of feeling. This means thinking about the process through which Europe, and especially Britain, colonized much of the world and, in doing so, created hierarchies of wealth, power and race, and how the current crisis is part of a much longer trajectory. Violent ignorance is not new – in fact it is historical – and this chapter shows how: both that violence and deliberate ignorance of it are not new, but also how history itself is often a process of violent forgetting. Drawing on specific instances including the destruction and concealment of files which detailed the torture and systematic mistreatment of Kenyans by British colonial forces, and the disregard of documentation for the Windrush Generation of post-war Caribbean arrivals in Britain, this chapter shows how important resistance to dominant ignorance is to the power struggles of today.

History – and deliberate forgetting and ignorance – also has a habit of coming back to haunt the present. Chapter 5 takes this to a more personal level, asking how violence is remembered or ignored in familial histories. Between the desire of Hollywood stars to ignore and erase slave-holding forefathers and the grappling of descendants of Nazi leaders with their legacy, I also explore some of the ways that present history has reignited meanings of my own ancestry. While many seek meaning in family history, others wish to disown and ignore particularly shameful elements – but if such connections *are* meaningful, how can they be reckoned with, without refusing more difficult knowledge and risking reigniting the violence of the past? By engaging with complex stories of how global history is personal, I start to tease out some ways that choosing an alternative to violent ignorance might be possible and bearable.

Chapter 6 continues this exploration of the relationship between responsibility and violent ignorance. What is the responsibility of those trapped in systems of violence, where they may be at once victim, perpetrator and bystander, to challenge the systems that use ignorance to dehumanize others? Looking at instances of resistance by immigration detention centre officers in present-day Britain, and teachers and civil servants in Nazi-era Germany, suggests that critical, adaptable, imaginative thinking is essential to resistance to oppression and to violent ignorance. This might mean avoiding an easy – or heroic – option and instead working within the mundane, at the edges, with ambiguity. Blame can also be a form of violent ignorance, where blaming others simplifies and obscures the complex ethical and power-laden dilemmas that are often at stake in situations of structural violence.

After this journey through the sites of discomfort and attempts to confront them, Chapter 7 finally attempts to set out clearly an alternative to the consensus middle ground of cosy picnics to deal with the crises of our current political moment. It asks instead that we look carefully, directly and with compassion at uncomfortable situations of injustice, disagreement and unequal power, and even at questions that seem unanswerable. Drawing on the lessons learned from previous chapters, the book concludes with a manifesto for personal, institutional and governmental ways of taking on the challenges posed by this discomfiting, volatile, politics of violent ignorance.

2

Puncturing violent ignorance

Sometimes it takes an image to wake up a nation
From its secret shame.

–BEN OKRI, *GRENFELL TOWER, JUNE 2017*[1]

[T]hat which one only sees / In nightmares[2]

In the early hours of 14 June 2017, a fuse blew in a domestic fridge-freezer in central London, and seventy-two people died. Hundreds of homes became uninhabitable, burnt out or poisoned by smoke and chemical pollution. Countless people were traumatized. Of course the real cause of this disaster was not a faulty kitchen appliance, but an organized lack of care for the lives of the people who lived in Grenfell Tower where the fire spread. This lack of care has lasted lifetimes. It has been called 'institutional indifference'.[3] It has been – wilfully – ignored. But as the sun rose on 14 June 2017 on Grenfell Tower's smoking horror, it seemed it could be ignored no longer. As poet Ben Okri wrote: 'When you saw the tower it no longer felt like an abstract disaster on television or in the newspapers. It felt like a tragedy in the family. It became in some mysterious way personal.'[4]

The immediate response was one of hurt and mourning; it was not a polite sorrow but an angry one. Young people – children – cried and shouted on national TV for the needless deaths of their close friends and relatives. Crowds gathered and demanded responses from elected officials, who initially refused to appear in public. The prime minister attended the scene to meet with firefighters but did not meet with residents in front of the cameras. More anger. Reporters were challenged by residents about where they had been before the fire. Calls were made by the leader of the opposition for luxury homes nearby, which were sitting unoccupied, to be made available to those made homeless by the fire. Supplies were sent and donations and support organized. Residents in similar blocks were pre-emptively evacuated in other parts of London while safety checks were carried out.[5] People throughout the country living in similar blocks felt unsafe. People evacuated from their homes because of the fire faced not just the loss of their homes, but the loss of their neighbours in the most horrible way and the knowledge they could have also died. People replayed phone messages they had received from people trapped in the building saying goodbye. People demanded something should change, and they were heard. But how long could the momentum of this image keep people awake to this 'secret shame'?

Would the same wake-up call have been received if the burning building and lives lost had been in Wigan or Cardiff – or Dhaka or Uyo?[6] Surely part of what made the image so difficult to ignore was the presence of global celebrities among the immediate neighbours, the familiarity of the area to the journalists who covered it – and the very visible division in wealth and life experience within such a small geographical space.

Within hours of the fire, there were public calls for independent investigation into how and why the Grenfell fire occurred, particularly in the light of previous similar fires in Melbourne, Dubai and London, including a deadly one in Camberwell, London, in 2009 at Lakanal House where six people died. There were competing calls for either an independent inquiry or a coroner's inquest. Legal advisors and campaigners favouring a coroner's inquest pointed out that survivors and the bereaved would be more central to this process, with the ability to ask questions of witnesses and the coroner – though they would not be entitled to support with legal fees. Concerns about the use of a public inquiry centred on the ability of the government to set the terms of reference, the possibility that the terms of reference could be so wide that an inquiry may take years to report, and the more limited ability of survivors and the bereaved to take an active part in the inquiry. Ultimately, a public inquiry was ordered by Prime Minister Theresa May, which did allow survivors and bereaved to be listed as 'core participants' and have legal representation and also allowed the scope to be wider than a coroner's inquest would be, and investigate the wider public housing issues that contributed to the fire.

In the days after the Grenfell fire, many noted the strength and generosity of local communities, and donations and support from people elsewhere in the country and around the world. Some note was taken – though not enough – of the fact that, because it was the fasting month of Ramadan, many local Muslims were awake in the early hours and first on the scene to offer help. Community members organized to set up places for people to rest and distribution of donated supplies. This was all while the local authority appeared to be largely absent. As with the response to the photograph of Alan Kurdi's toddler body washed up on a Turkish beach in 2015, people distant from the crisis did feel touched by the horror of what had happened at Grenfell and sent resources: money, food, clothes, offers of holidays for survivors. The kindness of these acts is important. But does it address the question of justice, which is what Grenfell survivors demand?

People asked – how could this happen? In one of the richest boroughs in one of the richest cities in the world? When all of the information that would have prevented it was readily available? But that it happened is not a contradiction. It is the essence of how our society is organized and sustained. It is organized around a deliberate will to look away from the problems that cut to the heart of the comforts of everyday life. Because to look directly at the problem might mean addressing it, and addressing it would mean giving up comfort.

Grenfell was a tower of social housing, built in 1974. At twenty-four storeys high, it was prominent in the views from the more expensive and genteel surrounding neighbourhoods of Kensington and Chelsea – one of the richest neighbourhoods in the world, home to pop stars and royalty. Its original exterior was concrete. Cladding was added to soften its appearance during a renovation implemented in 2015/6. This was to improve the view from the outside – to make it easier to ignore. There were no benefits to the residents of Grenfell. Far from it – the cladding that was used was unsafe and highly flammable. When one flat ignited, it was expected that the internal structures would have contained the fire within one dwelling, and residents were therefore advised to stay in their homes rather than evacuate. But the cladding was not safe. It took the fire up the outside of the building. It was cheap and faulty. It was installed to protect the view of wealthy neighbours, and it had deadly consequences for the people living in Grenfell.[7]

This was not unforeseen. Several Grenfell residents had raised concerns about the cladding, and other problems with the building such as the lack of escape routes and problems with gas pipes, on numerous occasions.[8] One of the problems raised was the frequent and dangerous power surges, one of which is thought to have been the cause of the original fridge fire in flat 16. These residents were ignored. They were not only seen as a nuisance by local authorities; they were also ignored by local press – an area where corporate buyouts have reduced on-the-ground reporting and its support for democratic accountability to a bare minimum.[9] Similar cladding had also been responsible for previous fires in tower blocks. But no action was taken – because Grenfell was only visible to decision-makers as an eyesore that needed covering with cosmetic cladding, not as a home for hundreds of people who deserved safety and decency.

The effect of seeing the tower on poet Ben Okri was such that he felt moved to write a powerful, eloquent poem full of rage and sadness, analysis and calls for justice and action. The terror of the burning tower, for Okri, is 'an image to wake up a nation':

> It has revealed the undercurrents of our age.
> The poor who thought voting for the rich would save them.
> The poor who believed all that the papers said.
> The poor who listened with their fears.
> The poor who live in their rooms and dream for their kids.
> The poor are you and I, you in your garden of flowers,
> In your house of books, who gaze from afar
> At a destiny that draws near with another name.
> Sometimes it takes an image to wake up a nation
> From its secret shame. And here it is every name
> Of someone burnt to death, on the stairs or in their room,
> Who had no idea what they died for, or how they were betrayed.
> They did not die when they died; their deaths happened long
> Before. It happened in the minds of people who never saw
> Them. It happened in the profit margins. It happened
> In the laws. They died because money could be saved and made.[10]

This extract from Okri's poem ranges over the central ideas underpinning this chapter. The ongoing violence of these 'deaths

[that] happened long / Before ... in the minds of people who never saw / Them'. The understanding that these living deaths of fears and dreams are foretold and seem inevitable because 'money could be saved and made' by ignoring and devaluing them. The understanding that this could happen because those living more comfortable lives could simply 'gaze from afar' while this indifference was enshrined in institutions and laws. And finally, the understanding that this indifference was somehow broken through – even if just for a moment – by the shocking sight of the burning, burnt tower block.

The point is, the tragedy waiting to happen on 14 June 2017 was already known and, in fact, was already happening. Residents gave evidence to the tribunal about the attempts they had made to report dangerous faults with the building and the accommodation of several people with mobility impairments in unsuitable flats on high floors. Residents did know; it is not Grenfell residents who exhibited violent ignorance, but they are people who experienced and are still experiencing its violence. Rather, ignorance was practised by those who could turn away from a problem apparently too difficult and intractable to solve and one that would seem to impact them little, or even benefit them, while being left to fester.

In the stanza above, 'you and I' are not the residents of the tower. The poet recognizes it is not his life that has been ruptured by this perfect storm of neglect and greed. He is addressing 'you and I' in our 'garden of flowers', 'house of books', with our 'secret shame' that this tragedy was already known, already predicted before that fridge burst into flames. Not only 'could have been predicted', but *was* predicted: by Grenfell residents, some of whom died in the fire, who had been warning that the tower, like many others, was at risk of such a tragedy, just as there had been a high-rise tower block fire in Lakanal House in Camberwell in 2009 in which six people died.

This chapter is about moments that puncture the skin of violent ignorance. We have already seen how powerful and comforting ignorance can be, while it enables systems of violence and injustice. Ignoring what is right in front of us ought to be difficult, but experience shows it is surprisingly easy – because facing up to difficult, complex questions about power, fairness and exploitation is much more difficult for many people than leaving things be. But there are certain moments, often captured in striking images, in which it seems impossible to look away from systematic violence we have been ignoring. The night of the Grenfell fire provided one such moment, as Okri suggests. Another was crystallized in a photograph of a dead toddler, Alan Kurdi, washed up on a Turkish beach in 2015, which momentarily focused public opinion on the human cost of the European border crisis. Looking at these two moments in particular, in this chapter I discuss how it is that 'an image [can] wake up a nation / From its secret shame' – and what happens after that. I think of this as puncturing the skin of violent ignorance, exposing the wounds. Often, that skin grows back quickly.

Puncturing violent ignorance

What happens when people see something they are usually so good at ignoring? This chapter is concerned with thinking through some of the moments when violence that is usually ignored while in plain sight comes to be visible and prominent. Thinking through the unfolding response to the Grenfell fire in 2017, and a key moment in the European border crisis in 2015, the focus of this chapter is on moments in which a crack in violent ignorance can occur, moments when – for perhaps only a moment – the violence which is usually ignored becomes visible to all. To talk about these moments, I have found it useful to adapt an idea derived from the French intellectual Roland Barthes: the idea of the *punctum*.

Barthes, in considering the ways we react to photographs, used the Latin word 'punctum' to describe the element of a photograph 'which rises from the scene, shoots out of it like an arrow, and pierces me ... that accident which pricks me (but also, bruises, is poignant to me)'.[11] His argument was that while many photographs may be interesting from an intellectual point of view, and might depict things in which the viewer is interested, very few photographs grab the viewer's attention in a visceral and compelling way. The broad field of photographs which are vaguely interesting he called 'the studium' ('of the order of *liking*, not of *loving*').[12] But those which 'pricked' the viewer had to also contain what he called a 'punctum'. For Barthes, the punctum was a detail which caught the viewer's attention in a way that connected with them deeply and emotionally, recalling personal memories or feelings. This might be something quite banal – a necklace or a hand gesture. In Barthes's work, it is clear that many of the details he identifies as having this power are entirely personal to him (he emphasizes, that which 'pricks *me*') – not something that would necessarily affect someone else in the same way. What I find useful in his idea of the punctum is the sense of a (usually unpredictable) detail which can *puncture* the viewer in a way that makes them notice not just the image, but ideas beyond it, in a profound way.

Thinking back to the assassination of Jo Cox MP discussed in the previous chapter, there was no sharing of violent images of her death. Yet there were images that punctured the public's imagination in powerful ways. Think back to the front pages of the newspapers, both on the day after her death and the day after her killer was sentenced – the smiling, white, pleasant-looking woman, in her wedding dress or looking capable in a red suit in front of the House of Commons –

presented alongside the news of her violent death. The image echoes those of well-presented middle-class women and mothers of Britain; it is of someone with whom one is meant to identify, aspire to be or want to protect. It is easy then to mobilize this as a loss which a national community must rally around, in a way that an image of a racially minoritized, disabled, poor or less 'respectable' victim might not be.[13] This image punctures because it asks for a reaction to the *person*, but what is then left out is the recognition that the assassination was not aimed at the person and family and friends of Jo Cox (the person), but at the institutions and political priorities she was seen to represent.

In thinking about how images or moments can puncture violent ignorance, I think it is important to push Barthes's thinking further (and to use plainer language). So I want to talk about *punctures*, rather than *punctum*. The moments that *puncture* our violent ignorance are not only found in photographs and images, though many of the examples I give here do relate to specific, searing images that have made visceral, haunting connections with their viewers. It is not that each of these images or moments (the burning Grenfell Tower, Alan Kurdi's body on the beach, the assassination of Jo Cox) was unique or unconnected to what had already been happening or to *what was already known*. Rather, they had a specific power to *puncture* the skin of violent ignorance – to break through in a visceral, bodily way which demanded longer attention. We might link this to other metaphors that have been used to understand the function of ignorance in the sense that I mean it (of knowing but refusing to know), like that of the 'veil' which can be torn. If we think of ignorance as having violent consequences, we might also think that there is a kind of violence to breaking through it or at least some form of concerted force. Thinking of these moments as ones when the skin of violent ignorance has been punctured, then, allows us to imagine that force, and that there is some sense of trauma exerted on those forced to confront their ignorance by such moments. What it also demands is that we recognize that, like living skin, ignorance can scab over, can reseal its wounds. The puncture caused by a moment like the shock of the assassination of a national politician can be quickly healed over by the ointment of 'Great Get Togethers' or half-hearted selective promises on refugee safety. The political crisis it signified can continue to be ignored, even if a scar remains.

That scar might remind us that something terrible happened – but what does it mean? American writer and philosopher Susan Sontag suggests that '[p]erhaps too much value is assigned to memory, not enough to thinking.'[14] In her evocative book *Regarding the Pain of Others*, Sontag discussed the politics and ethics of looking at shocking photographs of violence and war. Gruesome images, whether of the Spanish Civil War of the 1930s, or casualties of the American military in Iraq in the 2000s, can, Sontag says, act as a wake-up call: 'The photographs are a means of making "real" (or "more real") matters that the privileged and the merely safe might prefer to ignore.'[15] Sontag forcefully reminds us that while postmodernist philosophers might reflect on the artifice of photographs and media images as if they represent a distancing effect, a turning of 'reality' into 'spectacle', such an attitude is 'breathtaking' in its short-sightedness: 'It universalizes the viewing habits of a small, educated population living in the rich part of the world, where news has been converted into entertainment.'[16] That is, the complaint that images of real-life violence have lost meaning, and the associated discussion of 'compassion fatigue', can only be considered universal by erasing those actually living through that violence from the universe.

Sontag emphasizes throughout her book how shocking war photographs, and discussions about them, seem to create a split between those depicted and the viewing audience. The viewer becomes a universal 'we', the ones who see and can act – or can't and don't. For Sontag, it is important to remember that the 'we' of the viewing public is multiple and is not universal. Much of the world does not 'have the luxury' of treating painful reality as a choice.[17] And so when discussing the viewer who turns away from a shocking image, or is pierced by it, as 'we', there needs to be clarity about who is included in that 'we' and how specific 'our' position is within the world.

Recognizing this, there is still a value in focusing on the 'we', the relatively safe and privileged viewing audience, of whom I (the writer), and many of the readers of this book, inevitably form a part. When 'we' view the pain of *others* – whether experienced through war, neglect, bureaucratic violence, or climate catastrophe – are we simply exploiting this pain? What could possibly make it acceptable to compromise the dignity of a family drowning in the Mediterranean Sea by gazing at their faces and then absently turning the page? Sontag engages with these questions of compromises of dignity and power in the transmission of images of pain and violence. And yet she concludes that there is an importance to creating, sharing, and contemplating them:

> Such images cannot be more than an invitation to pay attention, to reflect, to learn, to examine the rationalizations for mass suffering offered by established powers. Who caused what the picture shows? Who is responsible? Is it excusable? Was it inevitable? Is there some state of affairs which we have accepted up to now that ought to be challenged?[18]

Asking such questions, she argues, is more important than a response of 'sympathy': 'Our sympathy proclaims our innocence as well as our impotence,'[19] an analysis echoed in Gloria Wekker's analysis of

White Innocence discussed in Chapter 1. Remember, this is the idea that being 'innocent' of historical racial violence – the sense of not knowing about it or not intending to reproduce it – exempts (white) people from taking responsibility for the consequences of their own actions and the reasons for the unequal distribution of power in the present.[20] Likewise, in Sontag's analysis, feeling sympathy for others experiencing trauma is a way of declaring one's virtuous instincts, but also a way of refusing to reflect on one's own implication in their trauma. A more appropriate, and politically responsible reaction, for Sontag, would be:

> a reflection on how our privileges are located on the same map as their suffering, and may – in ways we might prefer not to imagine – be linked to their suffering, as the wealth of some may imply the destitution of others.[21]

And yet, she adds, 'painful, stirring images supply only an initial spark' for such a task.[22] But what might it take to provoke such a spark of reflection? 'For photographs to accuse, and possibly to alter conduct, they must shock',[23] but '[h]arrowing photographs … are not much help if the task is to understand'.[24] All photographs are framed by narratives, which make sense of the image we see and its causes – we know, for example, when we see the image of the burnt-out Grenfell Tower that people lived in there, that they did not escape, that things could have been very different if more care was taken about their lives and their survival. The narrative might become framed differently depending how much or how little the viewer knows about what they are seeing, about what unfolded and why. But even while those different narratives fight for space around a specific image, what particularly piercing photographs do remains important: 'they haunt us'.[25] They keep asking us to remember, and when they connect with us completely, they keep returning to us and demanding we keep that image and what it represents in mind – and ask questions.

Alan Kurdi

Alan Kurdi was a happy three-year-old toddler with an older brother and a mother and father who wanted him to be safe and healthy. He became world famous as a corpse washed up from the sea.

When Alan Kurdi died, someone took a picture. Thousands of others like Alan have died on the journey from Syria to Europe, and their pictures were not taken. Some were not even seen as they slipped into the water. Many others did have their desperate journey recorded, including babies clutched by the parents with little to protect them from the hostile ocean. But this time, someone took a picture.

It was not enough to save Alan. The pictures taken were of his dead body, inert on a Turkish beach. Alan was three years old. He had travelled from Syria to Turkey and was attempting to reach Greece. His parents, Abdullah and Rehan, and his older brother, Galib, were travelling with him. Alan, Galib and Rehan died attempting to reach Greece from Turkey, on a boat carrying sixteen people but designed for only eight. They had tried to apply for a visa to join family in Canada as an escape from the deadly war in Syria. But they were refused, and saw the best chance for their family as a treacherous journey by sea towards imagined safety in Europe. As the poet Warsan Shire writes in her poem *Home*:

> no one leaves home unless
> home is the mouth of a shark
> …
> you have to understand

no one puts their children in a boat

unless the water is safer than the land.[26]

But the image of Alan's body travelled much further than his family's hopes for their living child. The picture appeared on newspapers and televisions around the world, but especially in Europe. The picture burned into people's brains. It shifted imaginations, sympathies and commitments. It briefly changed the conversation on migration and refuge in Europe.

The most widely seen image of Alan was of him alone, face-down on the beach, the water lapping at his pale skin and soaked hair. He is wearing a red T-shirt, blue shorts and trainers. This image became a turning point. Published on newspaper front pages and shared on social media around the world, this image became near-impossible to dispute as a representation of the brutal consequences of the Syrian war and the dangerous journeys taken to escape it and other conflicts. News outlets and politicians who previously had some of the most hard-line opposition to the rights of refugees and migrants expressed sympathy and horror for Alan's fate – largely as a result of this photograph. It was a moment at which popular sentiment of sympathy broke through for those making treacherous, unofficial journeys to imagined safety in Europe and elsewhere. In the UK, questions were asked in Parliament, there were widespread offers of rooms in people's homes for refugees, and supplies of food, clothes and household items were collected for distribution at refugee camps on an unprecedented scale.[27]

This image of Alan Kurdi was far from the first image of the brutal consequences of the European border regime. Images of people drowning, including families and children, had been taken and circulated in popular media. But none of them had the same, singular effect that Alan's image seemed to. Why is that? Some argued it was because of the paleness of Alan's skin, the way he looked like any 'ordinary' (read: white) European boy in his trainers and T-shirt: 'He looks like he could be any of our children.'[28] The fact that he was so young, his face turned away, and lying on a beach where consumers of the image might imagine their own children playing and paddling. That in the image he is on his own, isolated, and so vulnerable and yet no injury (which would have been more difficult to look at) is visible.[29]

It is hard to know what singular aspect of a photograph might break through the urge to ignore its violence or make a personal connection and deeply felt response to an image. All the elements might be there which would be imagined to shock the (safe) viewer: vulnerability, fear, desperation, threat, the juxtaposition of everyday items of clothing with the dangers of the sea, the broken boats and human bodies. Yet most of these images, for the disinterested news consumer, remain easy to ignore; they know they are important, but they do not shift their thinking or behaviour in any dramatic way.[30]

Perhaps for this reason, the photographer who took this bruising image of Alan, Nilüfer Demir, was accused by some of 'staging' the photograph.[31] Indeed, there were several images of Alan's death which circulated at the time. The most prominent (see Figure 2.1), of him lying alone; and another, of him cradled in the arms of a Turkish police officer. For her part, Demir said that when she came upon Alan lying on the beach, 'There was nothing left to do for him. There was nothing left to bring him back to life … I thought, "This is the only way I can express the scream of his silent body,"' and she took the photograph.[32] Alan's father, Abdullah, said he wished people would instead share an image of Alan when happy and smiling, the boy he had been, but of course, it is the image of the tragic waste of his life which was the one which cut through the world's ignorance, if only momentarily.[33]

Figure 2.1 *Alan Kurdi. Photograph by Nilüfer Demir, © AP Archive.*

Perhaps the accusations of 'staging' this image were a distraction from talking about the importance of what the image depicted and what it meant. It is not a new debate – as can be seen in essayist Susan Sontag's discussion of similar debates about important documentary photographs of the Spanish Civil War in the 1930s (some of which *were* staged).[34] Whether or not this image was framed and curated does not make it any less true that Alan Kurdi – and countless others – needlessly drowned while trying to reach safety in Europe. Whether captured purely by fluke or whether the lighting and framing was carefully judged, my question is, what can we learn from such moments and images that, with their power to provoke a visceral connection with others' struggles, puncture the skin of violent ignorance and force a wider population to look directly at the unjust contradictions of our social systems?

I also have a second question: how long can this reaction last, and what happens next? At the time of Alan's death, I wrote an article for academic journalism site *The Conversation*, identifying this shift in mood. It was a moment at which the dominant consensus – that people don't care about and are fearful of mass movements of populations from elsewhere – was fractured. The website editors gave the piece the title 'Public opinion on refugees is changing fast – and for the better'.[35] That wasn't my title – and it wasn't quite right. What that moment, and that connection with the death of Alan Kurdi, created was a possibility. It was a wake-up call that was heard. But it didn't take long for the moment to be re-domesticated into responses that better suited the existing common sense of looking away from uncomfortable sights.

As this 'new angle' on the border crisis (that one could have feelings other than fear or revulsion towards refugees) took hold of much of the British media, the prime minister, David Cameron, gave a televised statement on the situation. Cameron appeared on the screen, looking harried, standing in the street. He promised that the UK would provide homes for 20,000 Syrian refugees over five years (in December 2019, there were 5.6 million Syrian refugees living in countries bordering Syria).[36] Cameron's promise didn't look well curated or smoothly planned; it looked like someone forced into a corner of beginning to look uncaring and out-of-tune with public mood as even the most hard-line anti-immigration voices seemed to extend sympathy towards the victims of the border crisis. However, his promise did its job.

By 'did its job', I do not mean that 20,000 refugees reached safety because of it – because they didn't. Cameron's announcement was expressly designed to close down the demand that something be done to prevent deaths such as Alan's. The narrowness of the promise – to resettle only refugees already recognized as such by the United

Nations and only refugees from the war in Syria – was a political balancing act. Cameron and other politicians are often heard to argue that providing routes from the overcrowded refugee camps in countries bordering war zones is much preferable to granting refuge to those crossing the Mediterranean to Europe, because to do otherwise might 'encourage' such dangerous journeys.[37] Organizations and researchers working in these areas tend to disagree, arguing there is little evidence that measures taken by Western governments to cut off access to their territory via dangerous sea routes make anyone safer, or that increases in the danger of ocean crossings in unseaworthy boats have discouraged desperate people from making these attempts.[38] Likewise, the singular focus on *Syrian* refugees meant Cameron could be seen to be meeting the concerns of many of those disturbed by Alan's death, while ignoring those seeking safety in Europe from Afghanistan or Iraq (the second and third greatest countries of origin for asylum seekers in the EU in 2015, after Syria),[39] or Eritrea, Iran or Sudan (the three countries with the largest applications for asylum in the UK in 2015, above Syria).[40] Even with this limited promise, Cameron and his government were widely derided for time to come because this promise was made without any plan in place to implement it, and though it expanded an existing resettlement scheme, it took many months for the resettlements to begin to meet government targets.[41]

At the time, perhaps the prime minister's promise looked like an active response, a breakthrough which had forced the nation to look at the cruelty of the border regime and its consequences and respond. For those families who were resettled, it meant a lot. But on a wider scale, little changed. What the concession did was allow those who felt angry and unsettled by making the connection between the border regime, the death of Alan Kurdi and their own comfortable lives, to feel as if 'something had been done'. Ultimately, it became possible again to ignore the violent consequences of the border regime on a day-to-day basis and the skin of violent ignorance to grow back.

Counting the windows

Of his poem about the Grenfell fire, Ben Okri wrote that '[b]earing witness seemed the only thing to do'.[42] Central to his poem's message are questions of the violence of popular ignorance of daily inequity and violence – and of how the dreadful image of the tower is what forces us to look.

> But when you saw it with your eyes it seemed what the eyes
> Saw did not make sense cannot make sense will not make sense.
> You saw it there in the sky, tall and black and burnt.
> You counted the windows and counted the floors
> And saw the sickly yellow of the half burnt cladding
> And what you saw could only be seen in nightmare.
> Like a war-zone come to the depths of a fashionable borough.
> Like a war-zone planted here in the city.
> To see with the eyes that which one only sees
> In nightmares turns the day to night, turns the world upside
> down.[43]

'Did not make sense cannot make sense will not make sense'. In the first sessions of the government-commissioned independent inquiry into what happened at Grenfell, survivors, families and friends presented memorials to those who died as a result of the fire. All of these testimonies are wrenching. Okri's poem foreshadows one of the statements made, by Damel Carayol paying tribute to his family members Kadije Saye and Mary Mendy, Grenfell residents who died in the fire. During his testimony, Carayol presented to Sir

Martin Moore-Bick, the chair of the inquiry, a painting he had made of the burnt-out tower, as a reminder that justice must be done. He presented a similar painting to Prime Minister Theresa May, which she apparently said would hang in Downing Street.[44]

Carayol stated during his memorial of painting the image:

> It taught me one thing, or reminded me of one thing, which is no matter how angry you are, or the depth of expression, you still have to have a degree of measure in what you do. For I had to stop and measure the floors, and count things which I didn't want to do, I just wanted to throw the paint on there. This I hope will carry me, and yourself, and all of us through. With our depth of feeling we still need to stop and measure what are we looking for, the outcome of all this, on behalf of our family... for each other, for humanity, so if we don't care, take our eye off the ball, something like this could happen.[45]

In Okri's poem, 'you counted the windows and counted the floors', both to remember the dead and the traumatized and to try to convince 'yourself' of the scale of the damage. In Carayol's testimony, though 'counting the windows' does fulfil these purposes, it is also to a larger end; it is because that precision is necessary *to enable further action* for justice. Because though it '*did not make sense cannot make sense will not make sense*', sense has to be made and translated into justice.

Both Okri's and Carayol's images demand that the horror of the Grenfell fire is not only seen, but that it is engaged with. To paraphrase Susan Sontag, their demand is not only for memory, but also for thinking – and that thinking turn to action. Importantly, each window and each floor must be counted and considered to inform that action.

There have been many attempts to count and account for the losses of Grenfell, to treat its victims and survivors with dignity – as well as failures to do so. Images of the faces and names of those lost appeared in memorials around the tower, were recounted before the public inquiry, are repeated as names 'forever in our hearts' by many memorials and defiant protests led by the Grenfell community and others.[46]

Keeping wounds open

In November 2016, the Grenfell Action Group had predicted that

> only an incident that results in serious loss of life of KCTMO [Kensington and Chelsea Tenant Management Organisation] residents will allow the external scrutiny to occur that will shine a light on the practices that characterise the malign governance of this non-functioning organisation.[47]

After the fire, their warnings were acknowledged, but they came true because they had been ignored at the time.[48] And indeed, it is not clear that this foresight has entirely been achieved, because at the time of writing 'external scrutiny' has not yet been fully focussed on the governance of KCTMO or any of the other organizations responsible for the welfare of Grenfell residents. What was received, in the moment of the fire, was attention to the tangle of ignored warnings and lives which led to the deaths and trauma of the Grenfell fire – and that attention was not one that was easily or quickly turned away.

It was at the early stages of this inquiry that Damel Carayol presented his painting to Sir Martin Moore-Bick, the judge appointed by the prime minister to lead the inquiry. Many of the fears that had been expressed about the nature of a public inquiry continue to haunt this process: though announced by the prime minister on 15 June 2017, a day after the fire, the first phase of hearings did not begin until 21 May 2018, ending in December 2018, and the Phase One Report was released at the end of October 2019. This report dealt only with what happened on the night of the fire itself, focusing heavily on the actions taken by the London Fire Brigade, while questions of public housing, procurement, management and probity ('the circumstances and causes of the disaster') were left to Phase Two, hearings which began in March 2020, to be paused soon after as a result of the UK's lockdown measures in response to the coronavirus pandemic.

There is no doubt that the process of the inquiry is painstaking work – 619 core participants (including twenty commercial organizations and seven public bodies); more than 140 witnesses were heard from in Phase One; 500,000 documents were reviewed in Phase One and 200,000 are expected to be relevant to Phase Two.[49] The importance of examining in detail the questions before the inquiry – what happened and why, decisions made and actions taken in relation to the building, its construction and maintenance going back to 1974 – seems essential to finding some kind of justice for those who died and are traumatized by Grenfell and those still living in similarly unsafe housing.[50] And of course, such a task takes time.

But in the meantime, what has happened to the bereaved, survivors and residents of Grenfell, and those still living in unsafe housing? Nine months on from the fire, nearly half of the 202 households requiring rehousing as a result of the fire were still in temporary accommodation.[51] Twenty-four households were still awaiting suitable housing twenty-one months after the fire.[52] Hundreds of people are still grieving their loved ones, while also having to fight for justice. Unsafe cladding, identified as a cause of the fire in Phase One of the inquiry, remains in place on buildings around the country, including on a high-rise building of student accommodation in Bolton which saw a serious fire in November 2019.[53] As musician and activist Lowkey states in a lyric on Grenfell, produced with the survivors and bereaved who mouth his lyrics in the track's video: 'Witnesses to the crime we fear a whitewash is the end game.'[54]

In January 2019, with hearings for Phase One of the inquiry closed, Steve Reed, MP for North Croydon, accused 'a string of housing ministers' of being 'culpable' for the Grenfell fire because of failure to act on safety recommendations made after the Lakanal House fire in 2019, adding that if they had been working for a private company and behaved the same way, they would 'potentially be in the dock for corporate manslaughter'.[55] In December 2019, with Phase Two of the inquiry still to begin, Gavin Barwell, a Conservative housing minister between July 2016 and June 2017 (directly leading up to the Grenfell fire), was made a member of the board of Clarion Group, the UK's largest housing association, that is, a private organization providing social housing.[56]

As housing minister in the year before the Grenfell fire, Barwell had refused to act on letters or meet with MPs about housing safety concerns while he was the government minister in charge and refused to answer questions about whether Grenfell could have been avoided in the immediate aftermath of the fire and in his new role as Prime Minister May's chief of staff.[57] Another former minister, Liberal Democrat Stephen Williams, who as minister for communities had responsibility for housing standards between 2013 and 2015, responded to letters from concerned MPs who were pushing for a promised review of housing safety by saying he had 'neither seen nor heard anything that would suggest consideration of these specific potential changes is urgent' and said he was 'not willing to disrupt the work of this department by asking that these matters be brought forward'.[58] This seems like a clear case of institutional indifference and violent ignorance – should Williams, Barwell or any of the other politicians or officials who ignored these warning have had to live in homes without proper fire escape routes or with the types of risks documented in letters to them, it is hard to believe they would have 'neither seen nor heard' the urgency of acting.

Grenfell United and Justice 4 Grenfell are two local community organizations which organized both practical help and political demands following the fire. Yet Grenfell United organizers told journalists of how Conservative government advisers had tried to derail community organizing even then, by putting forward their own proposed community spokesperson and organization, 'Grenfell Bereaved and Survivors' Trust':

> '[The officials] were trying to say it would be easier, instead of having two organisations to talk to, [to] just have one,' [Shahin] Sadafi said. 'I remember Oliver [McTernan] saying: "What do you mean, it's easier for you? It should be easier for the community."'[59]

The people of Grenfell United refused to be pushed into a top-down organized group and held onto their own organization. They recognized that for their message to be heard, they had to be strong:

> 'This was government trying to simplify things for themselves,' said Sadafi. 'That woke us up. We knew people weren't coming to help us, but that people might be trying to jeopardise us and dismantle what we are doing. I was afraid of the people who should have been helping me.'[60]

Grenfell United constituted itself as a family association, with an elected committee, and opened a headquarters in February 2018 where survivors and the bereaved could go for counselling, health support and community with others who survived the fire. But they also organized for political change aimed at preventing anything like the Grenfell fire happening again, including through speaking out about the progress and conduct of the government-commissioned Grenfell Tower Inquiry.

Silence

On the 14th of every month, since the one-month anniversary of the Grenfell Tower on 14 July 2017, survivors, friends, relatives and supporters of the victims of Grenfell gather in Kensington and walk silently together in memory of what was lost in the fire and in search of justice for them and those in equally dangerous housing.[61] The Grenfell Silent Walk is powerful because of its sustained and dignified silence in the midst of noisy London streets. But this is not a passive silence or one without meaning or charge. It is a silence that cannot be easily ignored. Rather, the silence demonstrates both the determination for change and the unspeakability of the injustice of what happened to Grenfell residents. Many people carry banners and placards, some simply stating 'Justice for Grenfell', others decorated with green hearts which have become a symbol of solidarity with Grenfell, and still others with more explicit demands for safe housing or for criminal prosecutions. While those participating have a multitude of demands, of priorities, may see justice in terms of criminal prosecutions of individuals or in terms of changes to socio-economic structures, or may primarily want to keep the memory of their loved ones alive, the power of the walk is in their ability to unite in determined solidarity expressed through their shared silence and consistency. They are not going away.

In an essay on 'The Aesthetics of Silence', Susan Sontag considers the role of silence in relation to art. By 'silence', Sontag means both literal lack of sound and the silence that comes from saying, doing or making nothing. One example she uses is the composer John Cage's piece *4'33"*, in which an orchestra sits silently for four minutes and thirty-three seconds; another is the 'readymade' artworks by French artist Marcel Duchamp, who presented existing ordinary objects – such as a bottle rack or a urinal – in galleries as works of art. These 'silences', Sontag argues, exist in relation to other, more 'noisy' things:

> There is no neutral surface, no neutral discourse, no neutral theme, no neutral form. Something is neutral only with respect to something else. (An intention? An expectation?) As a property of the work of art itself, silence can exist only in a cooked or nonliteral sense. (Put otherwise: if a work exists at all, its silence is only one element in it.)[62]

In the same way, the silence of the Grenfell Silent Walk is an active silence. For previous governments, Grenfell residents were silent even as they did everything they could to have their voices heard; the authorities simply ignored them. The Silent Walk is eloquent because in their silence, the protesters speak volumes.

The monthly Grenfell Silent Walk is not the only time that silence has been used as a way of drawing attention to unspeakable, but widely ignored, violence. One famous example is the Women in Black movement, which began in Israel in 1988. From 1988 to 1994, a group of women met every Friday in public spaces in Jerusalem and other cities, dressed in black and standing in silence with signs simply saying 'Stop the Occupation'. They were protesting against the cycle of violence between the Israeli government and Palestinian people, and they drew much ire as well as much admiration for the stand they took. In writing about this movement, the sociologists Sara Helman and Tamar Rapoport emphasized another aspect of such silence: it enabled the women to stay united behind a single aim – to stop the Israeli occupation of Palestinian territories. Individual views among the movement about the specificities of problems, causes and solutions to be prioritized could vary, and critical debate about these questions was suspended within the Women in Black movement, meaning they could stay united in solidarity behind one aim – both simple and complex.[63] Something similar applies to the Grenfell Silent Walk – though each individual may be contemplating a different element of injustice, rage or mourning, and different desired outcomes – from jail time for housing developers to a change in political systems to safe housing for individuals – they are united in their shared respect and determination for Justice for Grenfell.

Their silence is shocking because it carries a message of determination and resistance. Silence also resists a glib reworking of demands for justice into soundbites that can be neutralized – the usual ways in which violent ignorance, once wounded, can heal over. Silence resists interpretation yet leaves open many possible demands.[64] While silence in the face of injustice may be framed elsewhere as indifference, in the case of the Grenfell Silent Walk it is quite the opposite. It is a demand, one which must be heard and which also highlights how far spoken demands have gone unheard. The 'silent indifference' of authority is 'countered with an active but soundless provocation.'[65]

The Grenfell Silent Walk is important because it keeps open the wounds that cannot heal, the deaths and losses of Grenfell and elsewhere, and demands we look at them and find a way to treat them that is more than just a bandage. It also keeps open the wounds which must not be allowed to heal, that piercing of the skin of violent ignorance which so easily scabs over with explanation and obfuscation. The silence shocks, and it also forces us to think about that shock and keep thinking. The silence is not the only response – it is in concert with the ongoing organizing and resistance of Grenfell United and others, summed up in the words of Ahmed Elgwahary, one of the Grenfell United members and organizers, talking about the ongoing struggle against the all-encompassing desire of officials to forget and paste over the rawness of the bereaved and survivors' experiences: 'Our families were burned and you have to remind them we are not a normal group. You have to do that to sensitise them.'[66]

And if we need a further reminder of the power of silence, of how an ignored plea can be all the more powerful once the worst fears that led to that plea have come true, we can think of the words of Nilüfer Demir, the photographer who captured the image of Alan Kurdi's lifeless body on the beach:

There was nothing left to do for him. There was nothing left to bring him back to life… I thought, 'This is the only way I can express the scream of his silent body.'[67]

3

Normal violence

It is unprecedented. And yet it is already normal.
– JOHN BERGER AND JEAN MOHR, *A SEVENTH MAN*[1]

In your face

In the spring of 2015, two experiences of the Mediterranean Sea clashed on the shore of Kos in Greece. Tourists from Northern Europe planning on a sunny beach holiday found themselves confronted with the exhausted and desperate arrivals of unseaworthy boatloads of people travelling from Turkey and Libya as the most recent step on their journey to refuge. Beach as idyllic getaway clashed with beach as life-saving pitstop.[2] Tabloid newspapers called it 'disgusting' and reported that 'British holidaymakers say their summer break has turned into a nightmare as migrants who are in Greece to claim asylum have turned Kos into a refugee camp'.[3]

The sight (and sounds and smells) of border violence was right in holidaymakers' faces. This did not act, for those whose experience was reported in British tabloid newspaper *The Daily Mail*, as a moment of revelation in which their sympathies were aroused for another human; it was too much and too disturbing. The response was a desire to push these lives and this knowledge away: to ignore.

It was a request – a demand – that the seawater paddle on a pleasant beach holiday not be polluted by a reminder that dead bodies floated in that same sea. Newspapers reported that holidaymakers' experiences had

> turned into a nightmare as penniless migrants who are in Greece to claim asylum sit outside their restaurant and watch them eat… Young Afghan mothers in head scarves, changing their babies and washing their children's clothes in the sea, share the promenade with tourists who sit uncomfortably on the beachfront… Local restaurants have erected a net barrier to block the sight of the makeshift camp, but workers complain that the tourists continue to stay away from this part of town because *they don't know where to look.*[4]

How, asked *The Daily Mail*, could people be expected to relax when such things were going on? People hungry, homeless, lost – and visible. Perhaps the answer is that people should not relax while such things are going on. But if they want to, they can do so by making sure such things go on in ways or in places that they can refuse to see: 'We won't be coming back if it's like a refugee camp again next year,' a 'British couple' told a reporter.[5]

A month before this report, a fishing vessel designed for a crew of fifteen sank in between Libya and the Italian island of Lampedusa, carrying an estimated 700–1,100 people also trying to reach European shores. Only twenty-eight survived. Four years later, artist Christopher Büchel brought the recovered vessel to the 2019 Venice Biennale for the art world to see, sparking a similar argument about the tastefulness of border violence being visible, this time among pleasure-seekers at one of the global art world's major events.

After the disaster, the Italian government had recovered the boat 'to give proper burial to our brothers and sisters who otherwise would have remained at the bottom of the sea', in the words of Prime Minister Matteo Renzi.[6] Almost 300 bodies were still inside the vessel; others did presumably remain at the bottom of the sea. This was a spectacular attempt at memorializing the casualties of border violence (the boat's recovery cost €9.5m). In parallel, violence continued as the EU introduced measures to push back boats attempting to enter Italy to camps in war-torn Libya, and reinforce border control within Libya, where migrants' rights and the right to asylum are not recognized, with a package of at least €46m agreed by the EU for this purpose.[7]

Once recovered, the boat was entrusted to the city of Augusta in Sicily and then loaned to Büchel, who transported it to Venice for the Biennale and mounted it on the harbour at the Arsenale, a busy part of the main exhibit.

The making of this death-boat into a monument raised questions. Some of these questions are part of a larger debate about the ethics of artworks which are based on real-life tragedy: to what extent are they exploiting the pain of others, and to what extent are they bringing this pain to public attention as a civic act?[8] What is the aesthetic or artistic value in such an act? And who has the right to profit from this? In the case of Büchel's work, questions were also raised about the specific incorporation of the 'work' within the Venice Biennale, where moments of contemplation and reflection are short, where visitors hop from artwork to artwork, where rampant conspicuous consumption is so close and obvious, where an encounter with the boat may become an Instagram moment rather than a recognition of deaths at sea? This was accentuated by the boat's placement alongside a busy seated café area, and without signage.[9]

But perhaps, thinking through a violent ignorance perspective, we might see this as exactly the point and the importance of this intervention. Placing it at the heart of wealth, power and imagination at such an art festival means it becomes possible to both see and ignore

– at the same moment – the violence of the world system that resulted in these deaths. Part of the artwork is the placing of this horrifying death trap next to the insouciant sipping of cocktails. That is what is possible in a world of violent ignorance. Hiding death and torture is not necessary; even when placed in full view, it can be ignored simply by staring it down (over a Campari and soda, perhaps). This artwork is not, then, the boat, but the reactions to it. The audience of the artwork is not the people on the Arsenale in Venice, but those observing them as they so easily assimilate, or straightforwardly ignore, its horror. And in seeing them doing this, recognizing this potential and practice in ourselves when we confront similar horrors every day but choose to turn away.

Barca Nostra is not simply a metaphor. It is, literally, the boat on which hundreds of people died when they could have been saved, and they died because of the unequal geographical and social distribution of safety and the means for a decent life, and of the power to deprive others of these.[10] People's ability to see, and perhaps appreciate this, but then to immediately continue with their enjoyable art appreciation tour is also not simply a metaphor, but a literal living out of a social process – violent ignorance. But we can also see this as a metaphor for how these processes play out in a variety of other ways throughout society – and that is where this becomes 'art'.

Coming face to face with people who have barely escaped drowning, or the boat on which hundreds died, forces a person to confront the violence of looking away, of not knowing where to look even if a 'net barrier' is erected around the restaurant to help with this. But there are other ways in which border violence is present in everyday lives, and rather than conspicuously looking away, these practices are incorporated as if they were 'normal' and not 'unprecedented'.

'The border' seems like it should be far away – at the edge of a nation. But in recent decades people's entitlement to be in a particular national territory has become something that is not only checked when crossing over a borderline or geographical boundary. 'Bordering practices', as many scholars call such inspection and control, occur in everyday interactions, such as checking documents before being able to rent a house, get a job, take part in education, receive healthcare, open a bank account, drive a car. Because these checks have become part of everyday life, everyday people with routine, seemingly non-border-related jobs (bank clerks, doctors' receptionists, university lecturers, people renting out their home) have become border guards. So the border is never far away in places that have implemented such controls – which includes most of the Global North.[11] People can be turned into numbers or into dirt which must be expelled or into problems which require nets, veils, walls and oceans to screen them from the view of the comfortable and keep us in our relative comfort. Even when those sheltering nets are torn, the violence that sustains our world can be easier to look away from than to confront. What would it take to change that?

This chapter considers some of the techniques through which violent ignorance is maintained by looking at examples of how the drama and violence of the global border crisis are ignored and able to proceed as if such extremes are normal. I begin by considering how the size of the problem of border violence – the sheer numbers of people who are unable to find a safe territory to live in – can itself become a factor in pushing observers to ignore the problem, when it seems too huge to even contemplate. The second technique of violent ignorance I explore here also uses numbers, but rather than numbers *of* bodies, bodies *become* numbers – whether literally marked with serial numbers or treated as units for processing rather than people. In this practice of dehumanization, it becomes much harder to see the consequences of the systems that reproduce border violence.

If these numbing numbering practices are a way of obscuring the human stories of border violence, a more straightforward way to completely obscure humans and their stories is to keep them out of sight. The third section of the chapter considers this practice in relation to offshore immigration detention and other forms of complete exclusion from mainstream society.

I close the chapter by asking if violent ignorance appears to be enabled both by hiding and by making known, then how can it be challenged? I suggest that an important element is the linking of feeling to knowledge and consider some ways in which artists and activists have attempted to do this, in order to achieve the connecting punctures in the skin of violent ignorance like those considered in Chapter 2. But the chapter begins by considering the scale of a problem – border violence – that seems so huge that no one *should* be able to ignore it.

Numbers of bodies

What does it mean when you read statistics like the following:

68,500,000 people in the world have been forced from their homes[12]
44,400 people per day are forced to flee their homes because of conflict and persecution[13]
6,280 people died or went missing while crossing borders worldwide in 2017[14]
2,275 people died or went missing crossing the Mediterranean in 2018[15]
24,700 people entered immigration detention in the UK in 2018[16]
30,000 people are in immigration detention in the USA on any given day[17]
85% of displaced people are hosted in developing countries[18]

It might make you see the size of the problem of border control and its violent consequences. And it is important to acknowledge the size of the problem. But it is difficult to *feel* the size of the problem in these abstract numbers.

One reason that the image of Alan Kurdi discussed in the previous chapter made so many people care deeply about deaths in the Mediterranean was that the image made him look like a person, not a number. Not just a person, but a vulnerable young child – and a vulnerable young white-European-looking child at that. Many people in Europe who had found the refugee crisis too worrying, too complicated or too threatening to engage with previously looked at that image and could see their own children, or children they cared about, in Alan's place.[19] When they were simply told that a toddler, or X number of toddlers, died each day attempting to cross borders to safety, they did not always make that connection.

One technique of violent ignorance takes advantage of the way that the massive numbers of people affected by border violence become hard to see simply because of the translation of their lives into statistics. We become accustomed to seeing not the individual ebbs and flows of different people's lives, but a set of numbers representing a large group of people, a technical matter rather than thousands of ethical and emotional challenges. A form of ignorance takes hold, moving the focus from the pain and joy of people's lives to the mathematical representation of populations. We might see the numbers, their size and patterns, but these numbers make it harder to recognize the lives they represent, as important and as nuanced as our own.

This is the context in which we might view the unprecedented, and yet normal, crisis of death at the borders of Europe and at many other borders around the world. Governments have the power to decide which lives become so barely alive that they are crushed, drowned, asphyxiated or simply disappear in the process of crossing borders.

The reasons people wish to enter Europe, North America, Australia, and the reasons that they are viciously prevented from doing so, are the same reasons those territories have become wealthy destinations: profiteering from exploitation, resource extraction and fear. Making people into numbers (individual numbers for processing or large unfathomable numbers of people travelling across borders or in need) makes this violence easier to ignore.

What does this mean in terms of violent ignorance? As discussed in Chapter 1, ignorance itself can be a form of power, for example, refusing particular knowledge if it would upset one's place in the world. Chapter 2 considered moments of crisis where violent inequities become impossible to look away from – if only for a moment. In this chapter, I will consider how it is commonplace to see border violence, its depth and extent, but to be able to ignore it. Here, I have suggested that the sheer weight of numbers can impress a particular kind of knowledge on an audience, but it can also make a situation seem too immense to change, while simultaneously removing the urgency of the individuals represented by those numbers. People experiencing border violence are not only made into aggregate numbers but are often (if they are counted) given individual numbers which can come to replace their identities, in terms of serial numbers given to people for processing or the quantification of a person's worth within a visa allocation system based on 'points'.

I am struck, for example, by two photographs from John Berger and Jean Mohr's 1975 book *A Seventh Man*.[20] When I see these images they puncture my sense of time and place.

What I see is a photograph of two rows of men dressed only in their underwear, bending forwards to touch their toes, while being inspected by a fully dressed man in a white doctor's coat. In the background, a woman sits behind a desk taking notes. In the second photograph, displayed on the facing page in Berger and Mohr's original book, is a photograph of a man's bare chest with the number '3' scrawled in felt tip above his right nipple. They are images of Turkish men being inspected by German doctors to decide their suitability for work in 1970s Germany. Berger's caption reads: 'Each man examined has his number marked in ink on chest and wrist.'[21]

The puncture which connects me viscerally to this picture comes from the resonance across time of writing numbers on other people's bodies in order to manage and control them. It is resonant with the way in which Nazis inked numbers onto prisoners in Auschwitz.[22] That is not to say that the medical checks on Turkish men entering Germany in the 1970s were *the same* as the horrors perpetrated by Nazis.[23] But it is to say that the pattern of treating other people's bodies as numbers, as items or stock, is dehumanizing; that writing a number on someone, rather than communicating with them, removes their agency; that in reducing someone to a naked body with a number, they are made less valuable and meaningful as persons in that context. And it is shocking, in part, because when this system of assessing the worth of newly arrived workers to Germany was taking place, the memory of the Holocaust was less than thirty years old.

This image punctures not only because it connects those practices of the 1970s to their recent past and suggests that memory can fade so quickly (for those who do not imagine themselves as becoming nameless, naked numbers). It also punctures through a connection to the present in which I am writing. In their visual, poetic documentary journalism of population movement in 1970s Europe, Berger and Mohr state: '[I]t is unprecedented. And yet it is already normal.'[24] This resonates with me as a description of the European border crisis that aroused international attention – sometimes sympathy, sometimes hatred – in 2015. In the longer passage from which this message from the 1970s comes, Berger writes of the process the migrant workers are undergoing:

He strips and lines up with many hundreds of other novice migrants. They glance hastily (to stare would be to show their astonishment) at the implements and machines being used to examine them. Also hastily at one another, each trying to compare his chances with those around him. Nothing has prepared him for this situation. It is unprecedented. And yet it is already normal. The humiliating demand to be naked before strangers. The incomprehensible language spoken by the officials in command. The meaning of the tests. The numerals written on their bodies with felt pens. The rigid geometry of the room. The women in overalls like men. The smell of an unknown liquid medicine. The silence of so many like himself. The in-turned look of the majority which yet is not a look of calm or prayer. If it has become normal, it is because the momentous is happening without exception to them all.[25]

Berger is writing of how normalized these mechanical treatments of bodies as pieces of machinery have become.

But turning of individual bodies into individual numbers is different from the aggregate population numbers discussed earlier, which overwhelm any sense of personhood with their size. In assigning numbers and quantities to specific bodies, the individual remains but only as a measurable entity for some outside use. This doesn't only occur through numbering with ink.

In the UK a common refrain in the immigration politics of the early 2010s was a call for 'an Australian-style immigration system'.[26] On the face of it, this refers to a 'points' system used by the Australian government to allocate work visas, identifying professions and skill shortages and giving preference to prospective migrants who could meet those needs (points towards a visa could also be allocated on the basis of other things such as age and language skills). The idea of points was appealing to parties on all sides, apparently because the measuring and quantification of skills and deserving characteristics was presented as a form of ensuring fairness. There was no discussion of how deserving characteristics would be calculated or weighted (perceived benefits to the economy and status of criminal records aside). The person behind the allocated number of points, their hopes, dreams, relationships and meaning were lost.

These forms of numbering are one way of obscuring the difficult and often violent consequences of border controls for human beings – violent consequences such as the ways in which some are prevented from ever entering territories while others can pass freely, where some people are assessed as useful and others as useless. They are of course also linked to more straightforward forms of looking away from violent consequences: hiding those consequences out of sight.

Out of sight

As noted, Australia's immigration system is often cited in British politics as a model of fairness to which the UK should aspire.[27] This ostensibly refers to the 'points-based system' for skilled worker visas. But Australia's border policies are not most marked by its points scheme, but by (a) its historical racism and (b) its contemporary system of offshore detention which flouts international law.[28] Australia as a nation was founded from British colonial adventures and ongoing genocide of the territory's original people.[29] At the federation of Australia, the Immigration Restriction Act 1901, which has always been popularly and politically known as the White Australia policy, was introduced. This was aimed principally at keeping out settlers from the nearest neighbouring countries in Pacific Asia and restricting immigration from Southern Europe to maintain a majority Anglo-

Irish population.[30] The White Australia policy was a way of ignoring the country's status as a settler colony in Pacific Asia, in which new arrivals would only be permitted if they could help to maintain the illusion of an outpost of northern Europe. It was a way of keeping out bodies that might act as reminders of the actual geography and history of the land mass of Australia.

The more current project of offshore detention or 'the Pacific Solution' has been in operation from Australia since 2001, with a short reprieve between 2008 and 2012.[31] This is the policy by which people seeking asylum in Australia are prevented from entering Australian territory by boat and placed in offshore detention in the neighbouring countries (and former German and then British/Australian colonies) of Nauru and Papua New Guinea. Not long after his defeat as Australian prime minister, Tony Abbott in 2015 argued this approach of 'offshoring' should be a policy taken up by all 'Western countries':

> It will require some force; it will require massive logistics and expense; it will gnaw at our consciences – yet it is the only way to prevent a tide of humanity surging through Europe and quite possibly changing it forever.[32]

Abbott's speech in London, given in honour of former British Conservative Prime Minister Margaret Thatcher, demonstrated that his support for border violence is based on a racist and xenophobic belief in preserving what he calls 'Western civilisation', which he believes is threatened by offering homes to people he describes in the same speech as 'living in poverty and danger'. The public argument for limiting asylum claims in Australia cannot be separated from this instinct that asylum seekers, however vulnerable, are a threat to the way of life of Australians.[33] Before offshore detention, the country already had a very restrictive regime, with mandatory detention of anyone claiming asylum. The immediate impetus for moving border

violence further out of sight was the increasing visibility of those
arriving in unsafe boats, piercing the collective ability to ignore the
human crisis of global inequality, insecurity and restrictive border
policies.

The 'Pacific Solution' was introduced in September 2001 after
the 'Tampa Affair'. On 24 August, a Norwegian freight ship, the
MV Tampa, answered a rescue call from 433 asylum seekers from
Afghanistan when their boat failed in the Indian Ocean. On
attempting to take them to Australian territory on Christmas Island,
the boat was refused entry and waited in limbo for eight days. The
Australian Liberal government sent troops to prevent the asylum
seekers disembarking and attempted to pass legislation giving them
powers to remove any foreign ship from Australian waters.[34]

The visibility of this incident was coupled with increasing numbers
of people travelling in smaller crafts, and washing up on Australian
beaches, or drowning at sea.[35] The violent consequences of being
unable to find safe passage, and being so desperate to reach shores
imagined as safe, became harder to ignore as Australians saw these
arrivals or heard of them. But rather than using this as a possible
turning point where leadership could have looked at ways of helping
people to survive, the government under Prime Minister John Howard
chose a policy of 'deterrence' (an approach then followed by successive
prime ministers of different parties). They argued that by making it
impossible to reach Australia by unofficial boat passage, they would
prevent people from bothering to make such treacherous journeys
and thereby 'save lives'.[36] The dead, the dying and those striving to
live would be pushed further out of sight and would remain numbers
rather than people.

To enable these policies, the map was redrawn and Christmas
Island was no longer considered Australian territory for the purpose
of asylum claims, so that those landing there in future would no longer

be recognized as having 'set foot on Australian soil', as Howard had vowed.[37] Australian immigration detention systems were instituted on Manus Island in Papua New Guinea and in Nauru. That is, the Australian asylum processing system was outsourced to sovereign territories of other countries, while also outsourced from the state to private companies. Alongside this physical removal from view, secrecy within the detention system was enforced by non-disclosure agreements for people working there including the Salvation Army, Save the Children, social workers, medical practitioners and outsourced security personnel for companies including G4S, Serco, Transfield/Broadspectrum and Wilson Security. These legal agreements prevented staff within the system from making public any abuse or malpractice they saw during the course of their work. This reached an extreme with the Australian Border Force Act 2015. That act threatened a jail term of up to two years for anyone working within the detention system who revealed details of what happened there to the media or any other person or organization.

This is an extreme and detailed form of governmental architecture expressly designed to make it possible *to ignore* both the knowledge and the feeling of the human violence of border controls – to avoid this knowledge 'gnawing' at the collective conscience. In the process of ignoring the desperation of those willing to risk their lives for life on another territory, it not only perpetuates but escalates that violence. It is in this context that those held in the detention camps – including children – could be subject to physical and sexual assault by guards that were recorded, but not reported. It is in this context that detainees were routinely driven to suicide attempts and self-harm, swallowing screws or razor blades, overdosing or refusing medication or food, slashing wrists. It is in this context that the Australian detention system's chief psychiatrist could define the detention process as 'akin to torture'.[38]

But it is not as if these practices are an exclusive Australian invention. EU countries have been playing with the idea of 'extraterritorial processing' since 1998.[39] In 2003, Tony Blair as UK prime minister suggested similar processes be used by the EU to prevent potential asylum seekers from entering EU territory, by processing them in another territory – his suggestions being Albania, Croatia or Romania, none of which were EU members at the time.[40] Blair's proposal was rejected. But perhaps a more brutal version of this scheme has been instituted since. In 2016, the enlarged EU made a deal with Turkey to send many people seeking refuge there back to Turkey, in return for easing of visa restrictions for Turkish citizens in the EU, renewed work towards Turkey's membership of the EU, and up to €6 billion for infrastructure towards managing refugees and borders.[41] This was a deal which defied the UN Refugee Convention.[42] In 2017, Italy signed an EU-backed deal with Libya which involved the Libyan coastguard 'pushing back' boats attempting to cross from there into the EU, in return for €46 million.[43] Frontex, the EU coastguard, has been involved in similar pushbacks, and they also occur at the EU's land borders.[44] All of this keeps the 'mess' of unmanaged movement of people out of sight, and out of mind, of everyday EU citizens. As legal commentator Anja Palm suggests, this seems to turn into reality 'the logic of shifting the burden of border and migration control to other countries (far away from the sight of the European public opinion and the reach of European lawyers and courts)'.[45] In turn, this makes the violent consequences of immigration and border regimes much easier to ignore.

Here the enforcement of ignorance is violent (deliberately sending vulnerable people back into war zones or into indefinite incarceration in immigration detention). By keeping border violence out of sight, it is possible to ignore not only the people who are its victims, but the reasons they are on the move. Vast sums of money are spent by governments on enforcing this border violence, whether through border patrols and security, pushbacks at sea or on land, detention within or outside the territory, and maintenance of asylum seeker monitoring systems within a territory.

Borders are profitable; someone will pay others to examine, constrain and move those bodies considered wrong or in the wrong place.[46] Even more so when there is a desire for the violent nature of border politics to remain out of sight. By outsourcing responsibility for the murky world of detention and border security to multinational private firms like G4S and Serco, governments feel able to deny knowledge – and responsibility – for many of the abuses that take place there.[47] They/We have created an institutional architecture for the express purpose of being able to deny knowledge of the violence committed inside it.

Resisting the new normal

If there are many ways in which the powerful have built structures to reinforce violent ignorance, there are also many ways in which others have sought to resist. This resistance seems most successful at sustaining a tear in violent ignorance when it goes beyond simply making knowledge visible and makes it imperative to pay attention – through an emotional, visceral connection.

There are many examples of people who have been directly targeted by the violent border regime making their pain (and its structural causes) visible to those who could choose to ignore it. Hunger strikes and sit-ins occur frequently and sometimes are reported by the outside world. Cultural theorist Imogen Tyler has written of ways in which people in the extreme conditions of indefinite immigration detention use their bodies to enact resistance and, in doing so, demonstrate viscerally how the system of border violence works on them. For example, in 2003, when Abas Amini, an Iranian Kurdish refugee had his successful asylum application appealed by the UK Home Office, he sewed up his eyes, lips and ears in protest. This was an act of desperation after experiencing and escaping torture in Iran, leaving his family, taking a terrifying journey eventually to arrive in Britain and going through years of government bureaucracy to have his asylum case accepted. Tyler argues that 'there was nothing exceptional about Amini's case or his protest, except for the extraordinary media attention it garnered.'[48] Indeed, similar protests came to public notice a year earlier in an Australian detention centre in Woomera, where seventy adults and three children sewed their lips together in protest at their conditions, with the message 'We want freedom or die.'[49] Nevertheless, these are protests that are so extreme that for anyone who does see them they will be unforgettable. The act of sewing up one's own face is so horrifying that it may lead anyone hearing of it to consider the circumstances in which such a desperate act seemed necessary. Yet such bodily resistances are so striking, so physically challenging and arresting, that they can make people feel disgust rather than connection. Perhaps in their extremity they encourage ignorance, being ignored.

More easily engaged resistance and making-known may be seen in the work done by detainees and former detainees, refugees and asylum seekers who share their stories as 'experts by experience'. There are many community and art projects which work around the idea of humanizing refugees, asylum seekers and migrants through social meetings with settled communities, with calls such as 'have a cup of tea with a refugee'. By having a cup of tea, it is thought, people will 'build bridges'.[50] But these projects are about tackling fear and unfamiliarity between groups of people. They are not about bringing into focus the violence of border controls, its causes and consequences.

That challenge is taken on though, by groups such as Detained Voices[51] and Freed Voices,[52] two groups of people who have been or are currently in UK immigration detention. Together, they have worked to make their experiences of border violence known to the general public and to decision-makers. This is often through the telling of personal stories, direct experiences of the border control system, by the person who experienced them. When such experiences are recounted in person, they are much harder to dismiss than a researcher or activist report. Groups such as Detention Action, the Detention Forum and Right to Remain have been at the forefront of supporting this recognition of the importance of 'experts by experience' in immigration detention in the UK. When politicians and managers who are responsible for those border systems have to hear what it is like for a human to experience them – and to hear it from a human whom they recognize as a *person rather than a number* – it can have a powerful political and ethical force. Can this continue to haunt someone in power too so that they find it harder to ignore the consequences of their actions?

If the acting out of violence on one's own body in spectacular response to border violence can be looked away from in disgust, perhaps the recognition of these human stories can be harder to look away from, at least in the moment. But they run the risk of invoking pity, rather than solidarity. Another way in which people have tried to forge understanding of border violence is through simulating it for themselves. 'Awareness raising' campaigns for many charities involve supposedly simulating the experience one wants to counter – think Sleep Outs to raise awareness and money for homelessness, for example.[53] In the case of border violence, international charities have organized the 'Ration Challenge' to 'show refugees we really are #inthistogether', and 'raise money' and 'awareness' by eating 'the same rations as a Syrian refugee living in a camp in Jordan' for a week.[54] These types of experience work on the body of someone who is not already targeted by the regime of border violence, and in doing so they are clearly well-intentioned efforts to make a difference. But in claiming to replicate the refugee experience while in a much safer space, they stop short of recognizing and dealing with the real violence at stake. Unlike the refugee in a camp, it's only 'down to you – and your conscience – to see it through' and 'you can earn extra ingredients ... by hitting fundraising targets'.[55]

When those who are relatively safe and comfortable wish to puncture the violent ignorance of the border regime, this might need to involve putting them/ourselves at risk too. If the aim is to draw the attention of those who are able to ignore border violence, and to keep that attention, maybe it involves making people see themselves as actually at risk too.[56] One such case might be the actions of the Stansted 15, fifteen activists who chained themselves to a plane to prevent it taking off on a flight that would have deported sixty people to Ghana, Nigeria and Sierra Leone.[57] In the ensuing court case, those activists faced prison, and they undertook the action knowing this could be a consequence. They were willing to take this risk in an effort to interfere with the certainty that others would be quietly removed from the UK, to uncertain fates. This action can be understood as relating to a violent ignorance framework in two ways: firstly, the activists defied all of the parameters set in place that would have made it easier for them to ignore the plight of those on the deportation flight and others like it. Secondly, they challenged the ease with which others could ignore the deportation flight – their intervention made the event into 'public interest' in a way that mundane deportation flights[58] are seen not to be; linked to this, the activists presented as (otherwise) respectable, mainly white, middle-class young people whose visible similarities to imagined 'ordinary' news consumers, voters and their families were harder to ignore than the experiences of asylum seekers and 'foreign criminals'. This is a response to a seemingly common expectation that only those seen as 'ordinary people' – or 'people like us' – can attract either sympathy or attention from a general public, at least in Britain.[59] Though the coverage was of their actions and subsequent trial and sentencing, the Stansted 15 and their supporters worked hard to keep the focus on the experience of people caught in the violence of border control which had necessitated their action.

From seeing to feeling

Artists have tried to make us feel the size of the problem through connection – through puncturing the veil of our ignorance. In 2018, artist Tania Bruguera installed a commission in the Turbine Hall of the Tate Modern in London. There were three parts to this piece. For one, the spectator would enter a side room off the giant Turbine Hall, perhaps after queuing; when they reached the door, an attendant stamped an ink number onto the participant's wrist or hand. This number was the sum of the number of people who last year migrated from one country to another, plus the number of migrant deaths recorded between the start of project and the day of the stamp.[60] The number was not necessarily explained to the participant unless they asked, as could be seen even in some art critics' reviews.[61] They then entered the side room, with all-white walls and ceilings, in which 'an organic compound' in the air was intended to provoke tears. Here, strangers might be prompted to cry by the tingling in the molecules of the air – again, not necessarily knowing why or feeling the usual emotions associated with tears. This seemed to suggest that one could read the emotions performed about deaths at sea as performances without being deeply felt, or perhaps it could be read as an opportunity to bond with strangers by exposing emotional selves in public (in the context of incomprehensible numbers of preventable deaths). Or perhaps it could be seen as the propensity of people to queue up for spectacles of which they have no prior knowledge. Bruguera called it 'forced empathy'.[62]

Outside this room, in the main space of the Turbine Hall, the floor was covered in heat-sensitive paint. Under the veneer lay an enormous photograph of the head and shoulders of Yousef, a young man who left Syria for London. This could be seen when the heat-sensitive paint was warmed up enough by body heat. The idea, explained in the accompanying panels if one sought them out, was that the only way to see the image in full was for many people to gather and warm the floor with their bodies at the same time (and in a systematic way). One might be expected to see this then as trying to drive home the importance of connection and togetherness in order to recognize the scale, importance and value of migration and reap its rewards.

Reading this whole installation through a violent ignorance framework suggests alternative angles on it. The stamp, like the numbers written on the bodies of men photographed by Jean Mohr, is again reminiscent of numbers written on the bodies of those entering the death camp of Auschwitz. In the Tate Modern installation, this action references deaths of others, less likely the fates of those visiting the gallery. So we might imagine this is re-inscribing them into the story of the crisis – demanding that they/we wear the stigma of being part of the border death machine (notwithstanding how easy it is to wash off this ink). In this, it echoes the renaming of the Lampedusa shipwreck as *Barca Nostra*; our boat, our stamp, our tragedy – not ours because we are drowning, but ours because we are implicated in its causes. Then, the forced tears of the side room – the denotation of emotion without feeling that emotion. The ease of wiping away those physiologically induced tears on exit, like removing the sight of the drowned or drowning bodies in our holiday destinations. And finally the face that won't ever emerge from beneath the grey paint and, even if in an organized feat it did emerge, would be quickly re-covered as the paint cooled. Even while the numbers of the border crisis are imprinted on our wrists, we can move on to the cafe and the gift shop.

***

The extremities of bordering practices and their racializing consequences, looked at face-on, seem so stark that they should be unbearable. Yet they continue and worsen. The extent of the violence of borders – uncountable deaths at sea or in transit, incarceration out of sight and without due process, lives trapped in limbo and poverty at the edges of territories, governments desperate to imagine desperate people as dangerous outsiders – none of this is new. And yet the scale and extent of the violence of borders continues to grow, in unprecedented ways, while the experience of living with these extremes becomes, increasingly, to be seen as normal – business as usual. There are occasions, like those discussed in the previous chapter, when an image or situation tears so strongly at public feeling that it cannot be ignored. But maintaining racial capitalism through border control – control of who and what can move, and under what circumstances, with whose authority – has so far remained paramount to governments. The well-being of unfortunate travellers caught in the border regime may be claimed as a reason for interventions such as the Stop the Boats campaign in Australia, but the extent of such interventions is often simply the moving of violence out of sight – a reinforcement of organized ignorance. The desire is not to solve the problem, but to turn away from it, because looking directly at it leads to realization that those looking are also entangled in the violence: in some ways as victims, but also as bystanders and perpetrators.

4

Enduring crisis

It has been dusk for four hundred years. If this past does not pass by it is because the future, the longed for, is not yet attainable. This predicament and this yearning are centuries old.

– SAIDIYA HARTMAN, *THE TIME OF SLAVERY*[1]

Violent ignorance is historical

In 1963, British imperial forces withdrew from Kenya after years of liberation struggle. As they did so, they carefully selected files from the mass of colonial government documents that they did not want the incoming government to see or to even know had existed. Some were marked 'for sight by "British officers of European descent only"' and removed from the country.[2] Other documents were so sensitive that they were destroyed. All reference to such files – referred to as 'watch files' – was also erased, so that their existence would be unknown to the new Kenyan government:

> The legacy files must leave no reference to watch material. Indeed, the very existence of the watch series, though it may be guessed at, should never be revealed.[3]

Similar practices were undertaken on the British withdrawal from thirty-seven colonies.[4] Aside from those archives 'migrated' to Britain, three and a half tons of documents were destroyed in Kenya alone in this process.[5] What could have been so sensitive that knowledge of it had to be so systematically eradicated?

The records that were concealed were, of course, records of colonial violence. They documented discussions between colonial officers 'right up to the Governor and beyond to the Colonial Office and Secretary of State in London' of policies that authorized systematic torture and abuse, with documents providing 'copious detail on the administration of torture and substantive allegations of abuse', including the burning alive of detainees by British officers.[6]

The plan to destroy these documents was called 'Operation Legacy', reflecting 'the British intention to shape the legacy of the empire at the moment of decolonisation'.[7] This, and the desire to cover up colonial violence and avoid independent investigations, is evident in contemporary documents including correspondence from Colonial Secretary Macleod deciding in November 1959 to 'draw a veil over the past' in relation to the abuses.[8] These decisions were taken at once to use ignorance to conceal violence – to create ignorance of violence – and in that act of enforced ignorance, further violent consequences ensued.

How did this decidedly literal enactment of violent ignorance come to light? The documents clearly contain instructions intended to keep the act of concealment itself concealed. Of course, nothing can ever completely be forgotten; people knew this had been done; people knew records must have been kept and destroyed. How did they prove it?

There were two pressures which meant this knowledge re-erupted. One was caused by an ongoing will to know and record, embodied in the practice of archiving. On the one hand, the 'will to know' can be a form of colonizing power, demanding explanation and confession. On the other hand, the listing, cataloguing and recording of those who wish to control knowledge can also become the source of challenges to the dominant versions of history.[9] As already noted, colonial record-keeping was what made these documents in the first place, apparently with a view that the understanding of them as documenting legitimate defence of property and territory would be an everlasting understanding. But the changing of regimes did not automatically destroy the desire of the archivists to record history for posterity. Whether that be motivated by a desire to record acts seen as glorious or shameful, or put forward as an objective documenting of facts, the drive to archive was retained.[10] The documents that survived complete destruction – including documents attesting to that destruction – were preserved in the archives of the Foreign and Commonwealth Office (FCO) in Hanslope Park, outside Milton Keynes. But they were preserved there without acknowledgement, to the extent that they were never disclosed to the Public Records Office or listed under the Freedom of Information Act, and their existence was denied to the civil servant searching for them in relation to legal action in 2011, until he insisted he would be coming to Hanslope Park to look for himself.[11]

The second crack in the facade of this enforced violent ignorance was the resistant memories of victims of the colonial regime. The hidden Kenyan archive included details and evidence of the British suppression of what they termed the 'Mau Mau uprising'. 'Mau Mau' was a name used to refer to resistance fighters against British colonial rule in Kenya. The Mau Mau rebellion, between 1952 and 1960, was a violent one on both sides. Thirty-two European settlers and 1,800 African civilians were killed by Mau Mau forces, and hundreds more disappeared. Meanwhile, between 12,000 and 20,000 Mau Mau rebels were killed by the British forces, and at least 150,000 people held in British detention camps during the period, usually without trial.[12] Collective punishment was used against whole villages, non-fighters and children. Brutal torture techniques were carried out systematically against suspected Mau Mau supporters.[13] The British regime kept detailed records of these decisions and actions, apparently (and arrogantly) without a thought at the time that this would be used as evidence against them should their reign of terror end. Once it did end, it became clear that these records needed to be removed. Without them, the victims and witnesses to the British state terror regime were unable to prove their case in court. This did not stop their campaigns and did not erase knowledge of the atrocities. When survivors of British torture in this period, more than half a century later, were able to bring their case to the High Court in London, their resistance and tenacity finally forced the British government to admit to the records that documented the systematic abuse carried out by the colonial regime.[14] After the court case led to the uncovering of the 'migrated' colonial archives, the British government failed in two procedural attempts to halt the legal case and in 2013 were forced into an admission and expression of 'regret' for torture and abuse of Kenyans, paying a settlement of £19.9 million to 5,228 claimants and building a memorial in Nairobi.[15] Without the persistence of the memory and knowledge of those survivors by then in their seventies and eighties, the British government would not have been forced to reveal its wilful ignoring of the detailed records of systematic violence.

A normal crisis lasts a long time

One thing we can learn from the stories in this chapter is that the past is not over. The other thing to recognize is that the 'crisis' of the abnormal, in which the power of violent ignorance is increasingly hard to ignore, is not something new or exceptional. For many people in the world, it has been abundantly clear for generations that those in power either refuse to know, or do not care, about the violence wrought by their everyday conduct. This does not necessarily mean that such violence goes unrecorded, but such records may remain silent, unincorporated into the narratives of history that dominate.

The quotation that frames this chapter is from an essay by scholar Saidiya Hartman, in which she reflects on the experience of 'slavery tourism' as an African-American woman visiting Elmina Castle in Ghana, identified as the embarkation point of no return for the transatlantic trade in people.[16] She names as 'dusk' – a dusk which has endured for over four hundred years – the hope and possibility of some kind of release or recovery from the inheritances of slavery, a hope and possibility which is always still-to-arrive. In this, Hartman alludes to the work of early sociologist W E B Du Bois who named his autobiographical theorization of race *Dusk of Dawn*, with the idea that, in 1940, at the age of seventy-two, he may be finally witnessing the eve of liberation and change for black Americans.[17] The point about this 'dusk before dawn' is that we are still waiting for dawn.

In making the link with Hartman's work on the ongoing legacies of slavery, I am pointing to a theme that has run through this chapter – that history is never over. The things that have happened come back to haunt us, but just as important is the selection of which things that have happened are remembered, and how, and by whom. The deliberate institutional 'forgetting', ignoring, erasure of colonial crimes in Kenya and elsewhere that was achieved through the destruction and migration of archival records did not mean that those violent crimes didn't happen or indeed that they had been entirely forgotten. The restoring of that violence to the public record, and the fight by the survivors of that violence to reverse the ignorance around it, meant a rewriting of history – but one based on reversing ignorance of what had really happened.

In parallel, this chapter will discuss what became known as the Windrush Scandal, in which the lack of a formal record of the status of British Commonwealth citizens who arrived in the UK in the mid-twentieth century was based on institutional decisions about what was important to document, which changed over time. Though governmental requirements for records from individuals changed, this did not mean that the facts of those individuals' histories had changed, and yet their histories suddenly came into question in dramatic and traumatizing ways in the present. The facts of what had happened had not changed; the archive of what happened had been constructed without valuing a record of what happened to them.[18] Once the narrative around their presence changed, these gaps in the archive mattered more. These gaps in the archive, and consequent ignorance, are increasingly vocally coming into question within educational settings through movements to 'decolonise the curriculum', and the resistance to this questioning also reminds us of the importance of knowledge (or ignorance) of the past to maintaining structures of often violent inequality. History is a process of remembering and forgetting, but it is never over.

History is a practice of remembering and forgetting

What is visible matters; what is remembered is a choice with consequences, even if it is not always a conscious choice. Governments and bureaucracies are tools of memory and tools of national memory in particular. Anthropologist Michel-Rolph Trouillot demonstrated one of the most (trans)nationally significant ways in which the construction of history has determined how the Haitian Revolution, an independence movement led by enslaved people to re-establish a nation independent from European rule, was largely omitted from mainstream historical and sociological accounts.[19] One consequence was the formation of pervasive ideas of European superiority (physical, military, economic, strategic, intellectual) being unchallenged by this defeat of European might by people they had oppressed and racialized as inferior. Another consequence was the widespread ignorance of the fact that the penalty enforced by France for Haiti's independence was the requirement that Haiti pay to France compensation of 150 million francs (estimated as $21 billion US dollars today). This was only repaid in full in 1947.[20] That is, the enslavers were paid back for the loss of their 'property' (i.e. enslaved people), whereas those who had been enslaved (and many generations of their descendants) effectively had to pay for their liberty.[21] Ignorance of these payments feeds ignorance of the conditions in which Haiti has remained an economically struggling country, despite its independence and resources, while France has not.

In his book *Silencing the Past*, Trouillot expands on the significance of the (forgetting) of the Haitian revolution in world history, to emphasize how *silence*, or rather *silencing*, is a key element of the writing and telling of history.[22] Whereas an uncritical understanding of history might define it as 'things that have happened', there are of course always some things that have to be left out of the telling of history. Those might be the 'insignificant' things. But who decides what is insignificant, and how?

For Trouillot, silences are introduced at four points in the creation of history:

Silences enter the process of historical production at four crucial moments: the moment of fact creation (the making of sources); the moment of fact assembly (the making of archives); the moment of fact retrieval (the making of narratives); and the moment of retrospective significance (the making of history in the final instance).[23]

Trouillot is clear that this does not mean full-on postmodernism (or 'post-truth') where *anything* can be said to have happened. History – meaning things that happen – leaves material traces, whether in written accounts and cultural products, in buildings, bodies, or monuments for example. These can't be invented out of nothing, but their importance or meaning can change or be exaggerated or diminished. Certain lives can be left out of the telling of history because they are not seen to matter by the teller or because the teller wishes they did not exist.

All of this may seem fairly pedestrian and obvious to many readers, perhaps a shock or abomination to others. The point is that the telling of *some* histories at the exclusion or distortion of others is itself a form of ignorance, often with violent consequences. Having your history erased is an act of violence in itself, if we believe that self-expression and identity are essential to human flourishing. Indeed, the originator of the legal concept of genocide, lawyer Raphael Lemkin, believed cultural genocide, or the destruction of a group's language, culture and institutions, should have been included in the international legal definition of the crime of genocide. This element of violent erasure was not included in the United Nations' 1948 definition of genocide under pressure from Britain, the United States, Canada, Australia and others, who recognized that this would bring those states' treatment of indigenous people into question.[24]

It is important to look at this more broadly too. This can't be an accusatory call against 'all history' as having to be rewritten, to include 'everything'. That is of course preposterous; to tell a story, to make sense of a situation, some information must be selected and other parts left out. The answer is not to try to cram everything in as if absence of ignorance was possible. Rather, it is to recognize that every story, every history, is *partial*; it can only include some things and will always be from a particular perspective, that perspective which tells the story having the power to choose what seems 'significant'. By the same token, ignorance is not avoidable; it is not possible to know everything, and if it were, it would not be possible to make sense of it all at once. The question, then, is how to be aware of what is being ignored, where the knowledge and the account are always partial. It is also important to note that what one person experiences as 'shocking' or a 'new' account is related to their own ignorances – whether complete lack of knowledge or lack of attention, whether deliberate or unrealized – and won't ever be universal.[25]

The question of what is deemed to be important knowledge, what is recorded for posterity, what is deemed worthy of mention from those records, and how these remembered and noted events are assembled and told together, is an ongoing discussion among professional historians. Feminist historians, sociologists and others have pointed to the neglect of women's lives in official records; working-class narratives have been reclaimed as important in understanding social history; the brutality of colonial treatment of indigenous people has been restated for official records.[26] None of these 'discoveries' have been uncontroversial; all of them have been contested by those practising existing forms of violent ignorance by excluding such knowledges – or deeming them unimportant. Refusing to see the lives of working people, of women, of oppressed minorities, as worthy of remembering is not just about dismissing the importance of those lives. It is also a way of blocking the passing on of knowledge about the ways those people survived, the political struggles they undertook and won, and the times they lost and what was taken from them. It denies that knowledge and those resources to the following generations. And when each generation seeks to recover histories of which they have been made ignorant, the backlash from defenders of the official canon is a clue to the importance of historic understanding and legitimizing – or challenging – present-day inequalities of power.

Decolonize and backlash: Violent ignorance is defended and defensive

'Is free speech in British universities under threat?'[27]

'The New Intolerance of Student Activism'[28]

'Politically correct universities "are killing free speech."'[29]

'Never mind Rhodes – it's the cult of the victim that must fall.'[30]

On 9 March 2015, students at the University of Cape Town, South Africa, took a stand – they no longer wished to have to look at the statue of the man who had wreaked the havoc of exploitation, stolen land and resources, dispossession and death, and its legacies including apartheid, on them and their ancestors. They demanded that the statue of Cecil Rhodes be removed from its pride of place on campus. Later that year, students at the University of Oxford were inspired by the South African protests and launched their own campaign, Rhodes Must Fall Oxford (RMFO).[31]

It was never disputed that Rhodes existed or that he was important to the history of the countries of southern Africa. Protesters never called for his memory to be erased or denied that he was significant. What they were protesting was the way that monuments to Rhodes presented his deeds as heroic and valuable. Those deeds included explicit white supremacism, enacted in his leadership in colonizing and violent governing of large swathes of Africa, and earning him comparisons in the 1940s to Hitler.[32] The protesters were asking for *more* attention to the detail, materiality, evidence and truth of history, rather than its erasure. They were asking that ignorance of Rhodes's violence be overcome.[33]

The response of some vocal historians, journalists and politicians was to accuse protesters of both being 'super-sensitive' and trying to 'rewrite history'.[34] One common refrain in such debates is to accuse protesters of neglect of historical context – that Rhodes was 'a man of his time' and should not be judged by 'today's standards'.[35] This is itself a form of wilful ignorance, as it is hard to find a time where 'everyone' thought that enslavement, murder or land grabs were acceptable – that is, if you take 'everyone' to include the people being enslaved, murdered or displaced.

Rhodes lived from 1853 to 1902, and in less than fifty years he stole land, ruled territories, ran a private paramilitary organization, and built up an exploitative global minerals business that controlled 90 per cent of the global diamond production by the time of his death. Some of the wealth he obtained in this way was used to support university education, through the Rhodes Trust set up in his will. This trust helped establish Rhodes University in South Africa and the famous Rhodes scholarship which provides support for overseas students to study at the University of Oxford. His statues in Oxford, Cape Town, and around the world are often claimed now as standing for this 'philanthropic' legacy: the inscription at the feet of the disputed statue at Oriel College in Oxford read (in Latin) 'Out of the splendid generosity of Cecil Rhodes'. This selective memory ignores Rhodes's more brutal history, from which he built the fortune that made this educational investment possible. Beyond this, it is also important to recognize that Rhodes and others like him were not simply sponsoring university education out of an interest in the life of the mind. The university system was set up to produce knowledge and power, and its dependence on money from people like Rhodes has helped to ensure universities' close alliance with the type of knowledge and power they would find acceptable – with its capitalist, patriarchal white supremacist underpinnings.

The difficult cultural work of removing the names of former rulers from liberated states has been documented around the world, from Paraguay to Russia, from Spain to Iraq. But removing statues of a brutal murderer from pride of place is just one demand of the student decolonization movement, albeit one which gave it an evocative name and slogan. Wider demands included examining which histories, thinkers and experiences are validated and taught in universities and who has the authority to decide.[36] Mainstream coverage focused on the statue issue, presenting this as trivial and childish. Infantilizing the demands of a liberation movement is a tried-and-tested oppressor tactic.[37] Recognizing the wider demands of the movement is important, but so is recognizing the significance of the symbolism of retaining the Rhodes statue in pride of place. This is not only about the experience of those who know that such statues revere a man who would have slaughtered them were he still alive and who dispossessed and attacked their ancestors. It is importantly also about the ongoing ignorance of the majority of people who see – or whose gaze slips right past – these statues of mass murdering criminals in our midst. But what would it mean to start focusing on these prominent reminders of the reasons for the current distribution of power, wealth and opportunity?

The Rhodes Must Fall movement is part of a wider call from students in many parts of the world to 'decolonise the curriculum' of schools and universities and to decolonize institutions. Put simply, this is a recognition that in most of the world, the accepted version of history taught in schools, universities, museums and other powerful institutions is a history 'written by the victors' – as put by Winston Churchill, one of the figures whose reputation this movement calls into question.[38] This is not only about the set of facts and stories that are remembered and repeated, but about the influence those histories have had, and still have, on the way that societies are structured – from accepted norms about who has power and who doesn't, what sort of behaviour is worthy of reward or punishment, and the expectations about what it is possible to change and what is not.

The call for decolonization is a call for recognition of (and the need to address) the fact that the current order of the world is only as it is because of centuries of war and violent oppression, torture and theft by the ancestors of many of those people who now hold power and wealth by 'birthright'. Some of the most simple – and probably the least controversial – steps to address this injustice would be the relatively modest proposals made by many decolonizing and anti-racist activists, to address imbalances in educational reading lists, so that students are made aware of literature and science from authors and traditions outside of the white, usually male and wealthy, Euro-American cannon. Even these claims though have been met with vehement opposition and ridicule.[39] Why might that be?

Perhaps it is not surprising that those who benefit from existing structures of power and knowledge (and associated ignorance) would want to defend the way things are. This would explain some of the headlines like those at the start of this section, which characterize the student movement's demands for the end of a reverence of Rhodes and his ilk as misguided attempts to 'erase the past'.[40] However, the aim of the Rhodes Must Fall activists, and the wider movement aiming to decolonize the curriculum, is precisely the opposite of this – it is about making the past known.

One area in which ignorance and its violence persist is the idea that the damage of colonialism ended with the end of European empires. As European empires withdrew their claims of sovereignty over other parts of the world throughout the twentieth century, national populations were able to, in varying degrees, establish functioning democracies and their own governments. However, in very many cases, the struggle for sovereignty could not be the end of colonial relations. Firstly, the damage wrought by European nations' struggles over land, resources and people had over centuries built up ethnicized divisions and unmanageable designations of land borders that meant damage to peaceful life could last for generations. Secondly, the withdrawing imperial powers often did so in a way that made their former colonies remain economically and diplomatically dependent on them for time to come. Finally, the tentacles of global capitalism established hand in hand with imperialism meant that global hierarchies of wealth and dependence were already established beyond the direct government of nation states.

In this sense then, decolonization – in the sense of dismembering the legacies of colonialism – remains an ongoing political project around the world. Given the breadth and depth of (post)colonialism's reach, it may seem odd to concentrate on the removal of statues and amendments to reading lists. Tackling these issues does not preclude other urgent issues such as the redistribution of wealth, rising sea levels and global temperatures, extinction crises, access to healthcare, sanitation and housing, or equitable decision-making. But it is also important in itself, because the mindset in which such changes to the global order seem impossible is brought about by only considering the world as it has been presented to us by institutional power. Established orders of history, knowledge and ideas are orders that exclude some knowledge and ignore the value of some – particular – lives. It is in this context that institutional indifference can lead to deadly consequences for those lives whose histories and archives are considered disposable or easy to ignore.

Destroying records, destroying lives: Windrush

In November 2017, Sylvester Marshall was referred to a London hospital for twelve weeks of radiotherapy as treatment for prostate cancer. When he arrived for his first treatment, he was told he must provide a British passport to the hospital staff or pay £54,000 to receive the life-saving treatment – which he had expected to be provided for free through the NHS for which he had paid tax and National Insurance for forty-four years. Sylvester wasn't just ill with a life-threatening illness, and it wasn't just that he had been refused treatment to which he was entitled (and for which he could not afford to pay anything, never mind such an exorbitant sum). He was also, suddenly, being told that he did not belong in the country where he lived, and had lived since he was nineteen.[41]

In October 2017, Paulette Wilson was arrested and taken to Yarl's Wood Immigration Removal Centre and held in a cell from which she heard women screaming throughout the night. She was detained there for a week and then moved to another detention facility at Heathrow Airport in preparation to be 'removed' to Jamaica, a place she had not even visited for five decades. It was the second time Paulette was detained, having been held for a few hours in August that year but released because the detention centres were full. This was the culmination of two years of receiving threatening official letters from the Home Office, telling her she must leave the country she had lived legally in since 1968, and that anyone renting her a place to live or employing her could be heavily fined; of being required to report weekly or fortnightly to a Home Office reporting centre 40 miles from her home; of living under constant threat with no income; of going without food and being supported by her daughter's part-time school dinner supervisor wages, but being told that any legal support to remedy the situation would cost as much as £5,000.

How did this happen to British citizens? As the widespread ignorance around the situation of Paulette, Sylvester and many others was punctured, they became referred to in shorthand as 'the Windrush generation', and their experiences as 'the Windrush Scandal'. The Windrush was the name of a ship remembered for bringing many of what are popularly known as the 'first wave' of Caribbean people to Britain after the Second World War.[42] Most of those affected by the hostile environment in what became known as the 'Windrush Scandal', like Sylvester and Paulette, were actually the children of that generation of Commonwealth citizens. They came to Britain as British Commonwealth Citizens – and they had that status because of the legacy of generations of British colonization. As the aphorism usually attributed to leading anti-racist intellectual Ambalavaner Sivanandan has it 'We are here because you were there'.[43] When they came, they were perfectly entitled to by British law – many, like Sylvester and Paulette, came to join their parents who had arrived in the immediate post–Second World War period to help with the reconstruction of Britain. Since their arrival though, British immigration law has gone through a succession of changes, meaning that while individual people may not have moved or changed their personal circumstances in any way, the British state has begun to treat them as if they had no right to live in the UK.

There were three stages to the process that led to this particular situation, and each are processes of enforcing/enabling ignorance and its violent consequences. We can also think of these stages in relation to Michel-Rolph Trouillot's stages of the production of silences in history (introduced earlier in this chapter).[44]

The first step was in the 1971 Immigration Act, which restricted the rights of Commonwealth citizens to settle in the UK. This was part of a series of laws which began in the 1960s, which tended to treat the unsettling 'coming home' of empire to the UK in the form of racially minoritized arrivals, as a problem to be solved on two levels.[45] On the one hand, there was the introduction of laws mitigating the ill-treatment of racially minoritized people. On the other, there was the restriction of further migration through new laws about entitlements to move, through successive Immigration Acts. The 1971 Act in particular was controversial and notorious because it included what became known as 'the patriality clause'. This was a statement that defined a 'patrial' as a citizen of Britain or its colonies who was born in Britain, or who had a parent or grandparent born in Britain, or who had previously settled in Britain and resided there five years or more.[46] Only people defined as 'patrials' had the right of abode in Britain and could enter Britain without special permission such as a work permit. Citizens of British colonies whose parents and grandparents were born in British territory, but not in mainland Britain, did not retain the right of abode in Britain once the Act came into force. In effect, this meant that the right to move to the UK was maintained or even increased for, in the vast majority, white citizens (particularly of countries such as Australia, New Zealand, Canada and South Africa, collectively known as the Old Commonwealth) while it was ended, in the vast majority, for Commonwealth citizens who were not white (from the other former British Empire territories or the New Commonwealth – so called because they achieved independence from colonial rule much later than the Old Commonwealth). Race was enshrined in immigration law and knowingly so.[47] However, what was important about the 1971 Act for Paulette, Sylvester and countless others was that it (a) effectively cut off new migration from Caribbean countries to the UK, while those who had moved before 1 January 1973 (when the 1971 Act came into force) remained entitled to stay, and (b) *no action was taken to document the status of those who had arrived before 1973*. In contrast to the pathological documenting of British exploits in Kenya and other colonies discussed earlier in this chapter, the documenting of those legally present appeared to be of little interest to the British government. It was this issue which caused problems decades later. We could see this failure to make a record of individuals' statuses as the production of a historical silence at the point of 'fact creation' or the 'making of sources'.[48] That is, the information – and the lives it related to – were not considered important enough to remember, so were ignored.

Many people who arrived from the Commonwealth before 1973 did subsequently seek paperwork that proved their entitlement to live in the UK, for example when applying for a passport. Because no certificates had been issued when they arrived (as their nationality at that point entitled them to British residence) or since (because this was not seen as an issue by British officials at the time), they had to be able to document their arrival before 1973. Passport officials became accustomed to identifying appropriate documentation, such as landing cards from Windrush and other ships, all of which were kept in the Home Office archive. However, in 2009, in a 'rationalisation' of records and office space, the then Labour government made the decision to destroy the old landing card records, for the sake of storage space. Little public attention was drawn to this internal matter at the time, though some Home Office officials said later that they had raised the potential problems this may cause and had asked that the transfer of the records to a public archive be considered.[49] In 2010, under new Conservative Home Secretary Theresa May, the plan was carried out and the landing cards were destroyed.

This was the second step of violent ignorance, and though it enacted some violence at the time, in the form of enforced ignorance – the destruction of the historical record and basis for official claims of many individuals – it was also apparently an act of ignorance in itself. The landing cards were not recognized as important; the relatively small numbers of people who might need them in future were not considered. And this all occurred at the same time as immigration officials in the Home Office were being deskilled and demotivated, and many with institutional memory were leaving the profession, so that the importance of those archives to casework was slowly erased from institutional memory.[50] This seems to fit with Trouillot's second stage of the production of silences in the making of history: at 'the moment of fact assembly (the making of archives)', when what evidence there was of Commonwealth citizens' arrivals was deemed not worthy of retaining in the archival record.[51]

The final action that led to the Windrush Scandal was the introduction of new powers in the Immigration Acts of 2014 and 2016. These were the major legislative interventions by then Home Secretary Theresa May which enforced the 'hostile environment' on immigration. It became necessary to check a person's right to residence in the UK before providing them with a home to rent, social services including welfare payments, a bank account or driving licence; severe fines and potential prison sentences were introduced, and then increased, for landlords, employers or others who failed to properly check the details of others. The apparent intention was to target foreign nationals, to make Britain hostile to their survival. But everyone's papers had to be checked, and this included British nationals and those with indefinite leave to remain. It also meant that many more people were involved in implementing the hostile environment. Suddenly, people who had lived decades or their whole lives in Britain were required to prove their right to do so, and if they did not have a UK birth certificate or a passport this proved difficult. This couldn't be solved simply by applying for a passport, because one of the key pieces of evidence that would prove their date of arrival had been destroyed in 2010. This was not the only problem though; even with the landing card, it was necessary to provide up to four items of documentary evidence for every year of residence since 1973, meaning national insurance records, school attendance and so on – things few people keep to document their entire life over decades and which can be hard to reconstruct retrospectively.[52]

As a result, many people were denied access to essential healthcare, to living support, to homes and work; some were detained; some were deported. This began happening to this group as the Immigration Act 2014 came into effect. But it was hidden. Few knew about it apart from the people involved.

In 2017, Guardian journalist Amelia Gentleman[53] began to publish a series of investigative pieces exposing the attacks of the hostile environment on the Windrush Generation. She told the stories of Paulette Wilson and Sylvester Marshall and of many others.[54] Gentleman's investigations demonstrated how the links in the chain outlined above enabled the state violence experienced by this group of people as part of the hostile environment. Her journalism and attention paid to the following up of these individual stories, and the highlighting of a much wider pattern of actions by the Home Office, was instrumental in puncturing the violent ignorance around what had become a systematic campaign of targeting vulnerable people who might be unable to provide the paperwork needed to meet new government requirements and lack the resources to challenge Home Office action.

Gentleman's newspaper articles began being published in 2017, and a national audience became aware of this situation. And yet it did not become headline news and a political crisis until 2018, leading eventually to Home Secretary Amber Rudd resigning over related issues on 29 April 2018. What was it that allowed this crisis to eventually break through the fortified walls of violent ignorance to require reparative action?

This puzzled me at first, because the action did not coincide with the initial making-public of the situation, nor with the community activism which tried to draw attention to the situation before that.[55] But what made it matter was a strategic, political, planned intervention that would require the British prime minister to confront the situation and the violence inflicted by her government head-on and in public and force a response. This intervention was enabled by Guy Hewitt, the High Commissioner of Barbados in London, who, like many including other Caribbean politicians, was frustrated by the lack of meaningful action by the British government to rectify their mistakes. It so happened that a regular Commonwealth Heads of Government Meeting (CHOGM) was due to take place in London in April 2018. For the Heads of many Commonwealth nations, this was an opportunity to use political levers. When the British prime minister, Theresa May, refused to meet privately with the Caribbean Heads of Government about the issue during their visit, Hewitt went public with this snub.[56] As a result, May was forced to explain at the CHOGM in public, in front of news cameras, what she was doing about the situation of effective statelessness she was putting lawful British residents into. Her 'apology' was limited to being 'genuinely sorry for any anxiety that has been caused', while also effectively admitting that the hostile environment she had implemented was responsible for the situation.[57]

This forced the government's hand, and a high-profile resignation followed. More meaningfully perhaps, an inquiry and a compensation scheme were introduced. Many lives remain wrecked by the violent ignorance that led to the Windrush Scandal: people who remain homeless, unemployed or indebted as a result of the wrongful disqualifications; people who have been deported; people who missed relatives' funerals. Wrangling continues over whether the compensation arrangements can be considered adequate, or what they might run to if they were; several victims of the scandal have died before receiving either apologies or compensation.[58] Nevertheless, this form of resistance *did*, for a moment, enable a rupture in the skin of violent ignorance that led to some change in the shape of the ongoing violence.

The fact that the Home Office's treatment of Windrush people became treated as a national scandal was in part because of how the arrival of British Commonwealth citizens had been incorporated into Britain's national story – what in Trouillot's framework would be called 'the moment of fact retrieval (the making of narratives)'.[59] For example, GCSE history syllabuses refer to this as when people from the Commonwealth came to 'help rebuild Britain' after the Second World War, during which much of the country's infrastructure had been destroyed, many people of working age had died, and much money and wealth had been spent.[60] Sometimes it is emphasized that these new arrivals came on the express *invitation* of the British government. Occasionally it is added that some of them also fought for Britain in the war effort. In one symbolic moment of nationalism, at the opening ceremony of the 2012 Olympics in London, a replica of the Windrush boat was included as part of the national story in the extravaganza of a dance and display of Britain's history which also included the workers of the industrial revolution, the NHS, suffragettes, the invention of the worldwide web and a multicultural/

mixed-race household as the culmination of modern Britain. Commonwealth – and specifically Caribbean Commonwealth – migration has, then, been accepted – through both processes of political struggle and of 'multicultural drift'[61] – as part of the British national story, but this has largely been about what that group can *give* to Britain, rather than an interest in their own personal welfare or stories. This latter aspect has been where some silences enter the narrative.

This is partly why the Windrush Scandal was recognized as so scandalous. The story was that many Black British people, people who had come to the country legitimately and as British subjects, and people born in the UK, people who had met the criteria for the 'respectable migrant' by 'working hard all their lives and paying tax',[62] respectable *British* people, even to the extent of being described by extreme social traditionalist and cartoonishly posh Conservative MP Jacob Rees-Mogg as 'as British as you or I',[63] were being made destitute, detained, and deported as part of regular immigration controls. The violence of immigration controls was made visible, but it was particularly made to matter because it seemed to be being applied to 'the wrong people'.

This idea that the 'Scandal' was that the effects of the hostile environment were being felt by 'the wrong people' recurs throughout discussion of what happened.[64] The things that were happening to members of the Windrush generation were wrong in the public mind, but they were largely wrong because these were (generally accepted to be) *British* people – not suspicious foreigners. Such an analysis enables an ongoing ignoring of the broader question of whether such treatment is acceptable when applied to *anyone*. Both anti-racist campaigners and the most anti-immigration politicians abided by this line, the latter using it to suggest that the problem was not the hostile environment itself, but its implementation. The alternative –

to stand by the visible institutional racism of this case – would be seen to be directly equating race and migration status. That might lose the hostile environment credibility, in a society where it remains taboo to stand by explicitly racist policies or views, even while carrying out or advocating for actions that enforce racialized inequalities, such as the operation of immigration controls.[65]

This separating off of the Windrush Scandal means that rather than drawing attention to the wide-reaching and racialized effects of the hostile environment, it is treated as an aberration. Indeed, the widespread outrage at the treatment of the Windrush group has been claimed as evidence that 'British people are not quite as racist as their government took them to be.'[66] This works from one angle: that there was public concern (including surprisingly from the right-wing, anti-immigration *Daily Mail*)[67] about the treatment of Black British Caribbean people was seen as evidence of a widespread understanding, otherwise feared absent, that Britishness does not necessarily equate with whiteness. However, the flipside of this was that the Windrush people were treated as British and therefore not deserving such hostile treatment, leaving it acceptable that such treatment be meted out to non-British people. It is also notable that discussion of the Windrush Scandal – including in Home Office statements and responses throughout – emphasized the 'contributions' made to Britain by British Commonwealth citizens, with an emphasis particularly on being hardworking and paying tax. This suggests that such inclusiveness in the British nation remains conditional on this type of respectable behaviour – what anthropologist Bridget Anderson has called being a 'tolerated citizen', someone who must prove their worth rather than being straightforwardly accepted as part of the nation.[68] A more secure, unconditional acceptance as belonging to Britain has always been more accessible for those racialized as white.[69]

***

This chapter has considered how violent ignorance is historical – in two senses. Firstly, violent ignorance is not something new; we have seen some of the ways in which the deliberate ignoring or concealing of 'difficult' knowledge took place in the past and continues to reverberate in the present. Secondly, violent ignorance is also a part of the practice of constructing history as we know it. The decision about what is worth remembering, and what should be ignored, is acknowledged by most professional historians as central to how we know what we know about the past (and the present). From recording and concealment of histories of colonial crimes in Kenya and elsewhere, to the erasure of records of British Commonwealth citizens' rights in the UK, this chapter has considered how official recording and social memory have roles in instigating and resisting ignorance, violence and the potential violence of ignorance as produced through history.

In Saadiya Hartman's reflections at Elmina Castle, Ghana, discussed earlier, she also considers the complexities of identifications of tourists with their ancestors who survived – or did not survive – the torture of kidnap, transport and slavery. While the pain of the inheritance of slavery endures, Hartman argues, the position of African-American tourists to Ghana is not a 'return' of the people who were stolen from Ghana originally. The visitors arrive generations later, with wildly different circumstances. And yet Hartman also feels the appeal of such an identification as it offers some kind of repair and belonging – but one which is never attained. The next chapter moves on to consider how this lingering and unfinished business of the remembering and forgetting of history, its processes of violent ignorance, matter even in our most intimate self-identifications as individuals and within families.

5

Haunting families

[B]etween us … and the worlds we encounter … are hauntings …
seething absences, and muted presences.

– AVERY GORDON, *GHOSTLY MATTERS: HAUNTING AND*
THE SOCIOLOGICAL IMAGINATION[1]

Ben Affleck's family secrets

In 2014, Hollywood star Ben Affleck appeared on the popular US ancestry-tracing television show *Finding Your Roots*. The broadcast episode included footage of Affleck discovering that his mother, Chris Boldt, had been an active civil rights campaigner in the 1960s. This fitted well with Affleck's well-documented interest in liberal social justice campaigns.

The following year, however, it became public that Affleck had chosen to follow only those branches of his family tree which fitted with his carefully sculpted public persona. When entertainment company Sony's emails were hacked and released by Wikileaks in 2015, this included an exchange about Affleck's episode between the *Finding Your Roots* presenter, Henry Louis Gates Jr, and Sony Entertainment executive Michael Lynton. These emails made clear that the search through Affleck's ancestors had also revealed that his great-great-

great grandfather, Benjamin Cole, had owned slaves.[2] Affleck had asked that this information not be included in the broadcast footage, and the company complied. An email from Lynton suggests that 'the big question is who knows that the material is in the doc and is being taken out. I would take it out if no one knows, but if it gets out that you are editing the material based on this kind of sensitivity then it gets tricky'. Gates replies that '[t]o do this would be a violation of PBS rules, actually, even for Batman' (Affleck was then starring as the superhero).[3] Nevertheless, the edits were made.

Lynton's assessment was correct – once the emails were leaked the news about Affleck covering up his ancestors' exploitation became a much bigger news story than the original revelation might have been. Affleck insisted that he had asked for the changes 'the same way I lobby directors about what takes of mine I think they should use', and this wasn't about covering up or privileged hiding of dirty secrets. 'I didn't want any television show about my family to include a guy who owned slaves. I was embarrassed,' he said in a public statement on Facebook. Affleck's statement emphasized that he wanted to distance himself from relatives who had profited from the slave trade and concluded his public statement with the assertion that 'we deserve neither credit nor blame for our ancestors'.[4]

What angered people about this episode did not appear to be that Affleck had been descended from slave-owners. Indeed, it might be an expected outcome of a family history search among wealthy white Americans, in a country built on the dispossession of indigenous lands and the enslavement of people kidnapped from Africa and elsewhere. As work by historian Catherine Hall and her colleagues has shown, many ordinary people in Britain and elsewhere may find themselves to be descended from slave-owners, as even the unspectacularly wealthy often held shares in other human beings' enslavement.[5]

Ben Affleck, like anyone else, has no control over who his ancestors are or what they did. In that sense, no one was trying to 'blame' him for his ancestors. The problem was his decision to ignore their history and what it might mean for his own life and his (and his family's) position in society. Though he says 'we deserve neither credit nor blame for our ancestors', his behaviour suggests that he believed the opposite – or at least that he would be given credit or blame for the ancestors he chose to remember. A civil rights activist in the family may indeed be something to be proud of, while a slave-owner is not. But what does it mean to only remember the 'good' and forget the 'bad'?

In part the problem with Affleck's actions was they seemed hypocritical. If we deserve neither credit nor blame for our ancestors, then why associate oneself with the civil rights hero? The suspicion of course is that Affleck was worried about public relations, that association with a slave-owner would tarnish his brand and thereby cost him money – and he was in a position of power to stop this happening. In doing so, he was also erasing the history of the people enslaved and exploited by his ancestor, who, directly or indirectly, contributed to his current wealth and power.

This is not to say that Affleck's revulsion and refusal of his ancestor's actions were not real or understandable. Many other people will choose particular branches of their family tree to remember or revere, whether for reasons of internal feuds, romantic exotic associations or excitement – while others are ignored as less interesting or more shameful.[6] The reason I am dwelling on Ben Affleck's dilemma and decision is that it brings three things to light: (1) the immediate relevance of history to our present social reality, (2) the desire to hide from painful histories and (3) the ways in which ignored, painful histories can and will rise up to haunt us in disruptive, violent ways – whether these are national histories or family ones.

Haunting and ancestors

Affleck's search was part of a wider popular interest in ancestry tracing, which has been boosted in recent decades by increasing ease of access to records through digitization of archives, online forms of connection and sharing of information (e.g. through Ancestry. com and others) and increasing use of DNA matching technologies to supplement historical record searches. Popular television shows like *Who Do You Think You Are?* (with versions in at least eighteen countries) and *Finding Your Roots* on which Affleck appeared, both spring from and encourage this trend. Academics fascinated by the ancestry tracing industry have asked, largely, what it means for people to do this. And many have found that an important part of the long-standing desire of many people to find out who their ancestors were springs from a desire to understand their own identity and place in the world.[7]

So it follows that this desire in itself is one that recognizes, at least implicitly, that history is important in shaping our present. But what happens when that history reveals some uncomfortable information about how we come to be who and where we are? This, essentially, is what happened to Affleck. And it is not uncommon. In research into 'family secrets' using data from the UK mass observation archive, sociologist Carol Smart found that many families have shared knowledge of their present and past that they choose to ignore and to avoid discussing. This might range from relatives being born outside marriage to personal grievances over money.[8] Whether these are 'secrets' discovered through archival searches, or from the more recent past and living memory, the desire to avoid thinking about them – to know while not knowing or to ignore – does not stop their influence or presence.

This is what we might call 'haunting', following the work of sociologist Avery Gordon.[9] The real ghosts that haunt us aren't made of ectoplasm. Gordon, whose statement opens this chapter, uses haunting to mean 'an animated state in which a repressed or unresolved social violence is making itself known, sometimes very directly, sometimes more obliquely'.[10] Drawing on psychoanalytical theory, Gordon argues that even what we cannot see can still determine our desires and actions. I would add that this is not simply a psychoanalytical effect, but a very material one too. Ben Affleck's life, like anyone else's, has been determined by the social status, wealth and power (or lack of it) that his ancestors had, and the interactions between those ancestors and the people around them.

While Affleck chose to actively ignore his shameful slave-owning family, that 'unresolved social violence [made] itself known', first through the researchers on *Finding Your Roots* and then more explosively through his attempt to repress this knowledge. As others have pointed out, there were other ways that Affleck could have approached this distasteful knowledge about his family in reparative, rather than repressive ways. For example, actor Bill Paxton, appearing on *Who Do You Think You Are?* in 2015, similarly found he was descended from slave-owners, but as a result chose to change the direction of his historical research to uncover and make known the history of one of the men enslaved by this ancestor. This approach recognized the wrongs of Paxton's ancestor, without celebrating the connection, but instead seeking in a minor way to repair the damage by understanding other histories that man had helped to erase.[11]

In this chapter, I want to build on the recognition in Chapter 4 that violent ignorance is part of writing histories, and that violent ignorance is an ongoing historical phenomenon, to look at how consequences of violent ignorance resurface – or haunt – the present in more personal ways, by focusing on the importance of family history and genealogy. In Ben Affleck's case, the 'hidden' history which he found shameful was the history of the power his ancestor had held as an oppressor of enslaved people. More commonly, oppressor histories are remembered and celebrated, even if their violence may become less emphasized in the retelling – think of the statues of men who slaughtered thousands standing in public squares around the world or the grand buildings of state and industry built on the back of enslaved populations in industries such as sugar and tobacco as well as slavery, which make up the grandeur of many European cities like Liverpool, Bristol, Marseille or Lisbon.

The histories that tend to be forgotten, or hidden, are those that were deliberately erased as unworthy or oppressed, as we saw in the previous chapter in relation to, for example, the behaviour of British colonists in Kenya. In more personal terms, individuals and families who have been convinced that their histories are shameful tend not to be those whose ancestors did something to hurt others (as with the Afflecks) but who were stigmatized and mistreated by others – for example, indigenous people robbed of their pasts, enslaved people forcibly transported around the world or families separated by institutions as a result of their abject poverty. When this shame resurfaces, are there ways of reclaiming this haunting as resistance?

While there may be a simplicity in agreeing with Ben Affleck that 'we deserve neither credit nor blame for our ancestors', the experience of many people is that ancestors have meaning and give meaning to their own lives. Even where this is not the case, or for people who do not know or have no interest in the lives of their ancestors, their inheritance – whether this be of wealth or of genetics or of social status or norms – does shape most people's lives. What does it mean to look to one's ancestors for explanations of one's own life, when doing so reveals the ways that racialization and national exclusions enabled or disabled their flourishing or the flourishing of others? Even if we are not deserving of credit or blame for our ancestors, should we take responsibility for them? What would this look like? This question may seem quite different for those who identify 'victims' in their history and those who identify 'perpetrators' – or bystanders. Is it different? What about those of us descended from both victim and perpetrator?

Discussing how people come to terms with their (family) pasts keeps coming back to the question – does it matter? Does it matter if we cannot see the relevance of those histories, and does it matter if we do confront them? And how can we confront them and break through the veil of violent ignorance?

Ancestral explanations

I first became fascinated with people's fascination with family history tracing when conducting an interview for my PhD fieldwork, on a completely different topic. I was interviewing UK local government officers about their views and experiences of implementing community cohesion policy.[12] At the end of the interview, I would ask each person whether their 'background or experiences' influenced the way they thought about community cohesion policy, to give an opportunity for them to reflect on how personal biography might impact on their work as bureaucrats or policy professionals. In one interview, I was struck by a senior manager's response:

> '[A] week ago I would have answered that a bit differently'. In the past week he had discovered ancestors who had been 'very active on interethnic and interfaith issues' in previous centuries, 'a strong tradition of serving the community and work in public service' in his family, which he now thought was 'part of the reason why

I've ended up in this job' because of 'values that have come down through my parents and my family'. I asked what he thought his answer might have been before he knew this history, and he said 'the bit about values would have been the same' but now he had 'the feeling that what I'm doing fit[s] so well with what some of my forebears did'.[13]

What I found intriguing about this answer was the way that this information seemed to have shifted the manager's understanding of his own personality and life history. Before he had that information, he had no idea that this ancestor existed or, it seemed, any inkling that his line of work came from a longer genealogical influence ('I would have given you a completely different answer'). Suddenly, his work made sense in a different sort of way, which, for him, situated him as directly connected to a long line of community workers.

Researchers working with family genealogists have found this kind of association to be common. While family history research often begins as a hobby or idle interest, for other people it can be a quest to track down a family legend or a desire to provide information for children or grandchildren about their origins. The quest often leads amateur genealogists to find particular affinities with some parts of their family tree, or particular figures, and to start to construct their own narratives of the connection between their characteristics, or the characteristics of relatives in living memory, with these long-lost ancestors.[14] Often benign, these stories can feel reassuring of one's place in the world – much as feeling belonging to a nation and its most proud version of history might feel reassuring.

With the growth of DNA technology and matching services, the amateur genealogist is no longer limited to dusty records when searching for familial connections. There are many services which will offer to tell a person the 'percentage' of different ethnicities in their blood, as well as seeking matches with other people who have had DNA tests. The geographic matching algorithms are questionable on many levels and have been criticized for their reliance on partial measurement and reification of racialized categories as if fixed.[15] Nevertheless, many people take these results very seriously and again can use them to reassess their own sense of identity and place in the world. Researchers Wendy Roth and Biorn Ivemark, interviewing US citizens who had received DNA test results for ethnicity, found that many then sought to incorporate this previously unknown 'heritage' into their identities, in varying ways including adopting a new ethnic or racial identity, learning new languages or dressing in the style of their newly discovered ancestors. Others, however, rejected test results which did not conform to their expectations or hopes.[16]

These ancestral 'discoveries' are different, I think, to an uncovering of or resistance to violent ignorance. In some cases, they reproduce a different kind of ignorance or refusal of uncomfortable knowledge. This could be seen for example in the row over the US Democratic Senator and potential Presidential candidate Elizabeth Warren's claim to indigenous American ancestry. While her intention in publicizing her DNA finding that 'between 1/64 and 1/1,024' of her ancestry was 'Native American' was variously characterized as an attempt at solidarity and recognition, or at political opportunism,[17] some indigenous scholars took a different perspective. As anthropologist Kim Tallbear explained, Warren's claims centre measures conducted and controlled by mainly settler-owned DNA testing companies and do not take into account the self-definition and self-government of the Cherokee Nation to which she claims belonging:

> Tribal governments establish regulations that do not use genetic ancestry tests, but other forms of biological and political relationships to define our citizenries.[18]

Warren's identification, while perhaps meant as an act of solidarity and recognition, played out instead as a colonial claiming of the right to an identity based in an ignorance of that identity. We might think of this as an instance of 'whiteness' as a form of property, identified and expanded on by legal scholars Cheryl Harris and Aileen Moreton-Robinson.[19] Thinking about whiteness as ownership, or entitlement to ownership (of people, property or rights), allows us to also see how this white entitlement can also encompass the expectation of taking on minority identities as property or as accessories that can be picked up and put down, rather than as experience and belonging.

Whereas Elizabeth Warren or the people in Roth and Ivemark's study were interested in exploring racialized parts of their identity that they never knew existed, the motivations appear as if they are all about the present, rather than about understanding the histories that produced the present. Taking ancestry as an outcome, rather than a process, is a form of violent ignorance that erases social interactions and meanings and instead takes on a shallow presentism about meanings of belonging. Rather than being 'haunted', this type of approach seems like the cheap thrill of a ghost-town fairground ride.

Post-generation trauma

Different images or promptings 'prick' the learned ignorance of different people differently, as we saw in Chapter 2. We notice different resonances because we have different histories, awareness, interests. But these noticings, or punctures, are real moments with power, consequence and histories of their own – and futures they may put in motion. They are important precisely because they seem ineffable or silent – because some people can ignore them while others cannot look away.

In September 2015, journalists reported refugees being crammed onto trains at the Hungarian border, told they were heading to Austria and Germany, to find themselves instead deposited at a Hungarian migrant reception centre. Some refused to disembark from the trains; others were pictured lying across tracks in protest.[20] This was reported widely as just another event in the tragedy of what was, that summer, termed 'the European migrant crisis'. But for me, the images of the crowded train, redirected by officials, bit into my awareness in a particularly visceral way.[21] It was partly the mirroring of how trains were used (including in that specific part of Europe) as tools in the Nazi genocide. It was also a specific, personal link I felt as the granddaughter of a German Jew who escaped on a passenger train in 1938, when he was a worried twelve-year-old angry to be leaving his home, kept in check by his parents fearful that their journey out of Nuremberg might be halted. This heritage is a troubling one to interpret; not only did my immediate family survive and thrive (while helping others to escape), but German laws on reparations to the descendants of those denied German citizenship meant I have been able to gain dual UK/German citizenship and remain 'in the EU' post-Brexit. 'Lucky you,' people say.

What I am most interested in here is the bringing together of the question of haunting and the question of violent ignorance. Is it possible that we can draw on the memories of (and disgust at) older examples of violent ignorance to mobilize a recognition of violent ignorance in the present – and to counter it? Could resonances with how previous generations initially ignored genocides and refugees, and the consequences of that ignorance, be a spur to action now?

Literature scholar Marianne Hirsch coined the terms 'post-memory' and 'post-generation' to talk about these ways in which the trauma of the European Holocaust of the twentieth century has woven itself into the lives of the children, grandchildren and other descendants of survivors.[22] Hirsch and many others turn to the 1987 comic-book memoir *Maus*, by Art Spiegelman, as a classic example of this cultural haunting.[23] In *Maus*, Spiegelman depicts his conversations with his father, Vladek, an Auschwitz survivor in the United States, about their life when Art was a child and the life before, in Poland, and Art's mother Anja's suicide. In the text, the Spiegelman family and other Jews are depicted as mice – or rather, as human-like creatures with mouse heads – while Nazis are cat-like creatures, (non-Jewish) Poles are pig-like creatures and so on. While the cartoon animal-like depiction is seen as a distancing technique, the text is full of pathos and vivid detail. The crux of its importance though is as a testament to the experience of being a *child of* Holocaust survivors.

Spiegelman tells the story of persecution, capture and escape as *his* story, while it is also his parents' story and not something that happened to him. And yet, in the text, he shows that its reverberations are still things that kept happening to him – his mother's depression and suicide, his father's fears and habits – while at the same time he never had to face the life-threatening, crushing and genocidal encounters they did. *Maus* is a classic, but far from the only text or cultural product that engages with the experience of the 'post-generation' in this way, of trying to make sense of a trauma that did not happen to the author, but to their parents or grandparents. Hirsch and others have documented and analysed such cultural products as a major wave of Euro-American literature and culture in the late twentieth and early twenty-first century.

The 'post-trauma' of those who were not survivors but the descendants of survivors of trauma is a controversial topic. In particular, a large proportion of this 'post-generation' (in which I could include myself) are in many ways socially privileged. Though Jewishness does not always equate to whiteness, the entitlements of whiteness are accessed by many of Jewish descent. Children of Holocaust survivors may well have lost large swathes of family, kin and friends, and the consequences of this for their childhood may have been severe. Though survivors, forced immigration is not a small matter. There are things to make sense of, and traumas to overcome, but how can this be related to the present? Is it a co-opting of ancestral trauma, a dwelling in the past? How can these understandings and experiences be honoured and respected in the present in relation to our current social situation, rather than an inherited one?

Cultural historian Saidiya Hartman's engagement with the legacies and reverberation of the transatlantic slave trade, and the ways in which descendants of slaves attempt to commemorate and come to terms with ancestral trauma, was mentioned in Chapter 4. In relation to people attempting to understand the impact of unspeakable crimes committed against their ancestors, Hartman asks:

> Can we mourn for those lost without assuming and usurping the place of the dead, and yet recognize that the injuries of racism tether us to this past? Does mourning necessarily entail the obliteration of the other through identification? Can we mourn the dead without becoming them?[24]

These questions, in relation to how to deal with being a descendant of enslaved people, are relevant to the discussions of Holocaust 'post-trauma'. But they also relate to coming to terms with being descended from perpetrators of such crimes. The tendency to see remembering of these pasts as a question of identification with one's ancestors leads directly to refusal such as Ben Affleck's, an insistence that one is not responsible for the actions of the past, and a refusal to 'know' this past. Hartman's questions are about the dangers of present generations overwriting the lives of their ancestors by claiming those past traumas as their own and, through this resignifying, losing the actual meaning and truth of those who suffered. She suggests instead that current generations seek ways to mourn those traumas, to recognize the present but *different* traumas that stem from them, and in doing so to neither ignore the past nor reinvent it.

Again, this is not simply about remembering, but about thinking and questioning – as we saw cultural theorist Susan Sontag suggest in Chapter 2 in relation to memorialization of tragedy. Further provocations from Saidiya Hartman help to make this explicit:

> Can monumentalizing the past suffice in preventing atrocity? Or does it only succeed in framing these crimes against humanity from the vantage point of contemporary progress and reason, turning history into one great museum in which we revel in antiquarian excess?[25]

Here, Hartman is questioning whether the memorializing of the slave trade in itself is enough of a reminder to prevent such horrors occurring again. As with the Holocaust, and with other wars and conflicts, many feel the imperative that 'never again' must this happen might be better secured by ensuring subsequent generations are aware of the scale of such atrocity. In this sense, we might think that public memorials, museums and education programmes dedicated to the memory of the Holocaust, the Transatlantic Slave Trade and other terrible crimes of human history are straightforwardly part of a project to combat violent ignorance, in the sense that such memorials counter ignorance of violence, with the aim of preventing future violence. However, Hartman's questions point to the risk that even such important projects can be sealed over with a film of violent ignorance, if they are treated as preserving such histories in amber, as artefacts from the past rather than as living history which reaches into our present and future.

Perpetrators in the family

The question for those considering their entanglement with perpetrators is differently nuanced. For them, the question is not about honouring one's ancestors, but learning from and understanding what they did and how those deeds relate to the present. Making such pasts felt in the present is unsettling – not least when they are already very close. While Ben Affleck's great-great-great grandfather was safely hidden in generations past until the television programme researchers uncovered him, for the children of genocidal criminals the pain of understanding how one's parents could be loved, or at least the people who made you, while also being inhuman monsters, could be the ultimate test of how to embrace or challenge violent ignorance.

Feminist researcher Susanne Luhmann has spent much time examining how the children and grandchildren of Nazi leaders deal with their family past. Where such descendants have tried to come to terms with their families' deeds through writing memoirs, one can see both how they try to look at and uncover such a past and yet how the desire to look away endures. Luhmann notes that

> these memoirs' very nature is such that these texts rarely can bear to acknowledge the entire extent to which beloved family members were perpetrators and the extent to which members of the extended family supported and sympathized with them.[26]

Sometimes, this can reach the extent of children of Nazi perpetrators presenting themselves as '"victim of the perpetrator father" tend[ing] to erase the identity of the real Nazi victims,' particularly where the story of the crimes is eclipsed by the focus on the familial struggles of the narrator in some accounts.[27] Discussing a memoir by Margaret Nissen, the daughter of Albert Speer, a Nazi armament minister, architect and close ally of Hitler, who was involved in the exploitation of forced labourers and concentration camp prisoners, Luhmann notes Nissen's description of how 'she did not want to know the specific details of what her father did' and that '[t]o maintain such a position of intentional ignorance throughout her adult life takes extraordinary effort'.[28] This was particularly so since Nissen spent over a decade working as a photographer for a memorial museum, which meant she had to reproduce images of Nazi violence and would come across images of herself as a child with her father within the archive. Luhmann draws attention to how Nissen would work with the photographs but refuse to engage with them and would 'actively "un-know"':[29]

> I took them [the pictures], enlarged them, saw them and still did not look at them. […] I did not want to think about the images, I wanted to avoid being confronted with things for which my father may have been responsible, or of which he had possibly known.[30]

While Luhmann notes Nissen's struggle and desire to understand how her life could have turned out 'normally', despite her father's terrible past, the answer to this question, Luhmann argues, is that Nissen was able to be 'normal' by ignoring, or refusing to know, the details of what her father did: '[H]er life's normalcy is a product not just of ignorance or of not knowing; normalcy springs from the refusal or the will to not know'.[31] What must be emphasized here is that Nissen's refusal to know about her father's crimes is almost masked by her endeavour of writing a book about him – or rather, about her relationship to him. While she seems to be looking at and attempting to understand her family history, the way this is approached remains a sealing up of violent ignorance at its heart as the actual crimes are kept out of view.

Does this – understandable – desire not to know about the horrible crimes of one's parents amount to violent ignorance (rather than just ignorance)? That is, what is the violence that is reproduced by refusing this knowledge? While internally families may suffer trauma and misery from repressing the knowledge of parents' crimes, the social consequences of the forgetting and ignoring of family perpetrator histories can also be violent and dangerous. If one is unable to understand – rather than just remember – what happened, how and why how is one to avoid its recurrence?

This is what preoccupies another descendant of a Nazi leader who has made it his life's work to examine and atone for what his father did. Niklas Frank is the son of Hans Frank, who was the head of the German government of occupied Poland during the Second World War, overseeing mass murder and extermination camps, accused of 'the execution of 200,000 Poles, the transfer of hundreds of thousands more to Germany and the creation of the ghetto'.[32] In 1987, Niklas Frank published a memoir about his father, *In the Shadow of the Reich*.[33] In more recent years he was interviewed by the lawyer and author Philippe Sands, for Sands's memoir *East West Street*.[34] Sands found Frank to be 'kindly, gentle but also steely, with his own temperament and agenda'.[35] In recent years, Frank has publicly compared the policies and rhetoric of the AfD (the far-right political party gaining ground in German elections in the 2010s) to that of the Nazi leadership, including his father. This includes a widely circulated essay in German newspaper *Der Spiegel*, which says it all in its title: 'Son of a Nazi war criminal on AfD rhetoric: That's my father talking!'.[36] Niklas Frank straightforwardly argues that lessons of the past must be learnt by recognizing the parallel and warning signs when they re-emerge in the present – and he takes on this upsetting task of reminding people as a mission that is his because of the crimes of his father.

Sands's interviews with Niklas Frank also led him to another son concerned with his own father's Nazi leadership: Horst von Wächter.

Horst's father, Otto von Wächter, was a high-ranking member of the German paramilitaries the SS, and among other things was Nazi governor of Krakow when 68,000 Jews were expelled from the city, keeping the remaining 15,000 within the Krakow ghetto from which attempted escape was met with being shot. According to the *New York Times*, 'Wächter's speciality was described as "the extermination of the Polish intelligentsia".[37] Sands found Horst von Wächter well aware of his father's crimes; indeed, he maintained a library of his father's books and documents.[38] Sands reports Horst as saying:

> I must find the good in my father ... My father was a good man, a liberal who did his best ... Others would have been worse.[39]

Like Margaret Nissen, Horst van Wächter might look directly at the records of his father's deeds but still refuses to know their depths. Whereas Nissen simply refuses to know, Wächter insists that he 'must find the good'. He does so even when confronted by Sands with documentary evidence that his father had known about and chosen to oversee the deportation and mass murder of Jews from the Warsaw ghetto in 1942, even when Heinrich Himmler, head of the SS, gave him the option to leave.[40] Even then, Sands describes how Horst would not condemn his father, and instead telling Sands:

> I have a responsibility for my father in some way, to see what really happened, to tell the truth, and to do what I can do for him ... I have to find some positive aspect. ... I know that the whole system was criminal and that he was part of it, but I don't think he was a criminal. He didn't act like a criminal.[41]

The conclusion Sands draws from this is that Horst remains reluctant to blame his father, even in the face of the evidence that he did have a choice and chose to continue directing atrocities. The shocking part of the statement from Horst above though might be his insistence that Otto 'didn't act like a criminal'. Though it is jarring, when he says this, he is not seemingly thinking of the orders to murder, maim and torture, but of Otto's behaviour at home: 'ski holidays, boating trips, family parties'.[42]

This struggle to understand how someone could be a loved and even loving family member, and yet also a perpetrator of some of the greatest crimes against humanity, is an extreme one facing people like Frank, Nissen and von Wächter. Yet it echoes too a more mundane struggle for many people – to understand how one can be 'a good person', and yet simultaneously implicated in violent systems of oppression, even as a 'bystander' who seems not to have taken direct action either way. The response of deliberate ignorance is understandable – and yet its invitation is also an invitation to ignore ongoing violence, as Niklas Frank has argued. The image of an 'amicable, gentle'[43] man struggling to reconcile himself with his family past which Sands presents of Horst van Wächter is thrown into relief by an account of another time they spent together. In 2014, Sands, Frank and von Wächter travelled to the Ukraine to make a film, *My Nazi Legacy: What Our Fathers Did*. Sands writes that

> the three of us attended a ceremony of remembrance to honour the dead of the Waffen-SS Galician Division, created by Otto von Wächter in the spring of 1943, still venerated by the nationalistic, fringe, Ukrainian group that organized the event. Horst told me that this was the best part of the trip, because men old and young came up to him to celebrate his father. Did he mind, I asked, that many of these men wore SS uniforms with swastikas? 'Why, should I?' Horst replied.[44]

The comma in Sands's rendering of von Wächter's comment does some work here, suggesting he is genuinely curious or surprised that Sands has taken exception to compliments from such men. It seems as if von Wächter has either become so engrossed in the matter of his father as an individual that he is grateful for anyone who has a good word to say about him, or else, he really has never taken in or accepted the full horror of the Nazi regime. Either way, his apparent blithe acceptance of the contemporary fascists' admiration suggests a concerted ignorance of the meaning of the history that otherwise seems to dominate his life.

Jennifer Teege

Jennifer Teege[45] has a different story, but one that still fits within much of the pattern of memoir by descendants of Nazi perpetrators, and the resurfacing of ignored violent histories in the present. Born in Germany in 1970, Teege's maternal grandparents were Amon Goeth, the man who constructed and ran the Kraków-Płaszów concentration camp, killing and torturing thousands of people, and Ruth Irene Goeth, who lived there in luxury with him during that time. Teege's mother, Monika Goeth, took her to a Catholic orphanage and put her in the care of the nuns, from where she was adopted. Despite her adoption, she stayed in touch with Monika and Irene until she was twenty-one. Teege only met her biological father when she was twenty-eight. He was Nigerian, meaning Teege herself is both an Afro-German and a descendant of Nazis, hence the title of the memoir she wrote on discovering her family history: *My Grandfather Would Have Shot Me.*[46]

Though Teege maintained contact with her biological mother and grandmother throughout her childhood, she did not know the reality of her grandfather's Nazi past until she happened to come across a book in the library at the age of thirty-eight. The book, a biography of Monika Goeth, published in 2002 and titled *I Have to Love My Father,*

Don't I?,[47] was concerned with Monika's relationship with Amon Goeth. This discovery shattered Teege, particularly because it pointed to the knowledge and involvement of her grandmother Irene, with whom she had maintained a warm relationship even during foster care and adoption. The process of dealing with and coming to terms with this discovery is the subject of Teege's own memoir.[48]

A particular aspect of Teege's story which may have contributed to it becoming a *New York Times* bestseller is that Amon Goeth appears as a character in the Stephen Spielberg film *Schindler's List*. The movie, based on Australian Thomas Keneally's 1992 non-fiction novel, *Schindler's Ark*, portrays the story of the German industrialist Oskar Schindler who eventually helped 1,200 Polish Jews to escape. In doing so, he is remembered as a hero, in stark contrast to Amon Goeth, who led the persecution, torture, exploitation and murder in the camp. And yet the men were friends who drank together, and Schindler was a member of the Nazi Party employing forced labour in his factory. It was Schindler who introduced Teege's grandparents to each another.[49] This is also part of Teege's story; in coming to terms with her beloved grandmother's continued involvement with such a man, she considers that perhaps a human can be many things, not simply good or bad. She seems to be able to come to this conclusion in a more sophisticated way than Horst von Wächter, in that this is not an attempt to rehabilitate a perpetrator but to understand their complicated reality.

> My grandmother was very liberal for her time: For a while she shared her flat with a transvestite called Lulu and went out on the town with him and his gay friends. My parents met when one of my father's friends, also African, was living as a lodger in my grandmother's house. Having an African man living in your house was far from normal in Munich in the 1960s and '70s. She was no racist.[50]

Likewise, Teege argues that the guilt of the parents must be distinguished from the lives of their descendants. She disagrees with the decision of Bettina Goering, great-niece of Hitler's chief of the Luftwaffe, to be sterilized so that she would not 'create another monster, not produce any more Goerings'. For Teege, this 'sends the wrong message. There is no Nazi gene'.[51]

Teege's story is not simply one of the eruption of understanding oneself as descended from, and having loved, someone implicated in terrible horrors. She also has a more complicated story – of aligning her understanding of herself and family through the process of adoption, the relationship between the family that brought her up and the family into which she was born. In some ways we might consider this to account at least in part for her rejection of the idea of 'a Nazi gene', knowing that family, relationships and identity are more than biology. On the other hand, many people who have been adopted, as with Teege herself, still find knowledge of their birth family and biological connections to be fundamentally meaningful to their sense of self.[52]

The other complication within Teege's life is her racialization as black, within white German society. All of her family that she knew growing up – both adoptive and biological – were white, and she describes being accustomed to being treated with 'amazement' when revealing her German identity. This caused double confusion and redrawing of assumptions when she was a student in Tel Aviv – long before she knew of her Nazi ancestors. Nevertheless, the connection with Germany and her presence in Israel were surprising to many, and all the more so because of her skin colour. Reading with concentration camp survivors in Israel as part of her volunteer role, she describes how she 'felt that I had to apologize for being German'. The very thing which usually made her stand out as an anomalous German was also a way to sidestep this discomfort sometimes: 'The color of my skin was good camouflage.'[53]

Perhaps it is in part this cacophony of meanings and ambiguities that enabled Teege to reach a position in which she can neither ignore nor embrace her grandparents and their deeds but can sit with their contradictions:

> None of this means that I agree with what my grandmother did, or that I want to cover for her. I renounce what she did, and sadly didn't do, in the camp. I renounce her explanations. I simply distinguish between the public figure, Ruth Irene Goeth, and my grandmother, Irene…
>
> My grandfather did not repent in the end; why else would he have raised his arm in a Hitler salute at the gallows? My grandmother never really repented either. She never really saw the victims; she walked through life with her eyes closed.
>
> Nonetheless, I still feel close to my grandmother. I will not try to justify the fact; I won't explain it either. That's just the way it is.[54]

Violent ignorance in the family

I am discussing post-generational trauma in an exploration of violent ignorance for three reasons. Firstly, the experience of post-generations is a reminder that knowledge of violent histories and ongoing oppression is not simply 'absent' but can be actively ignored by those with a stake in maintaining this ignorance. Secondly, mass cultural production on the memory and post-memory of the Holocaust is in one sense a way of protecting that atrocity from being ignored or forgotten. Yet its presence should also remind us that this is not the only or ultimate expression of unbearable violence humans have undertaken and should instead be a spur to recognize the knowledges of other post-generations (and current generations) experiencing genocidal violence, which seem easier to ignore from a white Euro-American perspective. Finally, the uneasiness of recognition of the European Holocaust as not simply a terrible historical event, but something which resonates with ongoing trauma and violence in which we are all (including members of post-generations) positioned, is one of the uncomfortable shiftings of perspective that must be undertaken in order to pry at the cracks of violent ignorance.

The memory of the European Holocaust must not be allowed to become a crystallized and fixed emblem of never-to-be-repeated horror. It was horror and should never be repeated. But it continues to be repeated – and indeed it in itself was a repetitive development of holocausts created by Europeans previously outside the continent of Europe.[55] The risk I am pointing to is that if this becomes a fetishized, no longer live history, then it becomes domesticated, like the response to Jo Cox MP's assassination, but on a grand scale. We can all publicly agree that the Holocaust was wrong, as we might all agree that 'we have more in common than that which divides us'. But this is barely a starting point, if such expressed agreement is used as a way of ending the discussion and refusing to see how the tendencies of oppression and violence remain the bedrock of how the global order currently functions.

As with 'more in common', and with Affleck's resistance to being associated with his slave-owning ancestor, wanting to distance oneself from violence is of course understandable and even laudable. However, to be politically effective and valuable, this distancing needs to be understood as a desire, and an ongoing process, rather than a fact. To engage in that distancing from evil as a process, it is necessary to recognize the different ways in which we might still be connected to that oppressive violence and even benefit from it – in order to work on overturning that. But to do so is, of course, a painful thing to attempt.

And what about my claim to recognition of resonances between the violence of the border crisis in Hungary and throughout Europe, and the horrors of Nazi deportation trains? Is it really correct to say that I notice that because I know part of my family history is tied up with escape from Nazi Europe? For most of my life I have resisted claiming my ancestry as an explanation for what I care about. Particularly since it is worth noting that there are other, equally valid versions of my family history that could be told: of two Protestant grandparents from Liverpool with Irish roots and class fortunes fluctuating between respectable working-class to home-owning; of two grandparents with degrees and professional jobs that took them, my mother and her siblings around the world; of having a very white British non-descript name and appearance and never really having any interest in or education about religion of any sort (other than festivals involving food and/or gift-giving).

Being an exile and refugee was not something my grandpa talked about to us or to my mum or (as far as I know) to his other children. My mum has described to me how when, as the oldest grandchild, I started learning about the Holocaust in history lessons at school, his first reaction was that we shouldn't know about that – we were too young. Mum said she talked to him about how important it is to know such histories to avoid them happening again. Later, she thought he came round to the idea, and he visited my school to talk to my classmates about Jewish culture and festivals (we were, as far as I know, the only Jew-ish family in that West Yorkshire comprehensive school).

Taking German citizenship was not something I had ever considered (or known I was eligible for) until the aftermath of Britain's referendum to leave the European Union in 2016.[56] In the atmosphere of intolerance and anxiety that surged with that campaign and has only increased since, the internet suddenly swarmed with people exchanging ideas for holding onto EU citizenship, and among them I noticed the Restoration of Citizenship process.[57] This was a rule introduced into the German constitution in 1949 as a form of reparation for the crimes of the Nazi government. Any German citizen whose nationality had been removed by the Nazi government between 30 January 1933 and 8 May 1945 was entitled to restitution of citizenship – and so were their descendants. This was the case even though, of course, if my grandpa and his parents and sister had not fled Germany, their descendants like me would not exist – either because they would have perished or, if the Nazis had not taken control, because they would not have left in the same way and met the same partners. Nevertheless, the principle of return and welcome was instituted.

Before the 2016 referendum, few people took up this opportunity, perhaps unaware it existed, or conflicted about having a desire to receive citizenship linked to such a violent past. Since 2016, the numbers applying have shot up, with 1,506 applications received by the German interior ministry for restoration of citizenship in 2018, compared to forty-three in 2015.[58] This parallels other applications for dual citizenship by Brits apparently rediscovering their multinational pasts, with applications for Irish citizenship increasing from 6,000 in 2015 to over 25,000 in 2018.[59] There has been sporadic news coverage of these trends, with many of the newly dual nationality British-German Jewish citizens professing their motivation to be one of retaining the right of free movement and access to faster passport queues in airports, while others emphasize a sense of history and connection to Germany.[60]

My motivation though was more one of anxiety; even as I felt it realistically unlikely that I/we would have to leave the UK, the opportunity for a backup plan did seem important. Relatedly, it seemed wise to play the border regime at its own game – to gather as many nationalities as possible. And yet this desire, no matter how rooted in anxiety and a real family history of persecution, remains one of privilege. I now have two of the most 'powerful' passports in the world.[61] At the same time, increasingly national governments are targeting dual nationals to make them more precarious, since one nationality can still be removed under international conventions without making such a person stateless. This is undoubtedly used in racialized ways, notably by the British government against 'British nationals *suspected* of engaging "in terrorism-related or other serious or organised criminal activity"'.[62]

In the case of reckoning with my relationship to family history, it is certainly not a question of the 'credit' or 'blame' for ancestors rejected by Ben Affleck. What this encounter with the eruption of seething absences and muted presences in my own family history – at a moment of the national schism of Brexit – shows is that the past remains live, but neither the present nor the past is clearly divided between the victim and the perpetrator, the good and the bad, the innocent and the implicated. It is also a reminder of how blurred and intertwined allegiance and belonging to both family and nation can be.

For each of the figures discussed in this chapter, we might think about how the descendants and beneficiaries of oppression and genocide come to terms with their place in the world. Each of them was children – or unborn – when their ancestors undertook well-documented violent crimes. There is no question that any of these children or grandchildren are 'to blame' for what their ancestors did. But for them, it is harder than for most to simply say that the Nazis were pure evil and distant from 'normal' behaviour. They knew their parents (or grandparents) as people they loved, and the reductive idea of 'evil genes' would mean that they themselves might be carriers. But to say that their parents were human beings, or people of their time, almost seems to defend their parents' actions. They do, in each case, seem to be understandably traumatized by their situation, but of course in a different way to the survivors and their descendants.

These descendants of perpetrators are haunted, but this does not necessarily take the form of unexpected eruptions (or punctures) – they hold their hauntings in their names, and in their immediate family tree, and in every memorial event held in their vicinity. They might attempt to reject or suppress the knowledge of their connection to ultimate violence and evil, but they are unlikely to ever escape that knowledge. So how can we learn from them about the workings of ignorance and implication for those of us more able to embed the knowledge of our implications in violence present and past in a cosy wrapping of ignorance?

We might see parallels between Horst von Wächter's pleasure in receiving praise for his father from men dressed in SS uniforms and the person who responds to news coverage of Decolonising Curriculum movements by stating 'Don't these people know we cannot place today's morals on history. So are we to criminalise our ancestors because their views were different to ours[?].'[63] Or between Margaret Nissen's refusal to engage with the photographs of her father's crimes and Ben Affleck's reaction to his slave-holder ancestor. But what about Jennifer Teege? How could we think through her example to unpick the experience of only existing because your perpetrator ancestor survived, and other ancestors loved them, alongside the sense that their driving philosophy was one that would lead to your own annihilation? If good and bad is not so easily separated, what does that mean for those of us who want to be good?

***

Belonging and nation are often described using metaphors of 'family' – the 'motherland' or 'fatherland', shared blood and kinship. Where national, imperial and territorial identities depend on histories that ignore or conceal their troubling aspects – as with the British withdrawal from Kenya discussed in Chapter 4 – families also choose which parts of their histories to remember and which to ignore or forget. In both cases, the parts left out or ignored can be too painful to contemplate or make sense of, particularly when such a strong sense of identity and entitlement can come from belonging to a family or nation. And yet those ignored or repressed histories can reappear, whether in the haunting of connection with political conflict in the present or in the emerging of new patterns of belonging or validation of different parts of a familial or national history – as in my own story. Ignoring the more painful or repulsive parts of one's family (or national) history can be violent because it prevents recognition of the consequences that painful history might have in the present, for example in the distribution of wealth and rights as an aftermath of slavery, and thus does nothing to prevent the perpetuation of those consequences. The answer is not to apportion 'credit or blame' for the actions of one's ancestors (whether familial or national); rather, it is to take responsibility for understanding how the consequences of their actions have benefited or hurt one's own life or the lives of others. This can only be done by confronting the tempting violence of ignorance.

6

Bystanders

In our age there is no such thing as "keeping out of politics".
All issues are political issues.

−GEORGE ORWELL, *POLITICS AND THE ENGLISH LANGUAGE*[1]

Whistleblower

Callum Tulley left school at the age of eighteen with a plan to become
a professional football referee. Looking for other work while he built
his career, he found a job near home, at Brook House Immigration
Removal Centre, where he thought he would be employed to 'help
people facing deportation'.[2] After a short time working at Brook
House, the reality of life in the detention centre seemed very different
to Tulley. Witnessing systematic abuse of the men held there, he
chose to become a whistleblower. Working with a team from the BBC
Panorama documentary series, Tulley began to wear hidden cameras
to work, to document the 'chaos, incompetence and abuse'[3] behind the
walls and fences in this leafy, suburban area of Surrey, near Gatwick
Airport in south-east England.

In one scene in the resulting documentary, Tulley enters a cell
that is covered in blood after a detainee has seriously cut his neck
and wrists and overdosed on heart medication, following a refusal

of his bail application; we see the state of the cell and the man shows Tulley his deep wounds some time later when he has recovered. Tulley describes the scene, as do other members of staff who saw the incident and cleaned up after it:

> I went into this cell and there was blood all over the floor, all over the bed sheets, over the shower curtains, in the corner of his room, there was just blood-soaked clothes, just lying there.[4]

Self-harm and suicide attempts are passed off by some officers as 'attention seeking',[5] while others express disregard for the lives of detainees, from making jokes in staffrooms and in front of detainees about them dying, to telling Tulley as he prepares to be part of a team forcibly removing a man with a heart condition (the same man who later self-harmed in his cell above) 'If he dies, he dies'.[6] Tulley later recounts this to camera:

> One officer said if he dies, he dies. I didn't wanna kill this guy you know, I didn't want to harm this man, I just wanted to go in there, do the job.[7]

The detainee at the centre of both the forcible removal and the bloody cell above has 'a history of violence, and … a conviction for attempted murder';[8] 'he's committed some horrific crimes, he's not a nice guy'.[9] And yet Tulley points to these episodes as evidence of a system that is hurting everyone, the detainees and the officers:

> [I]t's twisting him up on the way, staff are becoming disturbed as a result of his actions.[10]

After the deportation attempt in which Tulley feared a potential fatality, the detainee returned to Brook House the next day. He had complained of heart pains and the pilot of the charter flight refused to take him to Romania. This led to the subsequent bail hearing, refusal of bail and suicide attempt. The frustrations of officers who had put their safety at risk and (for some) feared hurting someone is plain. One officer says to Tulley of seeing the man return to Brook House after the failed deportation:

> All that effort and hard work everyone put in. It's fucking wrong innit? Don't make any sense.[11]

It is perhaps unsurprising that officers' frustrations translate into dehumanization of detainees when their working conditions leave little space for any other way of understanding the work they are being asked to do – and their own dehumanization.

This chapter is about blame as a tool of violent ignorance and a possible counter – taking responsibility. In seeing the violence occurring within the British immigration detention system – visible both as a result of the conditions in which men were being held and in direct encounters with staff – Tulley chose to take responsibility for countering this by documenting and publicizing the situation. Far more common responses within the system are either to leave or to turn a blind eye or even participate in this violence. Each of these latter options invokes violent ignorance as a survival technique, choosing to allow the violence to continue because it is too difficult to confront, even if one chooses not to be directly part of it – to remain a bystander.

But to confront this everyday violence is not an easy option, and this chapter considers some of the reasons that ignorance becomes how people cope in extreme situations, when cast as the oppressor. The key to this exploration is that settling 'blame' for violence on a particular source can also be a form of violent ignorance. Blaming someone (or some 'social force') ends the argument, the thinking and the searching. It allows someone (or something) to be condemned, perhaps removed (or perhaps further ignored). The wider reverberations of responsibility, culpability and conscience are lost from perception.

One person who attempted to understand how it could be that an ideology such as Nazism could take hold of otherwise reasonable and 'normal' people was Amy Buller, a teacher who, in the 1930s, led many cultural exchanges between England and Germany. As Nazism rose to power, she documented her encounters with the wide range of people she encountered in Germany, and the book she wrote serves as both a lesson in how people enact violent ignorance, and a counter to it, as she demonstrates the everyday choices that can lead to disaster and the difficulty of assigning singular or absolute blame. How might Buller's lessons be useful for understanding the behaviours of ordinary folk as they become implicated in more and more direct ways in the violence of racialized border control?

Darkness over Germany

I have always found Cumberland Lodge an uncanny place. It is in the middle of Windsor Great Park, a stately home that belongs to the Queen of England and is adorned with images of old white warmakers (including Lord Cumberland himself, famous as 'The Butcher' for leading a brutal military attack at the Battle of Culloden in 1745 and whose portrait – sword in hand – presides over the dining room). Since 1947, the lodge has been an educational charity, and I have attended several events there, as both a student and an academic, and enjoyed the plush surroundings and food as well as the time to think, discuss and reflect. The mission of the place – to 'embrace difficult conversations' – sometimes seems to jar with its material reality. There are sincere attempts at interfaith (and secular) connection and in discussing questions of national belonging and discrimination.

The question of slavery reparations arose once during a race equality seminar I attended there, and a query about the relationship between the proceeds of the slave trade and the buildings and property in which the discussion was taking place was met with a giggle and a nervous shudder from the assembled company. Is it necessary to suspend knowledge of those violent histories that made this place possible, or to stare directly at them, in order to talk about justice in such surroundings?

The educational mission of Cumberland Lodge stemmed from the work of Amy Buller. Buller was an Englishwoman who spent extensive time in Germany before and after the First World War. As a teacher and devout Christian and lover of German culture, she was keen to encourage cultural understanding between Germany and Britain and to understand 'how much opposition and criticism the Nazis would entertain'.[12] To this end, she took groups of academics and theologians on visits to Germany for Anglo-German discussion groups. On her trips Buller would also talk to the various people that she met, from high officials to teachers, from resistance fighters to army generals – though she does note that she came into contact with few 'ordinary workers'. Buller kept records of these conversations and found that there was interest from within Britain in understanding *how* fascism 'could have arisen'. She went on to write a book, *Darkness over Germany*, which was published in 1943 and republished in 2017. In 1947, King George VI and Queen Elizabeth the Queen Mother offered Cumberland Lodge to Amy Buller to set up an educational foundation that would foster learning and critical thinking, in line with her thinking emerging from *Darkness over Germany*.[13]

In Buller's book, we find a perhaps unique contemporary account of the changing political climate in Germany in this period. Many of her interlocutors were keen to speak with her because of her perspective as an Englishwoman familiar with and inclined to be friendly towards

Germany. In this, and being able to collect these accounts at the time rather than in the aftermath, her book is remarkable and deserves much more attention than it has received to date.

A striking encounter opens the book. Buller meets two cousins, both schoolteachers: Franz and Elizabeth. Franz begins by explaining to her that he, like Buller, is against the Nazi teachings but is now working in a school with a Nazi headteacher, where he is required to give their race lessons. The options he sees open to him are four. The first two courses of action, he noted, were only possible because he had money and connections – he could leave the country and go to America, or he could leave the school and stay in Germany, 'digging in my garden and writing books',[14] perhaps even books that could be useful for after the Nazis' fall. But he points out, as a form of resistance these would really only be of use to his feeling of personal morality; both options would please his headmaster, 'who is new and young and a very keen Nazi [and] … greatly hopes that I will leave'.[15] The pupils would simply be taught the same material by another teacher, perhaps a more enthusiastic one who believed in it. Either course of action might make him feel honourable, but in effect each would be a way for him to look away from the problem, while the violence continued.

The third possibility would be a more visible form of resistance: he could stay in his job and 'defy the headmaster and refuse to give Nazi lessons on race'.[16] He could even denounce Hitler in front of the whole school. But his view is that this would lead to him going to prison, 'and of course, some of my colleagues are already there'.[17] It would allow the headmaster to make an example of him and he would be removed from the school in any case. He is not even sure if the pupils would notice him taking a stand, and again, a more committed Nazi teacher would be recruited to fill his place. He comments on how a colleague who recently complained about Nazis discrediting German scholarship was thrown in the river by a group of boys, without censure from the headmaster. He suggests that this colleague might prefer to be in prison than teaching in such a situation, except that he would fear putting his dependants at risk.[18]

Therefore, Franz is sticking with the fourth option:

I must add that I am not happy and there is a constant strain. I remain on the staff and I pay lip service to all the Nazi school ceremonies and I do not show any open hostility, at least not enough to 'get the sack' as you say, but quite enough to make my position precarious and at times most unpleasant. I am trying through the teaching of geography to do everything in my power to give the boys knowledge and I hope later on, judgement, so that when, as they grow older, the Nazi fever dies down and it again becomes possible to offer some opposition, they may be prepared. I never refer to the Party or its teaching directly, and the boys are, I think, mostly unaware that I am trying deliberately to undermine it. There are four or five masters who are non-Nazis left in our school now, and we all work on the same plan. If we leave, four Nazis will come in and there will be no honest teaching in the whole school.

'Honest,' did I say – are we being honest I sometimes wonder? It is very exhausting as well as dangerous to live under the strain of a deliberate compromise with evil … But if I went to America and left others to it, would that be honest, or are the only honest people those in prison cells? If only there could be some collective action among teachers.[19]

Franz's cousin Elizabeth describes a similar course of action, making her mandated lessons on Nazi race theory 'very dull, whereas I try to make my other lessons as interesting as possible'.[20] She adds:

Of course, at times we get sick of the whole thing. After all, we only ask for freedom to teach decently and without distortion, but when I feel tired and think of giving it up, I remember that would mean handing my schoolchildren over to the Nazis.[21]

Both Franz and Elizabeth describe trying to undermine the Nazi system of indoctrination from the inside and see this as the only option (and indeed a personal sacrifice) as otherwise the system would become taken over completely by those who believe in its intentions. Yet they both recognize that in staying within the system, they may well be seen as collaborators. When Elizabeth adds that she hopes 'that my friends in England understand that there are many more than those in prison who try to fight Nazi teaching', Franz tells her she will be disappointed: '[Y]ou and I will be identified with the Nazis and perhaps lose for ever the friendship of those in England whose help we need.'[22] Rather than prioritizing a desire to escape blame for Nazi horrors however, the cousins both emphasize their responsibility to do what they can to counter what is happening, even if they are unlikely to receive praise or support from any quarter. On the walk home, Elizabeth confides again to Buller:

I do realize how terrible it all is, and I could talk all night about the bad and discouraging things. Sometimes I too see it as a losing battle and if it were a battle for my own generation then I think I would be tempted to give up, but when I get back to school and see the children I become angry again, and that helps me vow that I will not leave these children to the Nazis, and that I will fight in a way the Nazis will not discover.[23]

Though Buller does not cast doubt on the sincerity of Elizabeth and Franz, she later encounters others who suggest that such a claim of changing things from the inside may be a convenient excuse. On a trip to Austria, Buller bumps into a Dutch man she calls Dr

Holland and discusses the mass appeal of the Nazi programme, and the Hitler Youth in particular, with him and another English friend, Mr Langham. Holland suggests that the 'unemployed intelligentsia' attracted by promises of the future may not see their work within the Nazi project as a betrayal of 'their own intellectual integrity', but rather

> many of them may rationalize that by saying that if they are all in the movement they may influence it along sounder lines.[24]

This assessment from Dr Holland recalls Horst von Wächter's comments about his father, the Nazi Governor of Krakow and SS leader, Otto von Wächter, that he 'did his best … Others would have been worse'.[25] In the case of von Wächter, this is clearly an absurd attempt at such rationalization, since among other things he oversaw the execution of tens of thousands of Polish Jews.[26] For Franz and Elizabeth, however the choice to try to influence from their much less powerful positions as ordinary schoolteachers could be seen as a brave one, if we take them at their word. What strikes me particularly is Elizabeth's mention of her anger ('when I get back to school and see the children I become angry again'), which motivates her to 'fight in a way the Nazis will not discover'.[27] This reminds me of poet and theorist Audre Lorde's important injunction to use righteous anger as a source of power and energy for change:

> Every woman has a well-stocked arsenal of anger potentially useful against those oppressions, personal and institutional, which brought that anger into being. Focused with precision it can become a powerful source of energy serving progress and change. And when I speak of change, I do not mean a simple switch of positions or a temporary lessening of tensions, nor the ability to smile or feel good. I am speaking of a basic and radical alteration in those assumptions underlining our lives.[28]

Though Elizabeth can attempt only a stealthy fight, she can use the Nazis' own ignorance against them, to teach the lessons that may enable her students to see the truth of what is happening:

> I think it is important that we who oppose the Nazis should be cleverer than they are, and I am not giving in to them. It is difficult, but it can be done in lots of little ways. For instance, at all our summer camps we have fireside talks, which are often concerned with old German folklore. These Nazi women know only a very few stories, and they are the ones the Party suggests, and the teachers repeat them till the children get bored. I know a great many more stories and different ones... I try to make my stories exciting, and they teach quite different things from the Nazi stories.[29]

Though enticing children to pay attention to alternative folk tales might seem an inadequate response to the violence of the Nazi regime, it is an attempt by this teacher to work where and how she is able. Her use of folk tales points to the importance of imagination and narrative, as with the artworks discussed in Chapter 3, which might enable the young people to see past the violent ignorance being inculcated in them by the Nazi regime. Such interventions are not about 'a temporary lessening of tensions, nor the ability to smile or feel good', but about pushing and building towards 'radical alteration in those assumptions underlining our lives', even where this seems most unachievable.[30]

Faith and hope

The conversation between Buller, Langham and Holland is described in Buller's book as an attempt to understand the appeal of Hitler, particularly to young people, and while the Nazis' actions are clearly understood to be appalling, this does seem like a genuine attempt to comprehend, rather than to apportion blame. The conclusion, like Buller's overall conclusion throughout the book, is that Nazi ideology filled a hole left by lack of religious faith. Hitler's promises appealed to despairing and hopeless young (and older) people – and their consequences for others were easily ignored amid the dazzling possibilities. Buller records herself saying to her friends:

> It amazes me that some people in our own countries seem to imagine that Hitler stands up and describes all the beastly, sadistic orgies he can imagine and thereby attracts the wholehearted enthusiasm of youth. Were he to do so, he would be far less powerful, because he would then only attract the criminal or the pathological types, whereas now he gets the energy, the enthusiasm and the generous response of the best elements in the youth of the country.[31]

Where Franz had wished in vain for 'collective action' among teachers, Hitler appeared, in Buller's account, to easily mobilize ideas of collective action – built on the exclusion of undesirables. Buller describes at length some of Hitler's speeches and her attendance at some of the most frightening, and impressive, Nuremberg rallies. A conversation she has there confirms one of her main conclusions that the appeal of the Nazi movement was based on a desire for faith, and belief in greatness, for men who had previously had little success:

> I asked a middle-aged banker from Holland who was wearing a Nazi badge why he was a Nazi, 'I understand,' I said, 'how many Germans get caught up in this movement for various reasons, but your country has not passed through years of economic chaos and unemployment and your country has never been defeated in war.' 'I am a Nazi,' he said, 'because this Party has made me feel for the first time in my life that there is something big enough to

live for and that I have a part to play and also belong to a world fellowship of others with this same purpose.'[32]

While Buller's conclusions – that unemployment and despondency following Germany's defeat in the First World War were fertile ground for a charismatic leader offering 'hope', however violent its consequences – are not singular, her accounts from contemporaneous encounters with 'ordinary people' are unusual. It is surprising that they are not more widely known, particularly when reading them in the early twenty-first century can produce some very jarring moments of recognition.[33] Her conclusion, in aid of which she convinced the British Royal Family to donate Cumberland Lodge, was that it was a lack of critical thinking which led young and old to allow themselves to become part of the genocidal, amoral Nazi regime. Buller herself suggests strongly throughout her book that a lack of religious faith is also responsible for creating the space into which Hitler's promises could enter. I would suggest that it is not necessarily the absence of religious faith, but the absence of hope which she identifies as the space this ideology filled.

Of course, the starting point of looking to 'ordinary people' and how they might become embroiled in fascism lends itself to the idea that 'ordinary people' are not normally invested in such murderous regimes but can be swept along by them in particular circumstances. When Buller explains that Hitler's speeches do not publicize his 'sadistic orgies' because to do so would attract only 'the criminal or the pathological types', she is talking of an element of this movement which relied on violent ignorance – of both concealing and looking away from the ultimate aims and consequences of Hitler's regime. She could equally have been talking about proponents of empire and colonial projects within Europe, emphasizing riches and 'civilisation' but not murder, dispossession and exploitation.

In both of these circumstances there were also adherents of the powerful who were very much in favour of torture and mass murder of populations, whether or not they would use those terms or more sanitized ones. Buller met them too – she recalls a night in Munich when she was invited to coffee with a group of teachers and students, all members of the Nazi Party, to hear 'how happy the younger generation is about the revolution', as her host, Dr Hartmann, told her.[34] There, she was introduced to Karl Weber, as 'one of the most important younger Nazi leaders in our Ministry of Culture'.[35] This was a man with whom Buller had in previous years discussed Christianity and internationalism, and she suggested he faced a 'deep conflict' yet had now become 'a past-master in the art of rationalizing Nazi actions'.[36] As Weber explained how he perceived – not unlike Buller – that there had been a decline in faith, hope and guiding philosophy among German youth into which Hitler had stepped, he emphasized to the group 'the reality of race' and of 'cooperation within the family of the German race', while 'the youths in the group were drinking in all he said'.[37] Buller and her English friends interrupted to protest:

> 'But,' we said, 'in this family what is the place of the German Jew, and indeed what is the place of anyone who opposed the National Socialists?'[38]

While Buller still perceived Weber to be 'a traitor to himself' in his reply that 'even if we are thought ruthless or cruel, we must exclude all who would poison the life of the state',[39] she then observed that

> [e]ven the young boys joined in this part of the discussion and talked of the Jews as the great evil they must fight relentlessly. We realized that in an almost religious sense they had created their own devil against whom they must wage ceaseless warfare.[40]

From this encounter, Buller concludes that

[a]s far as I can see, the most cruel and ruthless elements in the Party are in the first place those who have seen in a movement based on force the chance for the free play of their own more brutal tendencies, and in the second place the intellectual who is a complete traitor to himself. The latter type is, I think, ve[r]y likely to become a cruel oppressor of anyone who makes him conscious of his self-betrayal.[41]

Considering this in a violent ignorance framework, Buller identifies the first group as those who might willingly embrace the brutality of a racist, murderous regime. The second group, in which she places Karl Weber and Dr Hartmann, is a group who might at heart see the brutality of concentration camps, mass extermination and deportation of specific populations as wrong or evil. Yet they have not had the courage or ability to resist becoming part of this regime and may indeed become instrumental in it. They can only live with this by either denying the knowledge of those violent crimes or by denying their moral repugnance – ignoring the violence, and in doing so, allowing it to continue – or accepting and justifying it.

'Their way of coping'

In Amy Buller's account, the teachers Franz and Elizabeth were aware that remaining as teachers and delivering lessons in Nazi ideology meant they would be viewed as part of that brutal system. And yet they remained in post because they believed this was the only effective way in which they could carry out their professional and ethical commitments to teach children critical thinking and in some way resist the harms of the Nazis. Their understanding of their implication in the system meant they recognized that despite their reluctance and resistance, they never claimed to be blameless bystanders – and in fact they rejected the idea of choosing a 'bystander' role of 'digging the garden' because they knew this would not absolve them of responsibility to challenge the Nazi regime.

In less extreme situations, we can also see that many people – teachers, social workers, civil servants – may find themselves working within systems or organizations with which they disagree. In some cases, organizations and professions as a whole can change during a person's career, or entering a profession people may find that the role does not meet the ethical standards that were part of their training and vocation.

This seems to apply to the situation of Callum Tulley, working for G4S and the Home Office in Brook House. His understanding of the role of a detention custody officer as a helping and caring profession might be surprising for people who have encountered the many accounts of brutality within the immigration detention system but is not unreasonable given his first encounter with the role would likely have been an advert like this one:

> We're looking for people with good communication skills, empathy and integrity … With a calm, firm but fair and non-judgemental approach, you'll also need to be a listener, team player, counsellor, peacekeeper and social worker … All you need is commitment to do the right thing and the ability to build rapport with just about anyone.…there is a real opportunity to make a real difference to people's lives.[42]

Despite this, once in post it was not long before Tulley witnessed and recorded scenes which ranged from the terrifying to the cruel. He highlights that staff are under-trained and under-resourced, overlooking illegal drug taking and its risks, physically abusing detainees, expressing contempt and racist verbal abuse with regard to the men in their care; these factors combine into a 'toxic atmosphere'.[43]

At the time of writing, provision of services in the UK detention estate is outsourced to the private firms G4S, GEO, Mitie and Serco,[44] with only one Immigration Removal Centre (Morton Hall) run directly by the state in the form of Her Majesty's Prison Service.[45] Among these, G4S is the world's largest security company and one of the largest private employers in the world, operating in 125 countries.[46] The Home Office's Detention Centre Rules are statutory guides to conduct within IRCs intended to ensure human rights and welfare of detainees, but there is much evidence, from detainees, staff and volunteers and the government's own inspectors, that they are not always followed.[47] There are periodic revelations of mismanagement by G4S in particular, including financial questions, deaths of detainees, problematic conditions inside detention centres, and physical and verbal abuse of detainees.[48]

A large number of detainees are, according to Tulley, involved in drugs and gang culture within the centre. He films one officer on the centre's induction wing describing how

> [y]esterday evening after dinner… it was like the walking dead in here. Everyone was zombied out. All walking around, all stoned off their nut.[49]

Tulley states that officers have asked management to move drug dealers off the induction wing and away from vulnerable new arrivals to the centre, but they were replaced by new dealers. There are multiple pieces of footage of detainees in extreme distress, rolling on the floor and unable to control their bodies, receiving medical attention or being physically restrained by staff. In Tulley's portrayal, there is neither widespread concern about the pervasiveness of drug culture (particularly Spice, a chemical alternative to cannabis), nor proper training or awareness of how to manage this. At one point he films a group of detention custody officers (DCOs) and medical staff discussing the latest medical emergency. They agree between themselves that 'there is no shadow of a doubt, someone will die' from drugs on the wing.[50]

The drug culture interacts with physical and verbal abuse from G4S employees in several sections of the film. In one example, Tulley's manager, detainee custody manager, Nathan Ring, is filmed during a medical response to a detainee 'out of it on Spice'.[51] The detainee is singing on his bed and clearly incoherent. Ring, as the supervising officer, laughs, jokes and insults the man while other staff attend to him:

> Does your face taste nice, as you appear to be chewing it off? ... lay still, you div... Scrotum ... Fucking leave him.

In light of this kind of leadership from management, DCOs face a choice of how to respond – how to invoke the 'empathy and integrity' they were told was central to the job? Political scientist Alexandra Hall's research inside immigration detention in the UK has led her to conclude that '[e]mpathy has the potential to profoundly disturb the logic' of the detention regime and that the 'emergence of empathy is an incongruous and disruptive emotional project' in this context, where it may begin to blur the distinctions between worker and detainee on which the violence of detention depends.[52] That is, though empathy might be suggested as an essential trait in working in such jobs, being able to see detainees as human can make sustaining the work there unbearable – and so it is easier to ignore or reject their humanity and trauma.

In another disturbing incident, a detainee called Mustapha Zitouni had been told that his expected flight to Algeria was cancelled because of missing documents from the Algerian government. He wanted to leave the UK but at the last minute was made to stay longer in Brook House, with no indication of when this would change. He protested by climbing onto the anti-suicide netting that runs between balconies on each floor of the centre, holding razor blades. An external team dressed in riot gear is brought in to retrieve him safely from the netting, but in the meantime a team of G4S Brook House officers prepare to be backup, including Tulley, who asks G4S restraint trainer John Connelly, who is supervising, for advice on procedure. Connelly tells him to use racist abuse:

> Tulley: 'John, just thinking mate, what am I doing? Just walking backwards in front of him and if he kicks off get his head down?'
>
> Connelly: 'Say, "Listen here, n*****. Listen to me."' [laughs][53]

Later, they wait in a stairwell dressed in their own riot gear for several hours, and after an officer says 'he [Zitouni] shouldn't be allowed to get away with this', Connelly responds:

> If he fucks about, we need to get him in here. Fuck him up around the corner. If he refuses, shove him in here. ... These stairs. That's our justification for fucking throwing him into that corner, and fucking dealing with him in that corner there.[54]

When another officer points out a CCTV camera ('camera there boss'), Connelly answers, 'I'll scrub the ****. No fucking problem.'[55] No one is recorded on camera protesting this plan to seriously assault a vulnerable detainee and destroy the evidence, in the same way that no one is recorded protesting against other similar threats or accounts of past behaviour made openly in staff rooms and corridors throughout the film. This callousness is clearly desperately wrong (and illegal) and involves both a belief that the abuse can and will be concealed/ignored and the maintaining of an ignorance of Zitouni's own humanity. The racist epithets may seem to make perfect sense when he is being treated not as a person, but as a nuisance and someone to be punished.

It is also worth noting that alongside framing the appalling culture and behaviour of some staff in this environment, Tulley recognizes that they too are under stress and vulnerable ('I don't know if that's their way of coping with the bleakness of Brook House') and are being traumatized by the harm they are witness to and part of through the nature of the institution. Tulley describes how there are 'often two officers just left to one wing, got to deal with 100 detainees'.[56] Detention custody officers are paid £10.36 per hour for a forty-six-hour week including night shifts.[57] Their training in how to deal with the desperate situations that can arise in detention custody in an ethical way, and how to cope with the challenges they face, leaves much to be desired.[58]

Throughout the film, Tulley demonstrates both vulnerability and violence among both detainees and staff. For both, it is suggested, there might be elements of finding means to adapt to the culture and context of the centre:

Alif Jan, former Brook House detainee	'In Brook House, if you are a very nice person, very cool-minded, you will become aggressive. Because you are facing aggressive things most of the time. The behaviour of the guys there, and the behaviour of the staff there. These are the two worst things.'[59]
Tulley:	'Some of the officers and managers, I don't know if that's their way of coping with the bleakness of Brook House, or because it's that they just hate the detainees and don't care what sort of state they're in.'[60]

However, it is also clear that there are officers in positions of seniority who model for other staff that the rules governing behaviour are not those of the government and G4S publicly available policy documents promising safety and empathy. The Home Office Detention Centre Rules state:

> The purpose of detention centres shall be to provide for the secure but humane accommodation of detained persons in a relaxed regime with as much freedom of movement and association as possible, consistent with maintaining a safe and secure environment, and to encourage and assist detained persons to make the most productive use of their time, whilst respecting in particular their dignity and the right to individual expression.
>
> ... Due recognition will be given at detention centres to the need for awareness of the particular anxieties to which detained persons may be subject and the sensitivity that this will require, especially when handling issues of cultural diversity.[61]

Safety, security, dignity and awareness of anxiety seem to have disappeared in the scenes depicted in Tulley's film. Though there is no way to excuse the behaviour of these officers, it is important not to ignore that they too are under pressure, and when faced with the traumatic and challenging behaviour of the pressurized detainees – self-harm, dangerous substance use – they apparently cope by ignoring the humanity of the men in their care and resorting to violence and disregard. This is also an outcome of the organization of the border and detention system itself, which treats some lives as less important than others, regardless of what is set out in documents like the Detention Rules.

The challenges faced in Brook House and other detention centres are not just about the abuse of the detainees, but the exploitation of staff. Dealing with the extreme situations they are placed in with little training or support,[62] it is perhaps unsurprising that a general response is to stop seeing the detainees in their care as human and worthy of that care. But what about professions where such an ethos of care has been central to their long-term training?

'We can't stand it anymore'[63]

The border crisis has infiltrated many aspects of life throughout the world. Throughout Europe, state welfare institutions are increasingly implicated not just in caring for those displaced by war and violence around the world, but in controlling and assessing their movements and rights to belong. In Sweden, researchers Lena Martinsson and Eva Reimers found that when, in 2017,

> Sweden deported unaccompanied refugee children, numerous social workers and teachers found themselves torn between acting as loyal civil servants or acting in accordance with their professional ethics.[64]

Responding to exclusionary decisions by the Swedish government around the closure of borders and acceptance of refugees, a group called 'Vi står inte ut' ('we can't stand it any more') formed in 2015. Documenting the activities of this group and related activists, Martinsson and Reimers have demonstrated how some teachers and social workers have been outspoken in cases when their professional ethics appear to come into conflict with official rules. Such activities challenge a more simplified activist view which might suggest that 'social workers' or 'the state' are the cause of restrictions placed on refugees. Such a simplified view ignores resistance within the workings of those 'black boxes', meaning challenges may be misplaced and alliances may be missed.[65]

Aside from publicizing the cruelty of government requirements to expel unaccompanied asylum-seeking children from the country and/or from education and support while in Sweden, some within the 'We Can't Stand It Anymore' movement also challenged the basis of immigration laws which came into conflict with social work laws. One social worker, Matilda Brinck-Larsen, publicly announced her resignation from the profession in order to work with asylum-seeking children living without their parents, through a non-governmental organization.[66] But were the protests of the 'We Can't Stand It Anymore' movement enough?

Social work scholar Andy Jolly identifies that challenging violence within systems of bureaucracy including social work requires understandings that go beyond individualized problems and engage with structures of oppression and that

> [a]t times, this might entail social workers having to make complex ethical decisions about whether to implement a policy which conflicts with social work standards, professional capabilities, values or ethics.[67]

That is, to maintain the standards of professional practice which social workers have been trained in necessitates challenging some laws and practices as the context evolves. Undertaking this at an organizational level may seem particularly daunting, but Jolly notes that there are precedents within the UK for local authorities refusing to implement changing provisions of immigration law which would have undermined their legal and ethical duty to care for vulnerable people. A provision in immigration law introduced by Labour Home Secretary David Blunkett was designed to remove subsistence and accommodation support from children whose families were 'considered to have failed to take reasonable steps to leave the UK voluntarily'. This would then mean that the families had no entitlement to any state support and may become destitute, in which case 'local authorities may use their statutory powers to take children into care', i.e. remove them from their birth families.[68] A pilot scheme to test out this new provision was planned for social work departments in Croydon/East London, Manchester and Leeds/Bradford in 2005.[69] However, the measure was opposed by the British Association of Social Workers and the Unison Trade Union, and ten Manchester local authorities refused to implement the policy on the basis that it was 'immoral' and contradicted human rights law.[70] The then government did not proceed with implementing this power.[71] Nevertheless, by 2017, and in the context of intensifying austerity and increasing hostility to migrants, there were wide reports that some social work departments were threatening to remove children from migrant parents made destitute by their inability to access any state welfare safety net.[72]

These struggles *within* systems as individuals and organizations struggle with different conceptions of justice not only show that resistance *is* possible, but also that it is hard – because violent ignorance is persistent. Finding ways to draw attention to the unfairness of 'following the rules' put social workers at some level of risk to their livelihoods, but the alternative would have been to ignore the injustice of rules that make families destitute and then break them up because they are destitute. In some cases, an organized response confronting the violence of these policies stopped them – but the onslaught of attacks from border regimes and austerity politics is such that maintaining attention is hard, and violent ignorance depends sometimes on the eventual exhaustion of those who oppose it as violence and injustice multiply.

Thinking

Recall Hannah Arendt's discussions of Nazi war criminal Adolf Eichmann which were touched on in Chapter 1. Her famous phrase to refer to him was 'the banality of evil'. Her point was that 'evil' is not exceptional, something embodied only in monsters, but everyday. Sociologist Les Back made a similar argument after an encounter with Nick Griffin, then the leader of the fascist British National Party, when he noted that to treat Griffin as an exceptional monster was to ignore the really insidious nature of his power and threat. In fact, Griffin and politicians like him *are* a lot like other people; it is that which we have to guard against.[73] But confronting this is dangerous and uncomfortable.

> The thing that was immediately striking about Griffin was how ordinary he looked in the ebb and flow of London life at rush hour... There was nothing to signal that this was a man on the margins of the political spectrum.[74]
>
> ... this encounter was also about uncomfortable resemblances... we were approximately the same age, university graduates, loving fathers.[75]

In this encounter, Back is face to face with his polar opposite politically. He describes how, in previous research into far-right networks, he had received abuse and threats which made him worry for the safety of his family as well as himself. This included being accused of being 'a traitor, a Jew'; he surmised that, though not Jewish, apparently this was the only way the people he encountered could make sense of a commitment to anti-racism from a visibly white person.[76]

The striking thing about this encounter is that Griffin seems so familiar, so 'ordinary'. He is a Holocaust denier, has brutal political views which he spread widely, and a past in a directly violent far-right street-fighting group, the National Front. But he is not an incomprehensible monster, someone who can be removed from the picture and therefore from the 'civilised' world, and for whom we do not need to face self-examination. In effect, expelling someone like this from the idea of 'people like us' is blaming that someone for racism and violence. It's too easy. It lets everyone else off the hook.

As many have pointed out, the 'blame' for racism and xenophobia in Britain is frequently assigned to 'the white working class'.[77] In the eventual consensus about the horror of the murder of the Black British teenager Stephen Lawrence in 1992 (and the police's failure to investigate it), the news coverage leaned heavily on blaming the 'white working class' for a culture of violent racism, where the 'message was that in looking for racism in the UK there was no need to look further'.[78] A similar move has been made in much discussion of the Brexit vote, with 'the north' and 'the white working class' seen as 'left behind' by multinational, multi-ethnic Britain, and thereby responding with a xenophobic vote to leave the European Union. Such analysis not only belies the facts[79] but allows a largely London-based media to leave unquestioned its own role in the exclusions and violence – both racist and class-based – associated with the causes and consequences of virulent anti-immigrant and racialized political culture.[80]

As with the desire to blame specific politicians for the vicious turns in political debate and policy,[81] the placing of the blame for everyday racism, or for extremes of inhumane violence like the Holocaust, is a form of violent ignorance. This is because situating the blame on the most extreme and hideous culprits means refusing to recognize that we are all part of wider systems of oppression. By blaming the 'bad apple', the less visible rot in the rest of the crop is not dealt with.

It is for this reason that simply referring to 'the system' or 'society' or particular organizations or sections of society is insufficient. Blaming particular detention centre officers, one detention centre or one management company does not address the problem. Straightforward answers are inadequate. This does not mean that individuals who directly commit harm should not be held to account. But it means that to focus only on them allows ignorance of other contributory factors and actions – and lack of action by 'bystanders' – to remain ignored. To understand, engage with and counter injustice and oppression, it is necessary to look at it directly, in fine-grained ways and without seeking refuge in easy answers.

7

Manifesto

what you know
can hurt
but what you do
not know
can kill.

– AUDRE LORDE, *BUT WHAT CAN YOU TEACH MY DAUGHTER*[1]

Throughout this book, I have tried to lay out a conception of the idea of 'violent ignorance', as something deceptively comforting, but dangerous, and something to be avoided. At times when I have been writing, and probably as you have been reading, it has felt overwhelming to look at these examples of violence in the world, to see the entanglement of that violence with apparently innocent everyday life. It has also sometimes felt exhausting and discouraging to recognize that many reactions intended to assuage some of that violence ultimately can simply reinforce both forms of ignorance and violence. But this isn't intended to be a hopeless or doom-laden book; I hope instead it is a book about seeing things differently – and by seeing things differently, being able to make the world different too. To that end, this final chapter provides something of a 'manifesto' for how we might act differently to avoid, and tackle, violent ignorance in its various manifestations.

To get there, this chapter first reviews the foundations I have set out for the concept of violent ignorance and how this concept helps us to see things differently. I then revisit some of the attempts to deal with violence which, I have argued, simply reinforce the tendency to look away from discomfiting facts. If that summary seems to reinforce the feeling of being overwhelmed, the rest of the chapter is devoted to possibilities, both utopian and concrete.

Drawing out threads from throughout the book of alternative approaches to confronting and combatting violent injustice, without laying blame or accepting defeat, I sketch out some lines of thought from which another way of being in relation to troubling truths can be conceived, always aware that the temptation to ignore difficult subjects will never go away. To avoid the pitfall of treating this only as a thought experiment, the book closes with a more concrete manifesto – a set of possibilities for beginning to enact these ideas at different levels of the social: as individuals and collectives, within institutions, and as governments.

Violent ignorance

Throughout the book I have emphasized the idea that ignorance is an active process. I did so jumping off from the growing body of work on ignorance studies and 'agnotology', work which has set out the importance of understanding 'what we don't know' and recognizing that while some knowledge is unreachable or unimaginable, much is neglected, refused or silenced. Largely developed from studies of scientific practice and research, works in ignorance studies have notably shown the ways that powerful interests can prevent certain types of research being done (such as that which would show a link between industry and climate change) or can reduce the public recognition of other research (for instance, on the link between cancer and cigarettes). In political and policy context, experts can guide by using ignorance, refusing to acknowledge information or experiences that do not fit with dominant world-framings.[2]

This book has focused mainly on issues of race, nation and belonging and, in doing so, has engaged with an area currently under-explored in ignorance studies. This is with the notable exception of the important work of Charles W Mills, on 'white ignorance'. Like other works I have mentioned, Mills demonstrates how particular gaps in the knowledge or world view of influential figures have shaped behaviour and knowledge in Western thought specifically, paying attention to his area of expertise of political philosophy.[3] What is especially important in Mills's work is that he identifies that this expression of ignorance is both an expression of power and a process of producing power, and his emphasis is on the expression and (re) creation of racialized power in the basis of foundational thinkers in Western philosophy. Kant and Locke were able to dismiss the humanity of large swathes of the world, not just because they didn't know better, but because they *chose* not to know. In justifying the violent divisions of humanity enforced through processes of invasion and colonization, they created alibis for others for the persistence of those divisions.

An important part of the idea of violent ignorance is of course not just the ignorance – the refusing to know – but the violence. Violence appears throughout the examples I have given in many forms, but the key element of the idea of violent ignorance is that it is an active turning away from uncomfortable knowledge, which in this refusing of knowledge produces (or allows) more violence. The violence I have discussed ranges from the most literal and extreme – genocide – to the smaller scale that is still painful for those experiencing it. The extreme examples, particularly relating to the recurring theme of the European Holocaust, are ones which have of course been analysed by many thinkers. They are brought together here because I hope some of the responses I have considered can be used to shed light on ways of responding to apparently more genteel, or more obscured, everyday violence and injustice today.

I have suggested that violence be thought of as often, but not only, physical violence – but nonetheless, all of the violence and injustice I have considered throughout has had material manifestations. This might be in the haunting of Ben Affleck's public persona by the history of his slave-owning ancestors and its potential reputational (and therefore financial) implications (as in Chapter 4). It might be in the destruction of written records of British Commonwealth citizens' movements which dismissed the importance of those events and later restricted their ability to prove a right of abode in their lifelong country of residence. It might be the refusal to address the physical safety of residents in social housing who were without financial or cultural capital to make themselves heard by the supposed democratic institutions that had a duty to keep them safe. Or it might be in the response to a political assassination which refuses to address the political cleavages which led to it and leaves them simmering instead.

A common thread within these examples of violent injustice is that physical and material bodies have been hurt, but also that the ways in which that has happened are tied up in knowledge and social relations. This is true in the banal way that slavery, border control, social housing, representative democracy and law enforcement are all social institutions which value particular kinds of knowledge, artefacts, status and interventions. But what I am really getting at is that, in each of these examples, both the violent injustice and the ignorance at stake are not easily pinned down to one event or individual, at least not at the time. They are situations in which many, if not all, are embroiled. And that also makes them harder to confront, because there are no easy answers.

While writing this book, I have experimented with a variety of metaphors to try to get at the essence of violent ignorance. It has been, variously, a skin (that can be wounded, but which scabs over, albeit leaving a scar in the ignorance skin), a wall (with cracks that can be pried apart or papered over), a veil (that can be torn, or seen through up close, or lifted and then dropped again), a film (that imperceptibly seals and secures) and a shield (that can be damaged and peered through with trepidation).

Of all of these metaphors, I think the idea of violent ignorance as a living skin is the most resonant. Ignoring uncomfortable truths keeps social order together, keeps shared meanings whole and coherent – for those inside the protective skin. Like a fleshy wound, a breach in violent ignorance can be painful, and it also can damage more than what is on the surface; making the extent of brutal injustice visible in the 'silent scream' of a toddler's corpse might lead to sufficient pressure to challenge violent border regimes and loosen the power of xenophobic fear, if only momentarily. This is the other important element of the 'skin' metaphor: the living, repairing nature of violent ignorance. Because it is one thing to make apparent the usually ignored, in a shocking moment of recognition such as the way that the Grenfell fire exposed the systematic exclusions, injustices and rejections of British systems of citizenship, housing, welfare and democracy. But to sustain that vision, to keep that clarity in sight, is much harder, because it is so painful. This doesn't happen immediately, but like living skin, violent ignorance can form a scab, repairing through acts of charity perhaps, until the injustices that were exposed are covered again, even if a scar remains to remind us superficially of what happened.

Scabs

Much of this book has been taken up with not only describing incidences in which painful knowledge of people's implication in injustice has been ignored, but also with considering moments when that knowledge could no longer be ignored. That is, moments when ignorance fails, or is wounded, and knowledge of violent injustice and its workings become evident to all. These are often moments of extremity – the assassination of Jo Cox, the fire in Grenfell, the image of Alan Kurdi, the exposé of abuse at Brook House – but in confronting each of them it is clear that they point to an everyday grinding reality of ongoing misogyny and hate, institutional neglect, border violence and incarceration. And yet, after each of these seemingly earth-shifting moments of shared recognition of injustice, things have continued on more or less as before. How could this happen?

It is not simply that people turned away callously, but that we are so protective of our ignorance that we continually find new ways to preserve it. When wounded, the would clots, blood dries, a protective scab is formed, the skin heals.

To heal the wound of a political assassination that showed the stark materiality of hateful backlash against the unfinished projects of addressing gendered, racialized and bordered power imbalances, we organize projects of shared food and togetherness. Doing so fails to confront the context in which this attack took place and the pattern of violence of which it forms a part. To heal the wound of seventy-two people neglected and burned alive in the most wealthy and well-resourced corner of the planet, we donate resources, organize an investigation and wait, while thousands continue to live in unsafe dwellings, or no dwellings at all, in rich cities where others pay millions to let homes stand empty. To heal the wound of the dead, solitary toddler on the beach, we send donations, offer homes, accept pre-sorted refugees from camps, but meanwhile thousands continue to drown and suffocate in their search for safety and comfort.

Perhaps criticizing these efforts seems sanctimonious. People are trying to make things better, and that is not to be condemned. The point I am trying to make is how powerful the desire and the drive to look away from violent injustice is – but particularly to look away from our own implication in it.

There is always going to be some ignorance, some not-knowing, and perhaps also some refusing-to-know. To make sense of the world, there is a need to make narrative, to single out the important parts and make connections. It's just that what we often choose to single out are the parts that absolve us or make us feel better.

The idea is not to feel bad. That serves no purpose at all. Perhaps feeling angry can help – we can use our anger as fuel, as poet and theorist Audre Lorde suggests.[4]

Some of the making-sense, though, is a filtering out of the connection between knowing and feeling. This too is a form of ignorance, of turning away. Reducing people to numbers – whether large numbers for population management or individual bar codes for sorting – allows an ignorance of their humanity. Understanding stories and feelings makes other humans harder to dismiss.

Finding someone or something to blame for injustice is another way of making sense, of filtering out noise – and knowledge. Identifying a villain means absolving the rest. But jailing Jo Cox's killer did not make other women, racially minoritized or anti-racist feminist politicians safe. Only confronting the white supremacist misogynist conditions in which the murder took place could begin to do that.

Possibilities

What are the possibilities for action that does not simply reinstate violent ignorance? We have glimpsed a few possibilities through the course of this book. Where Ben Affleck chose to deny and hide from his ancestral slave-owner, another actor, Bill Paxton, on finding a similar ancestor, explored instead the life of one of the people his ancestor had enslaved, thereby extending knowledge rather than ignorance. Where some children of Nazi war criminals dedicated their lives to condemning or redeeming their fathers, Jennifer Teege chose to neither reject completely nor justify her grandmother's actions, instead accepting the murky, conflicted life of horrific acts and of love for her. Where government advisers tried to smooth the way for post-Grenfell negotiations with simplified community engagement structures, self-organized groups of residents refused to abandon their own terms of engagement and their own voices, and Ahmed Elgwahary and other Grenfell United activists constantly had to return the immediacy of the situation to the forefront of government ministers' minds: 'Our families were burned and you have to remind them we are not a normal group. You have to do that to sensitise them.'[5]

Remembering: Past, present, future

Part of tackling ignorance and its violence is having the information to demonstrate its workings. The case of the hidden archives of British colonial crimes in Kenya shows both the power of documenting history and the power of concealing and reconstructing it with certain silences. Because the archives were kept, albeit secretly, it was eventually possible to prove the treatment of Kenyans by the British and for survivors to gain acknowledgement, apology and compensation. But the hidden records would not have been revealed if it had not been for the living memories and persistence of the survivors, and the campaigners and lawyers who supported them. The continuing importance of the past in determining the present and future is important to retain. Having records of the past is a form of witness that is often maintained by governments or state authorities, but many personal and activist archives exist too, and it is in the multiple sets of evidence and remembering that we may be able to tackle longer-standing widespread ignorance, through amplifying these pockets of knowing.

In discussing the power of images of war, photographer and cultural commentator Susan Sontag reminds us that it is not always enough simply to *remember* events, but important also to understand their meaning. This understanding might change over time, as more information is available – or as less context is remembered and meaning as well as memory fade over time. An example briefly touched on in Jennifer Teege's story was the understanding of Oskar Schindler as a hero, a story first made known worldwide by an Australian author in the 1980s and which is more challenging and less sugar-coated if we continue to remember that Schindler's bravery and heroism also followed using forced labour in his factories and friendship with some of the most brutal Nazi leadership. This does not take away from the historic story of rescue – perhaps it even enhances the bravery. But it makes a more complicated story.

Discomfort/indeterminacy

Violent ignorance protects those maintaining it from being exposed to, and confronting, discomfort. This discomfort is primarily of seeing one's own connection to (and perhaps benefits derived from) forms of everyday violent injustice. One form of evading this confrontation with discomfort is to work hard to identify another cause of injustice – for example, blaming 'ruthless people smugglers' for the dangerous conditions in which thousands of people cross international borders. Measures to tackle 'human trafficking' might well uncover forms of brutality and cruelty which should be stopped. But stopping such enterprises, even if possible, does nothing to tackle the conditions in which it is preferable for people to submit to dangerous journeys rather than stay where they are – the restrictions on moving across territories and the unequal distribution of resources, safety and dignity across and within borders.[6] Looked at this way, those championing the solution of tackling human trafficking may have to recognize that they are the beneficiaries of the underlying inequities which the border regime maintains. Rejecting violent ignorance means rejecting its seeming safeties and certainties; staying uncomfortable; refusing to play it safe, to look away from surprises or disturbance, or to act as if we already know who is to blame.

If blame is a form of ignorance, where should challenges to injustice be directed, and by whom? Who should be rewarded; who should be punished? These are the wrong questions. Rather than ignoring complexity because it hurts, the question is, how can we see that more than one thing can be true at once? That Jo Cox's death can be mourned as the tragic loss of a mother, sister, daughter, spouse and friend, but *also* as the outcome of an ongoing pattern of misogynist white supremacist outbursts. That human trafficking can be exploitative and cruel, but so can the practices of government bordering which enable it. That Nazi war criminals might have been perfectly lovely to their close family, but nevertheless committed, designed and sanctioned genocidal crimes. Holding these contradictions together is difficult – what resources might there be for doing so, and in doing so, challenging the temptations of violent ignorance that would have us dismiss these possibilities?

Feeling

When the Grenfell Tower fire, or the assassination of Jo Cox, or the humiliation and abuse of the Windrush Generation, or the death of Alan Kurdi, moved people to see the injustice that was in front of them, it was not because of an intellectual build-up of evidence. Information about the lack of safe standards in social housing, or the persistence of far-right attacks on politicians, or the arbitrary injustices of the hostile environment, or the death toll in the Mediterranean, were all well documented if anyone cared to look into them. In each of these instances, a dramatic event, image or well-told story forced a wider public to look directly at injustice – albeit briefly – and to feel that something was wrong.

The impulse to look away from suffering is not new, and often this has been explained by an innate refusal to feel compassion for those 'unlike' the viewer in some way – because of geographical distance, ethnic, national or racialized identity, or class position, for example. An argument often put forward is that, in order for the 'ordinary person' who is not in immediate danger to care, they must see those in danger as 'ordinary' too, like them. This is taken to mean that there must be an alignment in the social categories by which people organize themselves, or else perhaps how people want to see themselves – as hardworking, respectable, of good social standing. The implication is that an outcast, criminal, weirdo, shirker or otherwise distasteful and stigmatized character would not be the sort of person with whom 'ordinary people' would feel sympathy.

This of course means that in campaigns to raise public awareness of an injustice – to tackle ignorance – it is often thought wise to rely on 'respectable' faces for a campaign. This is behind the impulse, in the exposés of the Windrush Scandal, to portray this as a case of the hostile environment affecting 'the wrong people', 'hardworking'

British residents who had 'paid taxes'.[7] The Joint Council for the Welfare of Immigrants, a campaigning charity, responded to a similar impulse in the publicity they produced during the 2015 UK general election campaign, which attempted to counter the virulent anti-immigration tone of political debate at that time by depicting images of the faces of specific migrants with captions such as 'I am an immigrant. I am a brain surgeon. I have saved 2,000 lives.' As with the other examples of interventions which are well meant but which maintain the exclusions of violent ignorance, such moves are only reformist and not revolutionary. They may widen the circle of fellow-feeling, but they still rely on, or fail to challenge, an idea that there are some humans who are not worthy of sympathy – not hardworking enough, not valuable enough to society. These strategies are chosen because of a recognition that emotional connection is important to engender a powerful enough feeling to want to act on injustice. But they lack imagination, in that they stick with the idea that there are some humans who fundamentally cannot be recognized as worthy of dignity.

In some moments covered in this book, there have been glimpses of ways of expanding this feeling of connection so that it could include those more usually ignored. One powerful example was the artwork *Barca Nostra*, the moving of the boat on which over 700 people drowned near the Italian island of Lampedusa to the centre of the elite international art world at the Venice Biennale in 2019. The placing of this ship there was criticized as callous, as turning the deaths at sea into entertainment. I have argued, however, that the real consequence of this shifting of the context of the death-boat was to reveal the ease with which violent ignorance sustains itself. Those angry at the presence of the boat at the Venice Biennale had become angry at the artist, at the perceived lack of respect of tourists.

And yet the demonstration of how such a towering reminder of global networks of unjust power could become just another piece of art to view is what is remarkable: the ability to sip cocktails next to the death-boat and to view this from afar and become enraged in a way that reminds us – or does not – that the much more enraging tragedy is the ongoing border death toll. In this, the *Barca Nostra* does not require that the people who died are depicted as rule-followers or taxpayers, because the evidence of their terrible deaths, and the way their deaths are weighed against the value of glamour, style and wealth, are legible without that. Another moment at which a feeling of connection, a shared need to address injustice, is tangible is in the Grenfell Silent Walk.

Silence

Silence has reverberated in different ways throughout this book. The silencing of particular voices and histories is obviously central to the idea of violent ignorance, where ignoring can equate to silencing. The work of historian Michel-Rolph Trouillot has been influential in laying out how 'silences enter the historical record'[8] and how understanding such gaps – or spaces of ignorance – is essential to understanding how history is made and remade.

Of course, in many cases, people and stories that have been ignored have been far from silent. The residents of Grenfell Tower reported and recorded the neglect of their homes and welfare, using official and unofficial channels, and though they were loud and persistent, they were not heard – they were ignored. The power of institutional indifference to refuse certain voices is a violence in itself – but of course, the greater violence it enabled was the eventual tragedy that some residents had already, publicly, predicted might come about as a result of their concerns.

As those residents predicted, it was only such a tragedy and loss of life that made their voices heard, their predicament visible, and broke through the deliberate ignoring of the situation. Yet techniques of containment, alongside painstaking and essential investigations, have led to fears that this visibility is fading too soon. The delays in finding adequate accommodation for those displaced by the fire, the revelations that the flammable cladding which led to the fire is still in place on many residential blocks and the ease with which government officials who had responsibility for safety of housing have moved into further senior advisory positions, all suggest that this may be the case. And this is why the groups Grenfell United and Justice for Grenfell, and others, continue to devote their time and energy to changing housing policy and seeking redress, even while dealing with their own personal trauma. Alongside this, the Silent Walk for Grenfell, held on the 14th of every month, is a powerful symbol. In this shared, defiant, grieving, angry silence, there can be unity of purpose even where the details of what Justice for Grenfell may mean can differ between everyone present; those nuances can exist, but alongside a silent solidarity. The collective, reflective silence is something powerful which refuses noise, refuses to be pinned down by narratives that can be reinterpreted and refuses to be ignored.

Risk

The silence of solidarity that I suggest might be one avenue to forcing a recognition of what has previously been ignored is not the same as staying silent in the face of injustice. That, of course, is itself a way of ignoring, of not acknowledging. Sometimes, though, it can be a high-risk enterprise to speak out publicly against injustice – and indeed, even counterproductive to make 'speaking out' the primary act. I am thinking here of the schoolteachers, Franz and Elizabeth, encountered by Amy Buller in Nazi Germany. They describe a dilemma where in many ways they wish to take a public stand against the regime but fear that in doing so, their positions would simply be filled by Nazi enthusiasts – that is, the stand they might take that way would make them feel more honourable but would ultimately not challenge the Nazis or protect the children in their care. Instead, they choose to remain as teachers but undermine fascist teaching while supporting critical thinking among their pupils, hoping that by doing so they offer some resistance, but knowing too that they appear and will be treated as collaborators. The risk they take may seem less than taking a public stand and being imprisoned or executed, but it is a risk nonetheless, and one they believe will be more productive in countering the violence they confront.

Of course, there is an alternative, 'fifth option', which Franz hints at but seems to be unable to imagine putting into practice, that is, one of 'collective action'.[9] In many ways this was foreclosed by Nazi laws banning trade unions. The strength of resistance, though, whether in the form of public resistance or underground subversion, will always be greater when collective than individual.

The placing of oneself at risk, even as part of a collective, is perhaps essential in challenging violent ignorance. This might simply be the risk of dealing with the discomfort of recognizing one's privileged position. It could also be more active. The Stansted 15, a group of young British people who chained themselves to a deportation flight, is one example. Their act broke the law, and they were well aware that they were likely to face possible criminal records, fines and imprisonment as a result of these actions. They undertook the action to prevent other people being deported by the British government, many to countries they did not know. Though – as with the teachers Franz and Elizabeth – it was likely these actions would be undertaken anyway, on another flight at another time,[10] the public action was important more widely too. It challenged the organized ignorance of such deportations by making the event 'newsworthy'. Following the logic of 'ordinary people', these activists were seen as worthy subjects of news coverage, in a way that those inside the aeroplane were not. This despite the fact that it was the action that was extraordinary, and the deportation flight mundane. The actions of the Stansted 15 were an attempt to use the privileges of power differentiated by citizenship, class and race to draw attention to violence that would otherwise remain ignored.

Not everyone all the time

Alongside pointing out that ignorance is not always violent, and that some silences must always remain in order to make sense of the world, it is worth reiterating that violent ignorance is not something that is equally distributed. The violence and injustice of the world cannot, for most people in the world, be ignored in their everyday lives, where it will permeate in different, uneven ways. The ignorance I am primarily focused on in this book is the ignorance of the comfortable and particularly of those who are comfortable and do not wish to be disturbed by the idea that their comfort may have some relation to others' discomfort or lack of safety.

***

Manifesto

1. Information

i. Get information (in all forms)

If violent ignorance is about ignoring what is discomfiting or upsetting, and removing its evidence and evidence of its causes from view, maybe it can be challenged by gathering more and better information. Being hungry for information might mean being imaginative about what counts – facts and figures, fairy stories, life histories, soap operas, political speeches, business accounts, children's games, legal judgements, personal letters, dance, music, art and so on, all of this expands understanding, and consuming, experiencing and questioning all forms of information makes it harder to cut off meaning or make parts of the world invisible.

ii. Question information

Simply accepting what we are told risks ignorance; who knows if the person sharing information is right, or how they made their judgements or came by that information? Questioning doesn't mean disbelieving everything, but having reasons for believing something. Being able to change one's mind when new information or ideas emerge is another defence against ignorance; settled patterns of thinking can prevent seeing things we would prefer stayed hidden.

iii. Save information

Value, protect, create, share libraries and archives. Ideas and information come in many forms and can be easily lost, as the examples of the British colonial records in Kenya and the Windrush landing cards, discussed in Chapter 4, demonstrated. The fact that paper records were destroyed did not mean that all knowledge was lost; those who had lived through events knew what had happened, and other forms of record could be reconstructed. But this goes to show how important oral histories and folk archives are, alongside the more official or state-level archives, libraries and museums.

iv. Make information

Produce records of struggles, injustice, strategies, success. If history is a process of both remembering and forgetting, there is power in deciding what is remembered. Preserving records that might otherwise be lost can be done on personal, collective and institutional levels. Recording the lives of those lost to the violence of borders, or to the institutional indifference of the Grenfell disaster, is an important part of keeping those violent events from being lost in ignorance. Preserving the knowledge of how they came to lose their lives matters. It is important too to record that struggles against violence, and against ignorance, are what have challenged injustice in the past.

2. Imagination

i. Allow yourself to be surprised

The best way to see what is usually ignored is to be open to seeing new things and to allow ourselves to be surprised by what we see. Look at everything, wonder at it, explore meanings. Get beyond the obvious, even if that seems initially more satisfying. If someone is to blame for violence, is that the whole story? What else might matter?

ii. Connect meanings, feelings, ideas

Take that information you have collected, made, gathered and saved and work out what it means in new formations. Play with connections; think about why some things matter and some things don't seem to matter. What was it that made the image of Alan Kurdi make so many more people face up to the violence of borders and try to act? What other ways of connecting people to the meaning of distressing information that is around might help to harness anger into action? Stories, images and interactions can change the boundaries in which people usually think and make it possible to see ways out of a situation which violent ignorance obscures. They might even help us to imagine new ways in which the world could be organized, to help us escape the confines of what violent ignorance convinces us is inevitable.

iii. Find ways to communicate

Violent ignorance can be about oppressive silence, looking away, not talking about certain things and not thinking. Keeping questions, information, ideas and meanings live is a way of stopping ignorance from shutting down new connections. Communication doesn't have to be with words; it can be with images, art, actions. It can be loud or quiet. It is about listening – or looking – as well as telling and making (they are part of the same thing). It can be face to face and intimate, or public and anonymous. Interaction will keep changing information, ideas and meanings, raising questions, and new possibilities for a better way of connecting.

3. Risk

i. Understand, then bend, rules

The trick of violent ignorance is that it makes people feel safe, because it feels easier to ignore what is happening than to take action. But when injustice continues, no one is really safe; even those with the most power have to put their resources into protecting themselves and their position. Understanding that it is not safe to stay mired in ignorance may be the first step to being brave enough to take a risk to counter it.

ii. Find others, speak out

Use whatever privilege and resources you have. If you are not at the sharp end of the violent border regime, or have the resources to use the legal system to your advantage, maybe you can afford to take more risks than others. Maybe the resources you have are your ideas, your skills, or maybe they are the connections you have with other people. Taking risks together can make a movement more powerful. Learning about violence and injustice and its workings together is one thing. Recognizing one's own role in injustice is riskier – especially because it makes people feel unsafe and uncomfortable. Use that discomfort, and use your anger, to work together to find ways to keep trying to tackle unfairness and expose injustice, without needing to claim that you know all the answers or are infallible.

iii. Keep trying (fail again, fail better)

In many ways this book is a risk and this attempt at a manifesto is riskier. I certainly don't have all the answers, but I want to keep trying, so I am. Trying to work out why and how injustice continues, even when it is in plain sight and its harms are infiltrating the lives of millions, is a tough challenge. Trying to do something about it is harder and can seem doomed to failure before even beginning. But failing is a part of learning, and challenging the power of ignorance must, if nothing else, be about learning. So this is not the last word. But it is a set of suggestions about how to respond after understanding that we are all embroiled in systems of injustice, some with more power than others, and that such injustice is sustained by refusal to recognize it. Keep thinking, sharing and resisting.

Notes

Preface

1 Sontag, S (2003) *Regarding the Pain of Others*, London: Penguin, p.104.
2 Ibid., p.92.
3 E.g. Davies, W (2019) *Nervous States: How Feeling Took over the World*, London: Penguin; D'Ancona, M (2017) *Post-Truth: The New War on Truth and How to Fight Back*, London: Penguin.
4 Valluvan, S (2019) *The Clamour of Nationalisms*, Manchester: Manchester University Press.
5 Trouillot, M-R (1997) *Silencing the Past: Power and the Production of History*, Boston: Beacon Press.
6 Triggle, N (2020) 'Coronavirus: Testing, PPE and Ventilators – How Has the Government Done?' *BBC News*, 3 April, https://www.bbc.co.uk/news/health-52142083; Maclean, R and Marks, S (2020) '10 African Countries Have No Ventilators. That's Only Part of the Problem', *The New York Times*, 18 April, https://www.nytimes.com/2020/04/18/world/africa/africa-coronavirus-ventilators.html
7 Roy, A (2020) 'Arundhati Roy: "The Pandemic Is a Portal"', *Financial Times*, 3 April, https://www.ft.com/content/10d8f5e8-74eb-11ea-95fe-fcd274e920ca
8 Helm, T, Graham-Harrison, E and McKie, R (2020) 'How Did Britain Get Its Coronavirus Response So Wrong?' *The Guardian*, 19 April, https://www.theguardian.com/world/2020/apr/18/how-did-britain-get-its-response-to-coronavirus-so-wrong

Chapter 1

1 Arendt, H (1968 [2006]) *Eichmann in Jerusalem: A Report on the Banality of Evil*, London: Penguin Classics, p.288.

2 Jones, H, Gunaratnam, Y, Bhattacharyya, G, Davies, W, Dhaliwal, S, Forkert, K, Jackson, E and Saltus, R (2017) *Go Home? The Politics of Immigration Controversies*, Manchester: Manchester University Press.

3 See also Jones, H (2019) 'More in Common: The Domestication of Misogynist White Supremacy and the Assassination of Jo Cox', *Ethnic and Racial Studies*, 42(14):2431–49.

4 Frickel, S, Gibbon, S, Howard, J, Kempner, J, Ottinger, G and Hess, D J (2010) 'Undone Science: Charting Social Movement and Civil Society Challenges to Research Agenda Setting', *Science, Technology and Human Values*, 35(4):444–73.

5 Arendt, H (1968 [2006]) *Eichmann in Jerusalem: A Report on the Banality of Evil*, London: Penguin Classics.

6 Ibid., p.157.

7 For an overview, see Ezra, M (2007) 'The Eichmann Polemics: Hannah Arendt and Her Critics', *Democratiya*, 9:141–65.

8 Eichmann quoted in Arendt, H (1968 [2006]) *Eichmann in Jerusalem: A Report on the Banality of Evil*, London: Penguin Classics, p.88.

9 Ibid., p.89.

10 *The Guardian*, 6 December 2017, https://www.theguardian.com/society/video/2017/dec/06/heidi-allen-mp-tears-frank-field-impact-of-universal-credit-video

11 https://www.theyworkforyou.com/mp/25348/heidi_allen/south_cambridgeshire/divisions?policy=6670

12 Mills, C W (2007) 'White Ignorance', in Sullivan, S and Tuana, N (eds) *Race and Epistemologies of Ignorance*, Albany: State University of New York Press, pp.11–38.

13 Mills, C W (1997) *The Racial Contract*, Ithaca: Cornell University Press, pp.16–17.

14 Wekker, G (2016) *White Innocence: Paradoxes of Colonialism and Race*, Durham, NC: Duke University Press, p.17.

15 See also Ahmed, S (2008) 'Liberal Multiculturalism is the Hegemony – It's an Empirical Fact – A response to Slavoj Žižek', *darkmatter*, 19 February, http://www.darkmatter101.org/site/2008/02/19/%E2%80%98liberal-multiculturalism-is-the-hegemony-%E2%80%93-its-an-empirical-fact%E2%80%99-a-response-to-slavoj-zizek/; Srivastava, S (2005) '"You're Calling Me a Racist?" The Moral and Emotional Regulation of Antiracism and Feminism', *Signs: Journal of Women in Culture and Society*, 31(1):29–62.

16 Du Bois, W E B (1903 [2007]) *The Souls of Black Folk*, Oxford: Oxford University Press.

17 Ibid., p.157.

18 Ibid., p.162.

19 Gross, M and McGoey, L (eds) (2015) *Routledge International Handbook of Ignorance Studies*, 1st Edition, London: Routledge.

20 Proctor, R N (1996) *Cancer Wars: How Politics Shapes What We Know and Don't Know About Cancer*, New York: Basic Books; Proctor, R N and Schiebinger, N (eds) (2008) *Agnotology: The Making and Unmaking of Ignorance*, Stanford: Stanford University Press.

21 Frickel, S, Gibbon, S, Howard, J, Kempner, J, Ottinger, G and Hess, D J (2010) 'Undone Science: Charting Social Movement and Civil Society Challenges to Research Agenda Setting', *Science, Technology and Human Values*, 35(4):444–73.

22 Trouillot, M-R (1997) *Silencing the Past: Power and the Production of History*, Boston: Beacon Press.

23 Sullivan, S and Tuana, N (eds) (2007) *Race and Epistemologies of Ignorance*, Albany: State University of New York Press.

24 Du Bois, W E B (1903 [1994]) *The Souls of Black Folk*, New York: Dover Publications, Inc.

25 E.g. Sedgwick, E K (1990) *Epistemology of the Closet*, Berkeley: University of California Press.

26 To misquote Samuel Beckett.

27 Cobain, I, Parveen, N and Taylor, M (2016) 'The Slow-burning Hatred that Led Thomas Mair to Murder Jo Cox', *The Guardian*, 23 November, https://www.theguardian.com/uk-news/2016/nov/23/thomas-mair-slow-burning-hatred-led-to-jo-cox-murder. The article continues: 'In the days before the murder he sought out information about the Ku Klux Klan, the Waffen SS, Israel, serial killers and matricide.'

28 Brendan Cox quoted in Brendan Cox quoted in Addley, E, Elgot, J and Perraudin, F (2016) 'Jo Cox: Thousands Pay Tribute on What Should have been MP's Birthday', *The Guardian*, 22 June, https://www.theguardian.com/uk-news/2016/jun/22/jo-cox-murder-inspired-more-love-than-hatred-says-husband-brendan

29 It is worth noting that while political assassinations of elected representatives have been rare in the UK, they are much more common in many other parts of the world. The insistence that Cox's murder should have been taken more seriously does not contradict an awareness that living in a territory where political violence of this sort is rare is exceptional itself; rather I am suggesting this sort of peace is not something that should be taken for granted, as a minimizing of the significance of Cox's assassination risks doing.

30 Mr Justice Wilkie quoted in Mr Justice Wilkie quoted in BBC News (2016) 'Jo Cox Murder: Judge's Sentencing Remarks to Thomas Mair', *www.bbcnews.co.uk*, 23 June, https://www.bbc.co.uk/news/uk-38076755

31 Ibid.

32 Sims, P (2016) 'Murdered in Cold Blood', *The Sun*, 17 June, p.1.

33 Greenwood, C, Brooke, C and Dolan, A (2016) 'What a Tragic Waste', *The Daily Mail*, 17 June, p.1.

34 Cox, B (2017) *Jo Cox: More in Common*, London: Two Roads, p.212.

35 E.g. Falvey, D (2018) 'Theresa May Delivers Emotional Heartfelt Message to Jo Cox's Children About "Mummy"', *Sunday Express*, 18 January, https://www.express.co.uk/news/uk/906339/jo-cox-minister-for-loneliness-theresa-may-tracey-crouch-labour-mp-murder; Griffiths, B (2017) 'WIDOWER TELLS ALL Jo Cox's Husband Brendan Reveals Taking Kids to See Murdered Wife's Body "Was the Hardest Decision of His Life"', *The Sun*, 4 June; ITV (2017) 'Jo Cox's Children Set to Unveil Coat of Arms Dedicated to Mum', *ITV News*, 24 June, http://www.itv.com/news/2017-06-24/jo-coxs-children-unveil-coat-of-arms-dedicated-to-mum/

36 Annual, nationally co-ordinated but locally volunteer-organized street parties, picnics and other get-togethers 'inspired by Jo Cox'. See https://www.greatgettogether.org/

37 Jo Cox set up a cross-party Parliamentary Loneliness Commission with fellow MP Seema Kennedy, to 'run for one year and work with charities, businesses and the Government to turbo-charge the public understanding and policy response to the loneliness crisis'. After her death it was renamed the Jo Cox Loneliness Commission, published a report into loneliness and its implications, and led to Prime Minister Theresa May creating a Minister for Loneliness and a 'cross-Government strategy to tackle loneliness which set out a series of commitments to help all age groups build connections' in 2018. https://www.jocoxloneliness.org/

38 A training programme established by Cox's colleagues in the Labour Women's Network (which she chaired) and the Labour Party in her memory, to support and encourage women to take on leadership roles within the Party. https://labour.org.uk/members/jo-cox-women-leadership/

39 Cobain, I, Parveen, N and Taylor, M (2016) 'The Slow-burning Hatred that Led Thomas Mair to Murder Jo Cox', *The Guardian*, 23 November, https://www.theguardian.com/uk-news/2016/nov/23/thomas-mair-slow-burning-hatred-led-to-jo-cox-murder.

40 Smith, P (2016) 'Jewish MP Feared for Her Safety after Receiving 2,500 Abusive Messages a Day', *BuzzFeed News*, 5 December, https://www.buzzfeed.com/patricksmith/jewish-mp-feared-for-her-safety-after-receiving-2500-abusive?utm_term=.moxBv57P7#.clxvn6qwq

41 BBC News (2017) 'Jewish and Muslim Women MPs "Face Most Abuse"', *BBC News*, 21 March, http://www.bbc.co.uk/news/uk-politics-39339487; Dhrodia, A (2017) 'We Tracked 25,688 Abusive Tweets Sent to Women MPs

– Half were Directed at Diane Abbott', *New Statesman*, 5 September, https://www.newstatesman.com/2017/09/we-tracked-25688-abusive-tweets-sent-women-mps-half-were-directed-diane-abbott; Wheeler, B and Carter, A (2017) 'MPs Tell of Death Threats and Abuse at 2017 Election', *BBC News*, 18 September, http://www.bbc.co.uk/news/uk-politics-41237836

42 BBC News (2018) 'National Action: Men Jailed for Being Members of Banned Neo-Nazi group', *BBC News*, 18 July, https://www.bbc.co.uk/news/uk-politics-44873178

43 BBC News (2018) 'Darren Osborne Guilty of Finsbury Park Mosque Murder', *BBC News*, 1 February, http://www.bbc.co.uk/news/uk-42910051

44 Johnston, C (2018) 'Sadiq Khan Speech Disrupted by Brexit and Trump Supporters', *The Guardian*, 13 January, https://www.theguardian.com/politics/2018/jan/13/sadiq-khan-speech-disrupted-by-protesters-backing-brexit-and-trump-white-pendragons

45 TellMAMA (2018) 'Who Are the White Pendragons?' 15 January, http://tellmamauk.org/who-are-the-white-pendragons/

46 Musician.

47 Tennis player.

48 TV chef.

49 Footballer.

50 Actor.

51 Actor.

52 Actor.

53 Extract from Great Get Together (2017) 'The Great Get Together Aims to Unite Britain for Jo Cox', Video, https://www.youtube.com/watch?v=pgQf8JMX3_0; see also Jones, H (2019) 'More in Common: The Domestication of Misogynist White Supremacy and the Assassination of Jo Cox', *Ethnic and Racial Studies*, 42(14):2431–49.

54 Such as the think tank 'British Future' which also seeks to incorporate diversity but within a firmly, unquestioningly nationalistic imagery.

55 See also Back, L (2002) 'Guess Who's Coming to Dinner? The Political Morality of Investigating Whiteness in the Gray Zone', in Ware, V and Back, L (eds) *Out of Whiteness: Color, Politics and Culture*, Chicago: University of Chicago Press, pp.33–59.

56 Berglund, O (2017) 'Using Empty Luxury Homes to House Grenfell Tower Victims Is a No Brainer', *The Conversation*, 26 June, https://theconversation.com/using-empty-luxury-homes-to-house-grenfell-tower-victims-is-a-no-brainer-80025; Newbold, A (2017) 'Grenfell Tower Fire Inspires Generosity', *Vogue.co.uk*, 15 June, https://www.vogue.co.uk/article/grenfell-tower-fire-celebrity-reaction; Edwards-Jones, I (2017) 'Grenfell Tower has

United London's "Have and Have Yachts" Like I've Never Seen Before', *The Telegraph*, 15 June, https://www.telegraph.co.uk/women/life/grenfell-tower-has-united-londons-have-have-yachts-like-never/

57 Rawlinson, K (2018) '100 Households Around Grenfell Still in Temporary Accommodation', *The Guardian*, 29 March, https://www.theguardian.com/uk-news/2018/mar/29/100-households-around-grenfell-still-in-temporary-accommodation; Rawlinson, K (2017) 'There Are 1,399 Homes a Stone's Throw from Grenfell Tower Left Empty by Millionaires. Time to Move in the Victims', *The Independent*, 15 June, https://www.independent.co.uk/voices/grenfell-tower-fire-deaths-homeless-kensington-and-chelsea-luxury-properties-empty-a7791671.html; https://www.rightmove.co.uk/house-prices-in-my-area/marketTrendsTotalPropertiesSoldAndAveragePrice.html?searchLocation=w11+&sellersPriceGuide=Start+Search. There have of course been further mobilizations and more politically engaged responses to the Grenfell fire, some of which may lead to longer-term change in housing inequality; this will be discussed further in Chapter Two. Here, the point is that soothing interventions can help those comfortable enough to look away from tragedies such as Grenfell, to do so.

58 Thanks to Eiri Ohtani for drawing my attention to this.

59 McGoey, L (2016) *No Such Thing as a Free Gift: The Gates Foundation and the Price of Philanthropy*, London: Verso.

60 http://skoll.org/contributor/tim-dixon/; http://skoll.org/skoll-world-forum/pricing/

61 An international initiative to 'build communities and societies that are stronger, more united and more resilient to the increasing threats of polarisation and social division' through 'positive narratives' and 'connect[ing] people ... across lines of difference, through events and campaigns'. https://www.moreincommon.com/

62 A charity established 'to be part of practical efforts to advance the causes Jo championed' which has worked on causes including loneliness, the protection of civilians in conflict and supporting women to enter public life. https://www.jocoxfoundation.org/who-we-are

63 https://www.linkedin.com/in/brendan-cox-433b364/?originalSubdomain=au

64 Harris, T (2018) 'Metropolitans Tipped to Lead a "Centrist Party" are Undermining the Project Before It has Begun', *The Telegraph*, 23 October, https://www.telegraph.co.uk/politics/2018/10/23/metropolitans-tipped-lead-centrist-party-undermining-project/; Payne, A (2018) 'Anti-Brexit Politicians from all the Main Parties are in Secret Talks About Forming a New "Centrist" Movement', *Business Insider*,

8 August, http://uk.businessinsider.com/politicians-britain-political-parties-are-in-secret-talks-about-forming-a-new-centrist-movement-brexit-2018-8; Wallace, M (2017) 'Spring, Renew, Advance, Forward Together ... What Is behind the Flurry of Wannabe British Macrons?' *Conservative Home*, 8 November, https://www.conservativehome.com/leftwatch/2017/11/spring-renew-advance-forward-together-what-is-behind-the-flurry-of-wannabe-british-macrons.html; Wheeler, C (2018) 'David Miliband Eyes UK Return as Rumours of New Centrist Party Grow', *The Sunday Times*, 11 November, https://www.thetimes.co.uk/article/david-miliband-eyes-uk-return-as-rumours-of-new-centrist-party-grow-8fh7vrsxc; Savage, M (2018) 'New Centrist Party Gets £50m Backing to "Break Mould" of UK Politics', *The Guardian*, 8 April, https://www.theguardian.com/politics/2018/apr/07/new-political-party-break-mould-westminster-uk-brexit

65 Demianyk, G (2017) 'Centrist Campaign Group "More United" Crowdfunds £370,000 to Donate to "Progressive" Election Candidates', *Huffington Post*, 2 May, https://www.huffingtonpost.co.uk/entry/more-united-progressive-centrist-election-candidates_uk_5907940ce4b0bb2d08705a2a?393i; https://www.moreunited.co.uk

66 Giddens, A (1999) *The Third Way: The Renewal of Social Democracy*, London: Polity Press.

67 E.g. Levitas, R (1998) *The Inclusive Society? Social Exclusion and New Labour*, London: Palgrave; Lister, R (2001) 'New Labour: A Study in Ambiguity from a Position of Ambivalence', *Critical Social Policy*, 21(4):425–47; Newman, J (2001) *Modernizing Governance: New Labour, Policy and Society*, London: Sage; Poole, L and Mooney, G (2006) 'Privatizing Education in Scotland? New Labour, Modernization and "Public" Services', *Critical Social Policy*, 26(3):562–86; Vidler, E and Clarke, J (2005) 'Creating Citizen-Consumers: New Labour and the Remaking of Public Services', *Public Policy and Administration*, 20(2):19–37.

68 Hall, S (1998) 'The Great Moving Nowhere Show', *Marxism Today*, November/December, 9–14, p.10.

69 Back, L, Keith, M, Khan, A, Shukra, K and Solomos, J (2002) 'New Labour's White Heart: Politics, Multiculturalism and the Return of Assimilation', *The Political Quarterly*, 73(4):445–54; Hall, S (1998) 'The Great Moving Nowhere Show', *Marxism Today*, November/December, 9–14; Mulgan, G (2006) 'Thinking in Tanks: The Changing Ecology of Political Ideas', *The Political Quarterly*, 77(2):147–55.

70 Brennan, D (2016) *Femicide Census: Profiles of Women Killed by Men, Redefining an Isolated Incident*, London: Women's Aid and nia.

Chapter 2

1   Okri, B (2017) 'Grenfell Tower, June 2017: A Poem by Ben Okri', *Financial Times*, 23 June, https://www.ft.com/content/39022f72-5742-11e7-80b6-9bfa4c1f83d2

2   Ibid.

3   Lawrence, D (2018) 'Grenfell Inquiry Brings Painful Memories of the Fight for Justice for My Son, Stephen Lawrence', *The Guardian*, 2 June, https://www.theguardian.com/commentisfree/2018/jun/02/grenfell-inquiry-brings-painful-memories-of-fight-for-justice-for-my-son-stephen-lawrence; Lister, R (2018) 'From Windrush to Universal Credit – the Art of "Institutional Indifference"', *Open Democracy*, 10 October, https://www.opendemocracy.net/en/opendemocracyuk/from-windrush-to-universal-credit-art-of-institutional-indifference/

4   Okri, B (2018) 'The Tower and the Poem', *Financial Times*, 9 June, Life and Arts Section p2, https://www.ft.com/content/44484824-6a44-11e8-b6eb-4acfcfb08c11

5   Marsh, S, Rawlinson, K and Agencies (2017) 'Hundreds Evacuated from London Tower Blocks over Fears of Grenfell Repeat', *The Guardian*, 24 June, https://www.theguardian.com/uk-news/2017/jun/23/camden-to-evacuate-taplow-tower-over-fire-safety-fears-after-grenfell-disaster

6   BBC News (2013) 'Bangladesh Factory Collapse Toll Passes 1,000', 10 May, https://www.bbc.co.uk/news/world-asia-22476774; Al Jazeera (2016) 'Church Collapses in Uyo, Killing Dozens of Nigerians', 11 December, https://www.aljazeera.com/news/2016/12/church-collapses-nigeria-uyo-killing-scores-161211041437146.html

7   Moore-Bick, M (2019) *Grenfell Tower Inquiry: Phase 1 Report Overview*, London: APS Group, p.12, https://assets.grenfelltowerinquiry.org.uk/GTI%20-%20Phase%201%20report%20Executive%20Summary.pdf

8   Grenfell Action Group (2017) 'Grenfell Tower Fire', 14 June, https://grenfellactiongroup.wordpress.com/2017/06/14/grenfell-tower-fire/

9   *Local News: What Are We Missing?* (2017) BBC Radio 4, 22 November, https://www.bbc.co.uk/programmes/b09fy6g9; Newby, G (2017) 'Why No-one Heard the Grenfell Blogger's Warnings', *BBC News*, 24 November, https://www.bbc.co.uk/news/stories-42072477

10 Okri, B (2017) 'Grenfell Tower, June 2017: A Poem by Ben Okri', *Financial Times*, 23 June, https://www.ft.com/content/39022f72-5742-11e7-80b6-9bfa4c1f83d2

11 Barthes, R (1981) *Camera Lucida*, trans. Howard, R, New York: Hill and Wang, pp.26–7.

12 Ibid., p.27; original emphasis.
13 See e.g. BBC Trending (2014) '#BBCTrending: The Two Faces of Michael Brown', 11 August, https://www.bbc.co.uk/news/blogs-trending-28742301
14 Sontag, S (2003) *Regarding the Pain of Others*, London: Penguin, p.103.
15 Ibid., p.6.
16 Ibid., pp.98–9.
17 Ibid., p.99.
18 Ibid., p.104.
19 Ibid., p.91.
20 Wekker, G (2016) *White Innocence*, Durham, NC: Duke University Press.
21 Sontag, S (2003) *Regarding the Pain of Others*, London: Penguin, p.92.
22 Ibid.
23 Ibid., p.72.
24 Ibid., p.80.
25 Ibid.
26 Shire, W (n.d.) *Home*, https://www.care.org/sites/default/files/lesson_1_-_home-poem-by-warsan-shire.pdf
27 Jones, H (2015) 'Public Opinion on the Refugee Crisis Is Changing Fast – and for the Better', *The Conversation*, 4 September, https://theconversation.com/public-opinion-on-the-refugee-crisis-is-changing-fast-and-for-the-better-47064
28 Nicole Itano of Save the Children, quoted in Gurner, J (2015) 'Alan Kurdi: Why One Picture Cut Through', *BBC News*, 4 September, https://www.bbc.co.uk/news/world-europe-34150419
29 E.g. Gurner, J (2015) 'Alan Kurdi: Why One Picture Cut Through', *BBC News*, 4 September, https://www.bbc.co.uk/news/world-europe-34150419; Fisk, R (2016) 'Alan Kurdi Symbolised an Army of Dead Children. We Ignore Them at Our Peril', *The Independent*, 1 September, https://www.independent.co.uk/voices/a-year-on-from-alan-kurdi-we-continue-to-ignore-the-facts-in-front-of-us-and-we-ignore-them-at-our-a7220111.html
30 Boltanski, L (1999) *Distant Suffering: Morality, Media and Politics*, trans. Burchell, G, Cambridge: Cambridge University Press.
31 Dearden, L (2015) 'Katie Hopkins "Claims Aylan Kurdi's Drowned Body Was Staged on Turkish Beach"', *The Independent*, 25 September, https://www.independent.co.uk/news/people/katie-hopkins-claims-aylan-kurdis-drowned-body-was-staged-on-turkish-beach-10516423.html
32 Griggs, B (2015) 'Photographer Describes "Scream" of Migrant Boy's "Silent Body"', *CNN World*, 3 September, https://edition.cnn.com/2015/09/03/world/dead-migrant-boy-beach-photographer-nilufer-demir/index.html
33 I sought permission to reproduce an image of Alan such as his father described in the book, but this was not possible. However, family photos of

Alan and his brother Ghalib did appear widely in media coverage, which
the reader can find using a simple web search for their names.

34 Sontag, S (2003) *Regarding the Pain of Others*, London: Penguin.

35 Jones, H (2015) 'Public Opinion on the Refugee Crisis Is Changing Fast –
and for the Better', *The Conversation*, 4 September, https://theconversation.
com/public-opinion-on-the-refugee-crisis-is-changing-fast-and-for-the-
better-47064

36 UNHCR (2019) 'Syria Refugee Crisis', https://www.unrefugees.org/
emergencies/syria/

37 Wintour, P (2015) 'UK to Take up to 20,000 Refugees over Five Years, David
Cameron Confirms', *The Guardian*, 7 September, https://www.theguardian.
com/world/2015/sep/07/uk-will-accept-up-to-20000-syrian-refugees-
david-cameron-confirms

38 Amnesty International (2015) *By Hook or by Crook: Australia's Abuse of
Asylum Seekers at Sea*, London: Amnesty International; Heller, C and
Pezzani, L (2017) *Blaming the Rescuers*, https://blamingtherescuers.org/
report/; Médecins Sans Frontières (2017) 'Issue Brief: Humanitarian NGOs
Conducting Search and Rescue Operations at Sea: A "Pull Factor"?' August,
http://searchandrescue.msf.org/assets/uploads/files/170831_Analysis_SAR_
Issue_Brief_Final.pdf

39 Eurostat (2016) 'Asylum in the EU Member States Record Number of over
1.2 Million First Time Asylum Seekers Registered in 2015 Syrians, Afghans
and Iraqis: Top Citizenships', 4 March, https://ec.europa.eu/eurostat/
documents/2995521/7203832/3-04032016-AP-EN.pdf/790eba01-381c-
4163-bcd2-a54959b99ed6

40 Home Office (2016) 'National Statistics: Asylum, Updated 2 March 2016',
https://www.gov.uk/government/publications/immigration-statistics-
october-to-december-2015/asylum#nationalities-applying-for-asylum

41 Bolt, D (2018) *An Inspection of the Vulnerable Persons Resettlement Scheme
August 2017–January 2018*, London: Independent Chief Inspector of
Borders and Immigration.

42 Okri, B (2018) 'The Tower and the Poem', *Financial Times*, 9 June, p.2,
https://www.ft.com/content/44484824-6a44-11e8-b6eb-4acfcfb08c11

43 Okri, B (2017) 'Grenfell Tower, June 2017: A Poem by Ben Okri', *Financial
Times*, 23 June, https://www.ft.com/content/39022f72-5742-11e7-80b6-
9bfa4c1f83d2

44 Shropshire Star (2018) 'Grenfell Tower Painting Given to PM by Survivors
"Will Hang in Downing Street"', 11 May, https://www.shropshirestar.com/
news/uk-news/2018/05/11/grenfell-tower-painting-given-to-pm-by-
survivors-will-hang-in-downing-street/

45 Mair, E (2018) *The Grenfell Tower Inquiry Podcast with Eddie Mair: Episode 7: Commemoration: Day 2*, BBC, 22 May, https://www.bbc.co.uk/programmes/p067y12v

46 Bulley, D, Edkins, J and El-Enany, N (2019) *After Grenfell: Violence, Resistance and Response*, London: Pluto Press; Lowkey ft. Mai Khalil (2017) *Ghosts of Grenfell*, https://www.youtube.com/watch?v=ztUamrChczQ&feature=youtu.be; Lowkey ft. KAIA (2018) *Ghosts of Grenfell 2*, https://youtu.be/SQplVg9vE0I; Beaumont-Thomas, B (2018) 'Stormzy Asks "Theresa May, Where's the Money for Grenfell?" at Brit Awards', *The Guardian*, 21 February, https://www.theguardian.com/music/2018/feb/21/stormzy-asks-may-wheres-the-money-for-grenfell-at-brit-awards; BBC News (2019) 'Grenfell Tower Fire: "Agonising Memories" of Families and Friends', 14 June, https://www.bbc.co.uk/news/uk-england-london-48634630

47 Grenfell Action Group (2016) 'KCTMO – Playing with Fire!', 20 November, https://grenfellactiongroup.wordpress.com/2016/11/20/kctmo-playing-with-fire/

48 Newby, G (2017) 'Why No-one Heard the Grenfell Blogger's Warnings', *BBC News*, 24 November, https://www.bbc.co.uk/news/stories-42072477

49 Grenfell Tower Inquiry (2019) *Independent Grenfell Tower Inquiry Financial Report to 31 March 2019*, https://assets.grenfelltowerinquiry.org.uk/inline-files/Grenfell%20Tower%20Inquiry%20financial%20report%20to%2031%20March%202019.pdf; Grenfell Inquiry (2019) *Path to Phase 2 Hearings*, https://assets.grenfelltowerinquiry.org.uk/inline-files/Path%20to%20P2%20hearings%20English.pdf

50 Grenfell Tower Inquiry (2019) *Updated List of Issues*, September, https://assets.grenfelltowerinquiry.org.uk/inline-files/List%20of%20Issues%2025%20September%202019%20%281%29.pdf

51 Rawlinson, K (2018) '100 Households around Grenfell Still in Temporary Accommodation', *The Guardian*, 29 March, https://www.theguardian.com/uk-news/2018/mar/29/100-households-around-grenfell-still-in-temporary-accommodation

52 Taylor, D (2019) 'Grenfell Survivor in Legal Fight with Council to Get Home without a Lift', *The Guardian*, 25 February, https://www.theguardian.com/uk-news/2019/feb/25/grenfell-survivor-legal-fight-council-flat-without-lift

53 Simpson, J (2019) 'Bolton Fire: Combustible Membrane Pictured behind Cladding on Student Halls', *Inside Housing*, 22 November, https://www.insidehousing.co.uk/news/news/bolton-fire-combustible-membrane-pictured-behind-cladding-on-student-halls-64247

54 Lowkey ft. KAIA (2018) *Ghosts of Grenfell 2*, https://youtu.be/SQplVg9vE0I

55 Tanner, B (2019) 'Former Housing Ministers Could "Potentially Be in
    the Dock for Corporate Manslaughter"', *24 Housing*, 28 January, https://
    www.24housing.co.uk/news/former-housing-ministers-could-potentially-
    be-in-the-dock-for-corporate-manslaughter/

56 Tanner, B (2019) '"Grenfell" Housing Minister Joins Clarion Board',
    24 Housing, 17 December, https://www.24housing.co.uk/news/grenfell-
    housing-minister-joins-clarion-board/

57 Apps, P (2019) 'PM's Chief of Staff Did Not Act on Multiple Warnings
    about Fire Safety in Months before Grenfell, New Letters Show', *Inside
    Housing*, 13 June, https://www.insidehousing.co.uk/news/news/pms-chief-
    of-staff-did-not-act-on-multiple-warnings-about-fire-safety-in-months-
    before-grenfell-new-letters-show-61883; Sky News (2017) 'Gavin Barwell,
    Ex-housing Minister, Refuses to Answer Questions about Grenfell Tower
    – Video', *The Guardian*, 16 June, https://www.theguardian.com/uk-news/
    video/2017/jun/16/gavin-barwell-ex-housing-minister-refuses-to-answer-
    questions-about-grenfell-tower-video

58 Stephen Williams quoted in Apps, P (2019) 'PM's Chief of Staff Did Not Act
    on Multiple Warnings about Fire Safety in Months before Grenfell, New
    Letters Show', *Inside Housing*, 13 June, https://www.insidehousing.co.uk/
    news/news/pms-chief-of-staff-did-not-act-on-multiple-warnings-about-
    fire-safety-in-months-before-grenfell-new-letters-show-61883

59 Booth, R (2019) 'How Grenfell Survivors Came Together – and How Britain
    Failed Them', *The Guardian*, 11 June, https://www.theguardian.com/uk-
    news/2019/jun/11/how-grenfell-survivors-came-together-to-change-britain

60 Ibid.

61 The communal silent walk was paused on March 2020 as a precaution
    against spreading Covid-19. The walk began to be replaced by streamed
    videos of previous walks and forms of social media connection during the
    pandemic.

62 Sontag, S (1994) 'Aesthetics of Silence', in *Styles of Radical Will*, London:
    Vintage, p.7.

63 Helman, S and Rapoport, T (1997) 'Women in Black: Challenging
    Israel's Gender and Socio-Political Orders', *British Journal of Sociology*,
    48(4):681–700.

64 Ferguson, K (2012) *All in the Family: On Community and
    Incommensurability*, Durham and London: Duke University Press, p.81.

65 Back, L (2018) 'Silent Steps', *Streetsigns*, 26 January, https://cucrblog.
    wordpress.com/2018/01/26/silent-steps/

66 Ahmed Elgwahary quoted in Booth, R (2019) 'How Grenfell Survivors
    Came Together – and How Britain Failed Them', *The Guardian*, 11 June,
    https://www.theguardian.com/uk-news/2019/jun/11/how-grenfell-
    survivors-came-together-to-change-britain

67 Griggs, B (2015) 'Photographer Describes "Scream" of Migrant Boy's "Silent Body"', *CNN World*, 3 September, https://edition.cnn.com/2015/09/03/world/dead-migrant-boy-beach-photographer-nilufer-demir/index.html

Chapter 3

1   Berger, J and Mohr, J (1975) *A Seventh Man: The Story of a Migrant Worker in Europe*, Harmondsworth: Penguin, p.52.

2   See also Anderson, B (2017) 'The Politics of Pests: Immigration and the Invasive Other', *Social Research*, 84(1):7–28; Perera, S (2009) *Australia and the Insular Imagination: Beaches, Borders, Boats, and Bodies*, New York: Palgrave Macmillan.

3   Mail Online Reporter (2015) 'How Many More Can Kos Take? Thousands of Boat People from Syria and Afghanistan Set Up Migrant Camp in Popular Greek Island – with Holidaymakers Branding the Situation "Disgusting"', *MailOnline*, 27 May, https://www.dailymail.co.uk/news/article-3099736/Holidaymakers-misery-boat-people-Syria-Afghanistan-seeking-asylum-set-migrant-camp-turn-popular-Greek-island-Kos-disgusting-hellhole.html

4   Ibid.; emphasis added.

5   Ibid.

6   Tondo, L (2019) 'I Have Seen the Tragedy of Mediterranean Migrants. This "Art" Makes Me Feel Uneasy', *The Guardian*, 12 May https://www.theguardian.com/world/2019/may/12/venice-biennale-migrant-tragedy-art-makes-me-uneasy

7   Palm, A (2017) 'The Italy-Libya Memorandum of Understanding: The Baseline of a Policy Approach Aimed at Closing All Doors to Europe?' *EU Migration Law Blog*, 2 October, https://eumigrationlawblog.eu/the-italy-libya-memorandum-of-understanding-the-baseline-of-a-policy-approach-aimed-at-closing-all-doors-to-europe/; European Commission (2017) 'EU Trust Fund for Africa Adopts €46 Million Programme to Support Integrated Migration and Border Management in Libya', Press Release, 28 July, https://ec.europa.eu/commission/presscorner/detail/en/IP_17_2187; see also later in this chapter.

8   See e.g. Malik, K (2017) 'Kenan Malik on Cultural Appropriation', *Art Review*, December, https://artreview.com/features/ar_december_2017_feature_cultural_appropriation_kenan_malik/; Neshat, S (2018) 'When Does Political Art Cross the Line?' *The New York Times*, 5 December, https://www.nytimes.com/2018/12/05/opinion/shirin-neshat-political-art.html; Papailias, P (2019) 'Memeifying the Corpse: The Photograph and

the Dead Body between Evidence and Bereavement', in Kohn, T, Gibbs, M, Nansen, B and van Ryn, L (eds) *Residues of Death: Disposal Reconfigured*, London: Routledge, pp.169–83.

9 E.g. Earle, W (2019) '*Barca Nostra:* Is This Art?' *Spiked*, 23 May, https://www.spiked-online.com/2019/05/23/barca-nostra-is-this-art/; Itabaaza, S (2019) 'Remove *Barca Nostra* from Venice Biennale', *Change.org*, https://www.change.org/p/ralph-rugoff-remove-barca-nostra-from-venice-biennale; Pritchard, S (2019) '"Our Boat": Zombie Art Biennale Turns Venice into the Island of the Living Dead', 10 May, http://colouringinculture.org/blog/ourboat; Tondo, L (2019) 'I Have Seen the Tragedy of Mediterranean Migrants. This "Art" Makes Me Feel Uneasy', *The Guardian*, 12 May, https://www.theguardian.com/world/2019/may/12/venice-biennale-migrant-tragedy-art-makes-me-uneasy

10 This recalls Ruth Wilson Gilmore's much-quoted definition of racism: 'Racism is the state-sanctioned and/or extralegal production and exploitation of group-differentiated vulnerability to premature death.' In Gilmore, R W (2007) *Golden Gulag: Prisons, Surplus, Crisis, and Opposition in Globalizing California*, Berkeley: University of California Press, p.247.

11 Yuval-Davis, N, Wemyss, G and Cassidy, K (2018) 'Everyday Bordering, Belonging and the Reorientation of British Immigration Legislation', *Sociology*, 52(2):228–44. These functions are less remarkable in countries with long-established (and functional) national ID card systems such as Sweden, Germany, etc., where it is readily possible to exclude people from everyday actions without additional bureaucratic checks.

12 UNHCR (2018) 'Figures at a Glance: Statistical Yearbooks', 19 June 2018, https://www.unhcr.org/uk/figures-at-a-glance.html

13 Ibid.

14 IOM (2017) 'Migration Data Portal: Migrant Deaths and Disappearances', https://migrationdataportal.org/themes/migrant-deaths-and-disappearances, last accessed 2 June 2019.

15 UNHCR (2019) 'Six People Died Each Day Attempting to Cross Mediterranean in 2018 – UNHCR Report', 30 January, https://www.unhcr.org/uk/news/press/2019/1/5c500c504/six-people-died-day-attempting-cross-mediterranean-2018-unhcr-report.html

16 Migration Observatory (2019) 'Immigration Detention in the UK', 29 May, https://migrationobservatory.ox.ac.uk/resources/briefings/immigration-detention-in-the-uk/

17 Grierson, J (2018) 'Immigration Detention: How the UK Compares with Other Countries', *The Guardian*, 10 October, https://www.theguardian.com/uk-news/2018/oct/10/immigration-detention-how-the-uk-compares-with-other-countries

18 UNHCR (2018) 'Figures at a Glance: Statistical Yearbooks', 19 June 2018, https://www.unhcr.org/uk/figures-at-a-glance.html

19 Jones, H, Gunaratnam, Y, Bhattacharyya, G, Davies, W, Dhaliwal, S, Forkert, K, Jackson, E and Saltus, R (2017) *Go Home? The Politics of Immigration Controversies*, Manchester: Manchester University Press, p.7; Sirriyeh, A (2018) *The Politics of Compassion: Immigration and Asylum Policy*, Bristol: Bristol University Press, p.65.

20 Berger, J and Mohr, J (1975) *A Seventh Man: The Story of a Migrant Worker in Europe*, Harmondsworth: Penguin.

21 Ibid., p.50.

22 Identifying marks were also branded – burnt onto the skin – of enslaved people and people who had attempted to escape slavery in the United States.

23 For a discussion of ways of understanding the horrors of the present, colonialism and Nazism alongside, but not in competition with one another, see Rothberg, M (2009) *Multidirectional Memory: Remembering the Holocaust in the Age of Decolonization*, Stanford: Stanford University Press.

24 Berger, J and Mohr, J (1975) *A Seventh Man: The Story of a Migrant Worker in Europe*, Harmondsworth: Penguin, p.52.

25 Ibid., p.52.

26 An 'Australian-style' points-based system was introduced in the UK visa regime for non-EU nationals in 2008 by the Labour immigration minister, Liam Byrne, and Home Secretary, Jacqui Smith (the latter now Chair of the Jo Cox Foundation). Expansion of this system to EU nationals was in the 2015 manifesto of the far-right UK Independence Party, while hinted at by centrists such as then Labour Party Leader Ed Miliband. See Cooper, Y (2013) 'Yvette Cooper's Immigration Speech in Full', *politics.co.uk*, 7 March, https://www.politics.co.uk/comment-analysis/2013/03/07/yvette-cooper-s-immigration-speech-in-full; BBC News (2015) 'UKIP's Nigel Farage Calls for Immigration Visa Points System', 4 March, https://www.bbc.co.uk/news/av/uk-politics-31724979/ukip-s-nigel-farage-calls-for-immigration-visa-points-system

27 E.g. New Labour Minister Liam Byrne (Direct.gov) (2007) 'New Points Based Migration System to Start in the New Year', *Direct.gov*, 18 April, https://webarchive.nationalarchives.gov.uk/20100104234058/http://www.direct.gov.uk/en/Nl1/Newsroom/DG_067655); Conservative Prime Minister Boris Johnson (Staton, B and Wright, R (2019) 'Boris Johnson Eyes Australia-Style Immigration System', *Financial Times*, 25 July, https://www.ft.com/content/6afee982-af03-11e9-8030-530adfa879c2); MEP, UKIP and Brexit Party leader, Nigel Farage (BBC News (2015) 'UKIP's Nigel Farage

Calls for Immigration Visa Points System', 4 March, https://www.bbc.co.uk/news/av/uk-politics-31724979/ukip-s-nigel-farage-calls-for-immigration-visa-points-system).

28 Tavan, G (2005) *The Long, Slow Death of White Australia*, Carlton North: Scribe; McAdam, J and Chong, F (2014) *Refugees: Why Seeking Asylum Is Legal and Australia's Policies Are Not*, Sydney: NewSouth.

29 Moreton-Robinson, A (2015) *The White Possessive: Property, Power and Indigenous Sovereignty*, Minneapolis: University of Minnesota Press; Reynolds, H (2013) *Forgotten War*, Sydney: NewSouth.

30 The White Australia policy included such measures as a 'dictation test' which could be given in any European language decided by the officer and was often used to disadvantage those seen as not white or otherwise undesirable. The White Australia policy was officially abolished in 1973, under the Labor government of Gough Whitlam, though arguably that did not end its influence as a founding principle of the Australian nation; see Tavan, G (2005) *The Long, Slow Death of White Australia*, Carlton North: Scribe.

31 Gleeson, M (2016) *Offshore: Behind the Wire on Manus and Nauru*, Sydney: NewSouth.

32 Abbott, T (2015) 'Transcript: Tony Abbott's Controversial Speech at the Margaret Thatcher Lecture', *The Sydney Morning Herald*, 28 October, https://www.smh.com.au/politics/federal/transcript-tony-abbotts-controversial-speech-at-the-margaret-thatcher-lecture-20151028-gkkg6p.html; emphasis added.

33 Hage, G (2017) *Is Racism an Environmental Threat?* London: Polity; Perera, S (2009) *Australia and the Insular Imagination: Beaches, Borders, Boats, and Bodies*, New York: Palgrave Macmillan; Martin, G (2015) 'Stop the Boats! Moral Panic in Australia over Asylum Seekers', *Continuum: Journal of Cultural and Media Studies*, 29(3):304–22.

34 Eventually, the asylum seekers were taken to Nauru; 302 were processed there and 131 were sent to New Zealand. See National Museum of Australia (n.d.) 'Defining Moments: "Tampa Affair"', https://www.nma.gov.au/defining-moments/resources/tampa-affair

35 Phillips, J and Spinks, H (2013) 'Boat Arrivals in Australia since 1976', Canberra: Parliament of Australia, https://www.aph.gov.au/about_parliament/parliamentary_departments/parliamentary_library/pubs/rp/rp1314/boatarrivals; Hutton, M (2014) 'Drownings on the Public Record of People Attempting to Enter Australia Irregularly by Boat since 1998', 2 February, http://sievx.com/articles/background/DrowningsTable.pdf

36 For a discussion of this claim to compassion see Sirriyeh, A (2018) *The Politics of Compassion: Immigration and Asylum Policy*, Bristol: Bristol

University Press. For further stark evidence suggesting these policies do the opposite of saving lives at sea, see Amnesty International (2015) *By Hook or by Crook: Australia's Abuse of Asylum Seekers at Sea*, London: Amnesty International; Heller, C and Pezzani, L (2017) *Blaming the Rescuers*, https://blamingtherescuers.org/report/; Hutton, M (2014) 'Drownings on the Public Record of People Attempting to Enter Australia Irregularly by Boat since 1998', 2 February, http://sievx.com/articles/background/ DrowningsTable.pdf; Médecins Sans Frontières (2017) 'Issue Brief: Humanitarian NGOs Conducting Search and Rescue Operations at Sea: A "Pull Factor"?' August, http://searchandrescue.msf.org/assets/uploads/ files/170831_Analysis_SAR_Issue_Brief_Final.pdf

37 Mydans, S (2001) 'Which Australian Candidate Has the Harder Heart?' *The New York Times*, 9 November, https://www.nytimes.com/2001/11/09/world/ which-australian-candidate-has-the-harder-heart.html

38 Farrell, P and Doherty, B (2016) 'Nauru Files Show Wilson Security Staff Regularly Downgraded Reports of Abuse', *The Guardian*, 11 August, https://www.theguardian.com/australia-news/2016/aug/12/nauru-files-show-wilson-security-staff-regularly-downgraded-reports-of-abuse; Marr, D (2016) 'The Nauru Files Are Raw Evidence of Torture. Can We Look Away?' *The Guardian*, 10 August, https://www.theguardian.com/ australia-news/2016/aug/10/the-nauru-files-are-raw-evidence-of-torture-can-we-look-away; Marr, D and Laughland, O (2014) 'Australia's Detention Regime Sets Out to Make Asylum Seekers Suffer, Says Chief Immigration Psychiatrist', *The Guardian*, 4 August, https://www.theguardian.com/ world/2014/aug/05/-sp-australias-detention-regime-sets-out-to-make-asylum-seekers-suffer-says-chief-immigration-psychiatrist

39 Levy, C (2010) 'Refugees, Europe, Camps/State of Exception: "Into the Zone", the European Union and Extraterritorial Processing of Migrants, Refugees, and Asylum-Seekers (Theories and Practice)', *Refugee Survey Quarterly*, 29(1):92–119.

40 The Economist (2003) 'The Albanian Solution', *The Economist*, 13 March, http://www.economist.com/node/1632873

41 European Parliament (2019) 'Legislative Train 12.2019, 8 towards a New Policy on Migration, EU Statement and Action Plan', 20 September, http:// www.europarl.europa.eu/legislative-train/api/stages/report/current/theme/ towards-a-new-policy-on-migration/file/european-border-and-coast-guard

42 Kingsley, P and Rankin, J (2016) 'EU-Turkey Refugee Deal – Q&A', *The Guardian*, 8 March, https://www.theguardian.com/world/2016/mar/08/eu-turkey-refugee-deal-qa

43 European Commission (2017) 'EU Trust Fund for Africa Adopts €46 Million Programme to Support Integrated Migration and Border

Management in Libya', Press Release, 28 July, https://ec.europa.eu/
commission/presscorner/detail/en/IP_17_2187;

44 Grzymski, J (2019) 'Seeing Like a EUropean Border: Limits of the European
Borders and Space', *Global Discourse*, 9(1):135–51.

45 Palm, A (2017) 'The Italy-Libya Memorandum of Understanding: The
Baseline of a Policy Approach Aimed at Closing All Doors to Europe?' *EU
Migration Law Blog*, 2 October, https://eumigrationlawblog.eu/the-italy-
libya-memorandum-of-understanding-the-baseline-of-a-policy-approach-
aimed-at-closing-all-doors-to-europe/

46 Davis, A (1998) 'Masked Racism: Reflections on the Prison-Industrial
Complex', *ColorLines*, 10 September, https://www.colorlines.com/articles/
masked-racism-reflections-prison-industrial-complex

47 Birnberg Peirce & Partners, Medical Justice and the National Coalition
of Anti-Deportation Campaigns (2008) *Outsourcing Abuse: The Use and
Misuse of State-Sanctioned Force during the Detention and Removal of
Asylum Seekers*, London: Medical Justice; Sharman, J (2018) 'G4S Can Keep
Running Brook House Immigration Removal Centre Following Detainee
Abuse Scandal, Home Office Quietly Announces', *The Independent*, 4 May,
https://www.independent.co.uk/news/uk/home-news/g4s-brook-house-
choke-detainees-undercover-tinsley-home-office-contract-a8337051.html

48 Tyler, I (2013) *Revolting Subjects: Social Abjection and Resistance in
Neoliberal Britain*, London: Zed, p.79.

49 Marks, K (2002) 'Refugee Camp Children Sew Their Lips in Protest',
Independent, 22 January, https://www.independent.co.uk/news/world/
australasia/refugee-camp-children-sew-their-lips-in-protest-5362577.html

50 Not dissimilar to the Great Get Together and More in Common initiatives
in memory of Jo Cox MP, discussed in Chapter 1.

51 An organization which shares 'the stories, experiences and demands made
by people held in immigration detention centres in the UK or those who
have family members or partners in detention.' See https://detainedvoices.
com/about-2/.

52 A group of 'experts-by-experience committed to speaking out about the
realities of UK's immigration detention and calling for detention reform.'
See https://twitter.com/freedvoices.

53 See e.g. Sloan, A (2013) 'Sleeping Rough for Charity Hides the Real
Homelessness Crisis', *The Guardian*, 29 October, https://www.theguardian.
com/housing-network/2013/oct/29/homeless-sleep-out-charity

54 Ration Challenge (n.d.) 'Ration Challenge', https://www.rationchallenge.
org.uk/.

55 Ration Challenge (n.d.) 'The Rations Explained', https://actforpeace.
rationchallenge.org.au/the-challenge/the-rations-explained/

56   As philosopher Judith Butler puts it, 'If we ask why any of us should care
      about those who suffer at a distance from us, the answer is not to be found
      in paternalistic justifications, but in the fact that we inhabit the world
      together in relations of interdependency. Our fates are, as it were, given
      over to one another.' pp. 50–1, in Butler, J (2020) *The Force of Non-Violence*,
      London: Verso.

57   Iqbal, N (2018) 'Stansted 15: "We Are Not Terrorists, No Lives Were at
      Risk. We Have No Regrets"', *The Guardian*, 16 December, https://www.
      theguardian.com/world/2018/dec/16/migrants-deportation-stansted-
      actvists

58   De Noronha, L (2016) 'The Deportation Charter Flight – What's All the
      Fuss About?' *The Gleaner*, 11 September, http://jamaica-gleaner.com/
      article/focus/20160911/luke-de-noronha-deportation-charter-flight-whats-
      all-fuss-about

59   See pp.148–66 in Jones, H, Gunaratnam, Y, Bhattacharyya, G, Davies, W,
      Dhaliwal, S, Forkert, K, Jackson, E and Saltus, R (2017) *Go Home? The
      Politics of Immigration Controversies*, Manchester: Manchester University
      Press.

60   This was also the name of the installation, and so its name changed each
      day.

61   Searle, A (2018) 'Tania Bruguera at Turbine Hall Review – "It Didn't Make
      Me Cry but It Cleared the Tubes"', *The Guardian*, 1 October, https://www.
      theguardian.com/artanddesign/2018/oct/01/tania-bruguera-turbine-hall-
      review-tate-modern

62   Tate (2019) 'Hyundai Commission, Tania Bruguera: 10,148,451', https://
      www.tate.org.uk/whats-on/tate-modern/exhibition/hyundai-commission-
      tania-bruguera.

Chapter 4

1   Hartman, S (2002) 'The Time of Slavery', *South Atlantic Quarterly*,
     101(4):757–77, pp.759–60.

2   Sato, S (2017) '"Operation Legacy": Britain's Destruction and Concealment
     of Colonial Records Worldwide', *The Journal of Imperial and Commonwealth
     History*, 45(4):697–719, p.706.

3   Cobain, I (2013) 'Revealed: The Bonfire of Papers at the End of Empire',
     The Guardian, 29 November, http://www.theguardian.com/uk-news/2013/
     nov/29/revealed-bonfire-papers-empire. The 'watch series' was a code name
     given to files marked to be removed from the country or destroyed.

4   Badger, A (2012) 'Historians, a Legacy of Suspicion and the "Migrated Archives"', *Small Wars & Insurgencies*, 23(4–5):799–807, p.800.

5   Elkins, C (2014) 'Review: Huw Bennett. Fighting the Mau Mau: The British Army and Counter-Insurgency in the Kenya Emergency. (Cambridge Military Histories.) New York: Cambridge University Press. 2013. Pp. xii, 307. $29.99', *American Historical Review*, April 2014, pp.653–4, p.653. The term 'migrated' was used in official correspondence to refer to the archives moved to Britain in this process.

6   Anderson, D (2011) 'Mau Mau in the High Court and the "Lost" British Empire Archives: Colonial Conspiracy or Bureaucratic Bungle?' *The Journal of Imperial and Commonwealth History*, 39(5):699–716, p.710.

7   Sato, S (2017) '"Operation Legacy": Britain's Destruction and Concealment of Colonial Records Worldwide', *The Journal of Imperial and Commonwealth History*, 45(4):697–719, p.699.

8   Elkins, C (2011) 'Alchemy of Evidence: Mau Mau, the British Empire, and the High Court of Justice', *The Journal of Imperial and Commonwealth History*, 39(5):731–48, p.742.

9   El-Tayeb, F (2011) *European Others: Queering Ethnicity in Postnational Europe*, Minneapolis: University of Minnesota Press, p.173; Moore, N, Salter, A, Stanley, S and Tamboukou, M (2017) *The Archive Project: Archival Research in the Social Sciences*, London: Routledge; Pell, S (2015) 'Radicalizing the Politics of the Archive: An Ethnographic Reading of an Activist Archive', *Archivaria*, 80:33–57.

10   Sato, S (2017) '"Operation Legacy": Britain's Destruction and Concealment of Colonial Records Worldwide', *The Journal of Imperial and Commonwealth History*, 45(4):697–719, p.700.

11   Anderson, D (2011) 'Mau Mau in the High Court and the "Lost" British Empire Archives: Colonial Conspiracy or Bureaucratic Bungle?' *The Journal of Imperial and Commonwealth History*, 39(5):699–716, pp.708, 713.

12   Anderson, D (2005) *Histories of the Hanged: Britain's Dirty War in Kenya and the End of Empire: Testimonies from the Mau Mau Rebellion in Kenya*, London: Wiedenfeld and Nicolson, pp.4–5.

13   Anderson, D (2011) 'Mau Mau in the High Court and the "Lost" British Empire Archives: Colonial Conspiracy or Bureaucratic Bungle?' *The Journal of Imperial and Commonwealth History*, 39(5):699–716.

14   The court case was brought by Ndiku Mutwiwa Mutua, Paulo Nzili, Wambugu wa Nyingi, Jane Muthoni Mara and Susan Ngondi. For accounts of the brutal treatment for which they sought redress, see Anderson, D (2011) 'Mau Mau in the High Court and the "Lost" British Empire Archives: Colonial Conspiracy or Bureaucratic Bungle?' *The Journal of Imperial and Commonwealth History*, 39(5):699–716. Two lead complainants, Ndiku

Mutwiwa Mutua and Susan Ngondi, died before the full case could be heard by the High Court.

15 Hague, W (2013) 'Statement to Parliament on Settlement of Mau Mau Claims', 6 June, https://www.gov.uk/government/news/statement-to-parliament-on-settlement-of-mau-mau-claims

16 Hartman, S (2002) 'The Time of Slavery', *South Atlantic Quarterly*, 101(4):757–77.

17 Du Bois, W E B (1940 [1984]) *Dusk of Dawn: An Essay towards an Autobiography of a Race Concept*, London: Transaction.

18 See discussion of Trouillot, M-R (1995) *Silencing the Past: Power and the Production of History*, Boston: Beacon Press, which follows.

19 Bhambra, G K (2016) 'Undoing the Epistemic Disavowal of the Haitian Revolution: A Contribution to Global Social Thought', *Journal of Intercultural Studies*, 37(1):1–16; Trouillot, M-R (1995) *Silencing the Past: Power and the Production of History*, Boston: Beacon Press.

20 Sperling, D (2017) 'In 1825, Haiti Paid France $21 Billion to Preserve Its Independence – Time for France to Pay It Back', *Forbes*, 6 December, https://www.forbes.com/sites/realspin/2017/12/06/in-1825-haiti-gained-independence-from-france-for-21-billion-its-time-for-france-to-pay-it-back/

21 Similar to the ways that slaveholders, but not enslaved people, were paid compensation at the ending of slavery in the United States and Europe.

22 Trouillot, M-R (1995) *Silencing the Past: Power and the Production of History*, Boston: Beacon Press.

23 Ibid., p.26.

24 Mako, S (2012) 'Cultural Genocide and Key International Instruments: Framing the Indigenous Experience', *International Journal on Minority and Group Rights*, 19:175–94.

25 See e.g. Haraway, D (1988) 'Situated Knowledges: The Science Question in Feminism and the Privilege of Partial Perspective', *Feminist Studies*, 14(3):575–99; McGoey, L (2019) *The Unknowers: How Strategic Ignorance Rules the World*, London: Zed; Santos, B d S (2007) 'Beyond Abyssal Thinking: From Global Lines to Ecologies of Knowledges', *Review (Fernand Braudel Center)*, 30(1):45–89.

26 E.g. Oakley, A (1974) *Housewife*, London: Allen Lane; Reynolds, H (2000) *Why Weren't We Told? A Personal Search for the Truth about Our History*, Sydney: Penguin; Rowbotham, S (1973) *Hidden from History: 300 Years of Women's Oppression and the Fight against It*, London: Pluto Press; Thompson, E P (1963) *The Making of the English Working Class*, London: Gollancz.

27 Anthony, A (2016) 'Is Free Speech in British Universities under Threat?' *The Guardian*, 24 January, https://www.theguardian.com/world/2016/jan/24/safe-spaces-universities-no-platform-free-speech-rhodes

28 Friedersdorf, C (2015) 'The New Intolerance of Student Activism', *The Atlantic*, 9 November, https://www.theatlantic.com/politics/archive/2015/11/the-new-intolerance-of-student-activism-at-yale/414810/

29 Espinoza, J (2015) 'Politically Correct Universities "Are Killing Free Speech"', *The Telegraph*, 18 December, https://www.telegraph.co.uk/education/educationnews/12059161/Politically-correct-universities-are-killing-free-speech.html

30 O'Neill, B (2015) 'Never Mind Rhodes – It's the Cult of the Victim That Must Fall', *Spiked*, 28 December, https://www.spiked-online.com/2015/12/28/never-mind-rhodes-its-the-cult-of-the-victim-that-must-fall/

31 Rhodes Must Fall Movement (2018) *Rhodes Must Fall: The Struggle for Justice at the Heart of Empire*, London: Zed.

32 Gebrial, D (2015) 'We Don't Want to Erase Cecil Rhodes from History. We Want Everyone to Know His Crimes', *The Telegraph*, 22 December, https://www.telegraph.co.uk/education/universityeducation/12064939/We-dont-want-to-erase-Cecil-Rhodes-from-history.-We-want-everyone-to-know-his-crimes.html; Maylam, P (2005) *The Cult of Rhodes: Remembering an Imperialist in Africa*, Cape Town: David Philip.

33 Gebrial, D (2018) 'Rhodes Must Fall: Oxford and Movements for Change', in Bhambra, G K, Gebrial, D and Nişancıoğlu, K (eds) *Decolonising the University*, London: Pluto Press, pp.19–36.

34 O'Neill, B (2015) 'Never Mind Rhodes – It's the Cult of the Victim That Must Fall', *Spiked*, 28 December, https://www.spiked-online.com/2015/12/28/never-mind-rhodes-its-the-cult-of-the-victim-that-must-fall/

35 Anthony, A (2016) 'Is Free Speech in British Universities under Threat?' *The Guardian*, 24 January, https://www.theguardian.com/world/2016/jan/24/safe-spaces-universities-no-platform-free-speech-rhodes

36 See https://rmfoxford.wordpress.com/about/

37 Freire, P (2000 [1970]) *Pedagogy of the Oppressed*, trans. Bergman Ramos, M, New York: Continuum.

38 Attar, S (2010) *Debunking the Myths of Colonization: The Arabs and Europe*, Maryland: University Press of America, p.9; Mukerjee, M (2010) *Churchill's Secret War: The British Empire and the Ravaging of India during World War II*, New York: Basic Books.

39 Demianyk, G (2017) 'Daily Telegraph Admits "Decolonise" Cambridge Curriculum Story Was Wrong as Student Lola Olufemi Condemns

Newspaper', *Huffington Post*, 26 October, https://www.huffingtonpost.co.uk/
entry/telegraph-lola-olufemi_uk_59f1fe0fe4b077d8dfc7eaf9

40 Jenne, A (2015) 'Mary Beard Says Drive to Remove Cecil Rhodes Statue
from Oxford University Is a "Dangerous Attempt to Erase the Past"',
The Independent, 22 December, https://www.independent.co.uk/news/
education/education-news/mary-beard-says-drive-to-remove-cecil-rhodes-
statue-from-oxford-university-is-a-dangerous-attempt-to-a6783306.html

41 Sylvester Marshall was initially identified by the pseudonym Albert
Thompson in news coverage while his dispute with the Home Office was
ongoing; his story has subsequently been told using his real name. See
Gentleman, A (2019) *The Windrush Betrayal*, London: Guardian Faber,
p.87.

42 There were, of course, some Caribbean people living in Britain before this,
but this was the start of a significant movement which visibly changed some
neighbourhoods in Britain. See Fryer, P (1984) *Staying Power: The History
of Black People in Britain*, London: Pluto.

43 Younge, G (2018) 'Ambalavaner Sivanandan Obituary', *The Guardian*, 7
February, https://www.theguardian.com/world/2018/feb/07/ambalavaner-
sivanandan

44 Trouillot, M-R (1995) *Silencing the Past: Power and the Production of
History*, Boston: Beacon Press, p.26.

45 Solomos, J (2003) *Race and Racism in Britain*, Basingstoke: Palgrave
Macmillan, p.80.

46 Ibid., p.63.

47 In fact, the 1971 Act *increased* Old Commonwealth access to the UK
which had been restricted, along with the rest of the Commonwealth, by
earlier immigration acts; see Williams, C (2015) 'Patriality, Work Permits
and the European Economic Community: The Introduction of the 1971
Immigration Act', *Contemporary British History*, 29(4):508–38.

48 Trouillot, M-R (1995) *Silencing the Past: Power and the Production of
History*, Boston: Beacon Press, p.26.

49 Gentleman, A (2019) *The Windrush Betrayal*, London: Guardian Faber,
p.149.

50 Ibid., pp.145–62.

51 Trouillot, M-R (1995) *Silencing the Past: Power and the Production of
History*, Boston: Beacon Press, p.26.

52 While many other governments have long-standing ID card systems within
which such information would routinely be stored and checked, the UK –
for various reasons including concern for civil liberties and institutional
inertia – has no such coordinated system, so the challenge of proving
residence in this way is both onerous and impractical.

53   Incidentally, the wife of Conservative MP and sometime Cabinet Minister
     Jo Johnson, and sister-in-law of then foreign secretary, later Prime Minister
     Boris Johnson.
54   Now collected and expanded in Gentleman, A (2019) *The Windrush
     Betrayal*, London: Guardian Faber.
55   Refugee and Migrant Centre (n.d.) 'Case Study – Windrush', https://
     rmcentre.org.uk/casestudies/case-study-windrush/
56   Gentleman, A (2019) *The Windrush Betrayal*, London: Guardian Faber,
     p.201.
57   Ibid., pp.204–5.
58   The people who died after being mistreated as a result of the Windrush
     Scandal, and before receiving any apology or compensation, include
     Hubert Howard, Jashwa Moses, Sarah O'Connor and Richard Stewart. As
     of November 2019, a further fourteen people found to have been wrongly
     classified as immigration offenders died before officials contacted them
     about compensation. See Gentleman, A (2019) 'Windrush Victim Dies
     without Compensation or Apology', *The Guardian*, 12 November, https://
     www.theguardian.com/uk-news/2019/nov/12/windrush-victim-dies-
     without-compensation-or-apology
59   Trouillot, M-R (1995) *Silencing the Past: Power and the Production of
     History*, Boston: Beacon Press, p.26.
60   OCR (2017) *GCSE (9–1) Candidate Style Answers History B (Schools History
     Project)*, Cambridge: OCR, p.5, https://www.ocr.org.uk/Images/369892-
     migrants-to-britain-c.1250-to-present-candidate-style-answers.pdf
61   Hall, S (1999) 'From Scarman to Stephen Lawrence', *History Workshop
     Journal*, 48:187–97.
62   Dhaliwal, S and Forkert, K (2016) 'Deserving and Undeserving Migrants',
     Soundings, 61:49–61.
63   Jacob Rees-Mogg said this at the height of publicity for the Windrush
     Scandal, despite having five years previously addressed a dinner of the
     Traditional Britain Group which favoured the repatriation of black people
     from Britain. See LBC (2018) 'Jacob Rees-Mogg Lays into "Disgraceful"
     Home Office over Windrush Row', 16 April, https://www.lbc.co.uk/radio/
     special-shows/ring-rees-mogg/jacob-rees-mogg-disgraceful-home-office-
     windrush/; Fletcher, M (2018) 'The Polite Extremist: Jacob Rees-Mogg's
     Seemingly Unstoppable Rise', *New Statesman*, 20 February, https://www.
     newstatesman.com/politics/uk/2018/02/polite-extremist-jacob-rees-mogg-
     s-seemingly-unstoppable-rise
64   In Amelia Gentleman's important book on the crisis she uses this phrase
     repeatedly and seemingly uncritically, despite a critical interlude where she

examines the problem with this perspective on pages 189–91. Gentleman, A (2019) *The Windrush Betrayal*, London: Guardian Faber.

65 Ashe, S (2015) 'The Rise of UKIP: Challenges for Anti-Racism', in Khan, O and Sveinsson, K (eds) *Race and Elections*, London: Runnymede, pp.15–17.

66 Viner, K (2019) 'Foreword', in Gentleman, A (ed.) *The Windrush Betrayal*, London: Guardian Faber, pp.1–4, p.3.

67 Including condemnation from *Daily Mail* columnist Sarah Vine, who like Gentleman was also married to a member of the Conservative Cabinet which introduced the hostile environment (Michael Gove): Vine, S (2018) 'The Windrush Scandal Is yet Another Example of How Poorly Britain Treats Those to Whom It Owes a Great Debt and How Twisted Our Bureaucratic Morals Are, Says Sarah Vine', *Daily Mail*, 18 April, https://www.dailymail.co.uk/debate/article-5627811/Windrush-scandal-example-poorly-Britain-treats-owes-says-SARAH-VINE.html. For more on the *Daily Mail*'s usual line on race and immigration, see Collins, L (2012) 'Mail Supremacy', *The New Yorker*, 26 March, https://www.newyorker.com/magazine/2012/04/02/mail-supremacy; Philo, G, Briant, E and Donald, P (2013) *Bad News for Refugees*, London: Pluto Press.

68 Anderson, B (2013) *Us and Them? The Dangerous Politics of Migration Control*, Oxford: Oxford University Press.

69 See e.g. Byrne, B (2015) 'Rethinking Intersectionality and Whiteness at the Borders of Citizenship', *Sociological Research Online*, 20(3):16; Ware, V (2010) 'Whiteness in the Glare of War: Soldiers, Migrants and Citizenship', *Ethnicities*, 10(3):313–30.

Chapter 5

1 Gordon, A F (2008) *Ghostly Matters: Haunting and the Sociological Imagination*, Minneapolis: University of Minnesota Press, p.21.

2 Associated Press in Savannah, Georgia (2015) 'Ben Affleck's Slave-Owning Family: Records Sketch a Conflicted Past', *The Guardian*, 17 May, https://www.theguardian.com/film/2015/may/17/ben-affleck-slave-owning-family-tree-records

3 Email exchange between Henry Louis Gates Jr and Michael Lynton, https://wikileaks.org/sony/emails/emailid/140305; BBC (2015) 'Ben Affleck Slavery Row Leads to TV Show Suspension', *BBC News*, 25 June, https://www.bbc.co.uk/news/entertainment-arts-33267697; Oldham, S (2015) 'Ben Affleck Apologizes for PBS Slavery Censorship: "I Was Embarrassed"', *Variety*, 21

April, https://variety.com/2015/biz/news/ben-affleck-slavery-pbs-censor-ancestors-1201477075/
4   Affleck, B (2015) Facebook Post, 22 April, https://www.facebook.com/benaffleck/posts/849207928486969
5   If you are interested, you can check if you are a descendant of a slave-owner on their website, *The Legacies of British Slave-Ownership*, at https://www.ucl.ac.uk/lbs/search/
6   Kramer, A-M (2011) 'Kinship, Affinity and Connectedness: Exploring the Role of Genealogy in Personal Lives', *Sociology*, 45(3):379–95.
7   Holdsworth, A (2011) *Television, Memory and Nostalgia*, Basingstoke: Palgrave; Kramer, A-M (2011) 'Mediatizing Memory: History, Affect and Identity in *Who Do You Think You Are?*' *European Journal of Cultural Studies*, 14(4):428–44; Roth, W D and Ivemark, B (2018) 'Genetic Options: The Impact of Genetic Ancestry Testing on Consumers' Racial and Ethnic Identities', *American Journal of Sociology*, 124(1):150–84.
8   Smart, C (2011) 'Families, Secrets and Memories', *Sociology*, 45(4):539–55.
9   Gordon, A F (2008) *Ghostly Matters: Haunting and the Sociological Imagination*, Minneapolis: University of Minnesota Press.
10 Ibid., p.xvi.
11 Elliott, M (2017) 'The Inconvenient Ancestor: Slavery and Selective Remembrance on Genealogy Television', *Studies in Popular Culture*, 39(2):73–90.
12 Community cohesion policy was a dominant force in UK local government from around 2001 to around 2011.
13 Jones, H (2013) *Negotiating Cohesion, Inequality and Change: Uncomfortable Positions in Local Government*, Bristol: Policy Press, p.155.
14 Kramer, A-M (2011) 'Kinship, Affinity and Connectedness: Exploring the Role of Genealogy in Personal Lives', *Sociology*, 45(3):379–95.
15 E.g. Morning, A (2014) 'Does Genomics Challenge the Social Construction of Race?' *Sociological Theory*, 32(3):189–207.
16 Roth, W D and Ivemark, B (2018) 'Genetic Options: The Impact of Genetic Ancestry Testing on Consumers' Racial and Ethnic Identities', *American Journal of Sociology*, 124(1):150–84.
17 BBC News (2018) 'US Senator Elizabeth Warren Faces Backlash after Indigenous DNA Claim', *BBC News*, 16 October, https://www.bbc.co.uk/news/world-us-canada-45869804
18 Tallbear, K (2018) 'Statement on Elizabeth Warren's DNA Test', 15 October, https://twitter.com/kimtallbear/status/1051906470923493377?lang=en
19 Harris, C I (1993) 'Whiteness as Property', *Harvard Law Review*, 106(8):1707–91; Moreton-Robinson, A (2015) *The White Possessive*, Minneapolis: University of Minnesota Press.

20 Nolan, D and Graham-Harrison, E (2015) 'Hungarian Police Order Refugees Off Train Heading to Austrian Border', *The Guardian*, 3 September, https://www.theguardian.com/world/2015/sep/03/budapest-station-reopens-no-trains-running-western-europe-migration-crisis-europe

21 Much as the resonances of the images of the treatment of Turkish workers arriving in 1970s Germany struck a haunting chord – see Chapter 3.

22 Hirsch, M (2008) 'The Generation of Postmemory', *Poetics Today*, 29(1):103–28; Hirsch, M (2012) *The Generation of Postmemory: Writing and Visual Culture after the Holocaust*, New York: Columbia University Press.

23 Spiegelman, A (1987) *Maus: My Father Bleeds History*, New York: Pantheon.

24 Hartman, S (2002) 'The Time of Slavery', *South Atlantic Quarterly*, 101(4):757–77, p.771.

25 Ibid., p.773.

26 Luhmann, S (2009) 'Gender and the Generations of Difficult Knowledge: Recent Responses to Familial Legacies of Nazi Perpetration', *Women in German Yearbook*, 25:174–98, p.178.

27 Ibid., p.181.

28 Ibid., p.184.

29 Ibid., p.183.

30 Margaret Nissen quoted in Ibid., p.183.

31 Ibid., p.184.

32 Sands, P (2016) *East West Street*, London: Wiedenfel and Nicolson, p.248.

33 Frank, N (1991) *In the Shadow of the Reich*, trans. Wensinger, A, New York: Alfred A Knopf.

34 Sands, P (2016) *East West Street*, London: Wiedenfel and Nicolson.

35 Ibid., p.224.

36 Frank, N (2019) 'Sohn eines NS-Verbrechers über AfD-Rhetorik: Da spricht ja mein Vater!', *Der Spiegel*, 6 September, https://www.spiegel.de/plus/sohn-eines-ns-verbrechers-ueber-afd-rhetorik-da-spricht-ja-mein-vater-a-00000000-0002-0001-0000-000165813287, my translation.

37 Sands, P (2016) *East West Street*, London: Wiedenfel and Nicolson, p.248.

38 Ibid., p.243.

39 Horst von Wächter, quoted in Sands, P (2016) *East West Street*, London: Wiedenfel and Nicolson, pp.245–6.

40 Sands, P (2016) *East West Street*, London: Wiedenfel and Nicolson, pp.249–50.

41 Ibid., p.250.

42 Ibid., p.243.

43 Ibid., p.242.

44 Ibid., p.382.

45 I am grateful to Susanne Luhmann, whose paper 'Representing Familial Legacies of Nazi Perpetration: Postmemory and/or a "Move to Innocence"?' at the University of Warwick, 5 December 2018, first introduced me to Jennifer Teege's history and memoir.

46 Teege, J and Sellmair, N (2015) *My Grandfather Would Have Shot Me: A Black Woman Discovers Her Family's Nazi Past* ..., trans. Sommer, C, London: Hodder and Stoughton.

47 Kessler, M (2002) *'Ich muss doch meinen Vater lieben, oder?': Die Lebensgeschichte der Monika Göth, der Tochter des KZ-Kommandanten aus Schindlers Liste*, Cologne: Bastei Entertainment.

48 Teege, J and Sellmair, N (2015) *My Grandfather Would Have Shot Me: A Black Woman Discovers Her Family's Nazi Past* ..., trans. Sommer, C, London: Hodder and Stoughton.

49 Ibid., pp.27, 47–8.

50 Ibid., p.80.

51 Ibid., pp.140–1.

52 Lambert, C (2020) 'The Ambivalence of Adoption: Adoptive Families' Stories', *Sociology*, 54(2):363–79, https://doi.org/10.1177/0038038519880107

53 Teege, J and Sellmair, N (2015) *My Grandfather Would Have Shot Me: A Black Woman Discovers Her Family's Nazi Past* ..., trans. Sommer, C, London: Hodder and Stoughton, p.175.

54 Ibid., pp.94–5.

55 Césaire, A (1972 [1955]) *Discourse on Colonialism*, trans. Pinkham, J, New York: Monthly Review Press; Rothberg, M (2009) *Multidirectional Memory: Remembering the Holocaust in an Age of Decolonization*, Stanford: Stanford University Press.

56 See also Jones, H (2020) '"We Are the European Family": Unsettling the Role of Family in Belonging, Race, Nation and the European Project', *Open Arts Journal* (8) Summer 2020:15–27. https://openartsjournal.org/issue-8/article-1/

57 German Missions in the United Kingdom (n.d.) 'Restoration of German Citizenship (Article 116 II Basic Law)', https://uk.diplo.de/uk-en/02/citizenship/restoration-of-citizenship

58 Connolly, K (2019) 'Germany Citizenship Rules for Descendants of Nazi Victims Eased', *The Guardian*, 29 August https://www.theguardian.com/world/2019/aug/29/germany-to-ease-citizenship-law-for-descendants-of-nazi-victims

59 Collinson, P (2019) 'UK Applicants for Irish Passports "Face Excessive Delays and Costs"', *The Guardian*, 7 September, https://www.theguardian.com/politics/2019/sep/07/please-ireland-help-sort-out-my-eu-membership

60 BBC1 (2017) *British Jews, German Passports*, 2 May, https://www.bbc.co.uk/programmes/b08mfgsj; Harpin, L (2018) 'Surge in British Jews Applying for

German Citizenship since Brexit', *The Jewish Chronicle*, 21 October, https://www.thejc.com/news/uk-news/surge-in-british-jews-applying-for-german-citizenship-since-brexit-1.471269

61 Passport Index (2019) 'Global Passport Power Rank 2019', https://www.passportindex.org/byRank.php

62 Kapoor, N and Narkowicz, K (2019) 'Unmaking Citizens: Passport Removals, Pre-emptive Policing and the Reimagining of Colonial Governmentalities', *Ethnic and Racial Studies*, 42(16):45–62, pp.48–9; original emphasis; see also Jones, H (2020) '"We Are the European Family": Unsettling the Role of Family in Belonging, Race, Nation and the European Project', *Open Arts Journal* (8) Summer 2020:15–27, https://openartsjournal.org/issue-8/article-1/

63 'boltongirl', commenting on Hawken, A (2018) 'Oxford Suggests Creating a Second Cecil Rhodes Statue for Students to Write Explicit Graffiti on as University Makes Plans to Broaden Its Appeal to Minorities', *MailOnline*, 15 April, https://www.dailymail.co.uk/news/article-5618131/Oxford-University-suggests-creating-second-Cecil-Rhodes-statue.html

Chapter 6

1 Orwell, G (1946) 'Politics and the English Language', *Horizon*, 13(76):252–65.

2 Panorama (2017) *Undercover: Britain's Immigration Secrets*, TV, BBC1. 4 September. 2100 hrs, 00:00:51. This remains available via Box of Broadcasts (https://learningonscreen.ac.uk/; direct link https://learningonscreen.ac.uk/ondemand/index.php/prog/0F9CD9DD?bcast=124992158).

3 Ibid.

4 Ibid., 00:36:34.

5 Ibid., 00:22:58; see also Hall, A (2010) '"These People Could Be Anyone": Fear, Contempt (and Empathy) in a British Immigration Removal Centre', *Journal of Ethnic and Migration Studies*, 36(6):881–98, p.891.

6 Panorama (2017) *Undercover: Britain's Immigration Secrets*, TV, BBC1. 4 September. 2100 hrs, 00:32:43.

7 Ibid., 00:32:51.

8 Ibid., 00:32:21.

9 Ibid., 00:37:45.

10 Ibid., 00:38:01.

11 Ibid., 00:34:25.

12 Barling, K (2017) 'Foreword', in Buller, E A (ed.) (2017 [1943]) *Darkness over Germany: A Warning from History*, London: Arcadia Books, p.xvi.

13 Cumberland Lodge (n.d.) 'Darkness over Germany', https://www.
   cumberlandlodge.ac.uk/about-us/history-and-heritage/darkness-over-
   germany
14 Buller, E A (2017 [1943]) *Darkness over Germany: A Warning from History*,
   London: Arcadia Books, p.6.
15 Ibid.
16 Ibid., p.7.
17 Ibid.
18 Ibid., p.8.
19 Ibid., p.9.
20 Ibid., p.11.
21 Ibid.
22 Ibid.
23 Ibid., p.15.
24 Ibid., p.165.
25 Horst von Wächter, quoted in Sands, P (2016) *East West Street*, London:
   Wiedenfel and Nicolson, pp.245–6.
26 See Chapter 5.
27 Buller, E A (2017 [1943]) *Darkness over Germany: A Warning from History*,
   London: Arcadia Books, p.15.
28 Lorde, A (1997 [1981]) 'The Uses of Anger', *Women's Studies Quarterly*,
   25(1/2):278–85, p.280.
29 'Elizabeth' quoted in Buller, E A (2017 [1943]) *Darkness over Germany: A
   Warning from History*, London: Arcadia Books, p.10.
30 Lorde, A (1997 [1981]) 'The Uses of Anger', *Women's Studies Quarterly*,
   25(1/2):278–85, p.280.
31 Buller, E A (2017 [1943]) *Darkness over Germany: A Warning from History*,
   London: Arcadia Books, p.169.
32 Ibid., p.213.
33 For example, this description seems to bear some resonance with reactions
   to various current heads of state:

> I ... would go so far as to say that the single most powerful, and
> therefore most dangerous thing about Hitler, is his absolute belief
> in what he says at the moment he says it ... He seems to me to live
> entirely in the present and to have no capacity whatever for linking up
> what he is saying at the time with anything he has said in the recent
> past, or anything he is likely to say in the near future ... millions
> of Germans and many outside were prepared to accept the most
> bewildering contradictions and seemed to have been infected with the
> Führer's own power of forgetting the past.
>
> (p.223 in ibid)

34 Ibid., p.183.

35 Ibid., p.184.

36 Ibid., p.185.

37 Ibid., p.188.

38 Ibid., p.189.

39 Ibid.

40 Ibid.

41 Ibid., p.192.

42 G4S (2017) 'Detainee Custody Officer, Job Reference 5437, Closing Date Dec 11 2017', http://careers.g4s.com/jobs/job/Detainee-Custody-Officer/89863. The wages advertised for this post are £10.67 per hour for a forty-six-hour week of shift work including nights. For comparison, another G4S post as a Cash Transportation Officer advertised at the same time paid £12.68 per hour to drive a van delivering and collecting cash from businesses. Jobs working as a night cleaner in a pub at nearby Gatwick Airport paid £9.50 per hour (https://www.indeed.co.uk/viewjob?jk=79076c c6412c693e&tk=1c9n09j1j14ba1j9&from=serp&vjs=3)

43 Panorama (2017) *Undercover: Britain's Immigration Secrets*, TV, BBC1. 4 September. 2100 hrs, 00:3:17–00:3:32.

44 Silverman, S J (2017) *Briefing: Immigration Detention in the UK*, Oxford: The Migration Observatory, http://www.migrationobservatory.ox.ac.uk/wp-content/uploads/2016/04/Briefing-Immigration_Detention-2.pdf

45 Corporatewatch2 (2018) 'Immigration Detention Centres Factsheet: New Edition May 2018', https://corporatewatch.org/immigration-detention-centres-factsheet-new-edition-updated-may-2018/

46 DeCarlo, S (2014) 'The World's 10 Largest Employers', *Fortune*, 12 November, http://fortune.com/2014/11/12/worlds-largest-employers/

47 Home Office (2001) *The Detention Centre Rules*, https://www.legislation.gov.uk/uksi/2001/238/article/3/made?view=plain; Detained Voices (n.d.) Detained Voices Twitter Account, https://twitter.com/detainedvoices; Haoussou, K (n.d.) 'Survivors Speak OUT', https://www.freedomfromtorture.org/survivor_activism/survivors_speak_out; Medical Justice (2015) 'Mental Health in Detention: Written Evidence Submitted by Medical Justice to the Shaw Review', http://www.medicaljustice.org.uk/wp-content/uploads/2016/04/alHealthinDetention-SummarybyMedicalJusticeforShawReview.pdf; Shaw, S (2016) *Review into the Welfare in Detention of Vulnerable Persons: A Report to the Home Office by Stephen Shaw*, London: TSO; Shaw, S (2018) *Assessment of Government Progress in Implementing the Report on the Welfare in Detention of Vulnerable Persons: A Follow-Up Report to the Home Office*, Cm 9661, London: TSO.

48 Allison, E and Hattenstone, S (2017) 'G4S May Make More Profit than Allowed from Removal Centres, Figures Suggest', *The Guardian*,

13 September, https://www.theguardian.com/business/2017/sep/13/
g4s-may-make-more-profit-than-allowed-from-removal-centres-figures-
suggest; Hattenstone, S and Allison, E (2014) 'G4S, the Company with
No Convictions – But Does It Have Blood on Its Hands?' *The Guardian*,
22 December, https://www.theguardian.com/commentisfree/2014/
dec/22/g4s-convictions-deaths-employees-racial-overtones; Taylor,
D (2017) 'Brook House Asylum Seekers in Legal Fight over Lock-in
Procedures', *The Guardian*, 16 November, https://www.theguardian.com/
uk-news/2017/nov/16/brook-house-asylum-seekers-in-legal-challenge-
over-lock-in-procedures

49 Panorama (2017) *Undercover: Britain's Immigration Secrets*, TV, BBC1.
4 September. 2100 hrs, 00:09:15.

50 Ibid., 00:11:22.

51 Ibid., 00:15:35–00:16:57.

52 Hall, A (2010) '"These People Could Be Anyone": Fear, Contempt (and
Empathy) in a British Immigration Removal Centre', *Journal of Ethnic and
Migration Studies*, 36(6):881–98, p.895.

53 Panorama (2017) *Undercover: Britain's Immigration Secrets*, TV, BBC1.
4 September. 2100 hrs, 00:28:32.

54 Ibid., 00:29:00–00:29:23.

55 Word bleeped out in original film and subtitles; ibid., 00:29:30.

56 Ibid., 00:14:06–00:14:12.

57 G4S (2017) 'Detainee Custody Officer, Job Reference 5437, Closing
Date Dec 11 2017', http://careers.g4s.com/jobs/job/Detainee-Custody-
Officer/89863.

58 In his discussion of staff culture in his review of immigration detention
conditions, Stephen Shaw implies that he would favour more training and
leadership for ethical behaviour (103), more openness by staff about the
challenges they face and coping strategies (104), and closer involvement
and oversight of IRCs by the Home Office itself (113). However, it is only
this final area of change which is translated from the 'staff culture' chapter
into specific recommendations in the report. See Shaw, S (2016) *Review into
the Welfare in Detention of Vulnerable Persons: A Report to the Home Office
by Stephen Shaw*, London: TSO.

59 Panorama (2017) *Undercover: Britain's Immigration Secrets*, TV, BBC1.
4 September. 2100 hrs, 00:15:06.

60 Ibid., 00:16:55.

61 Home Office (2001) *The Detention Centre Rules*, https://www.legislation.
gov.uk/uksi/2001/238/article/3/made?view=plain

62 Shaw, S (2016) *Review into the Welfare in Detention of Vulnerable Persons: A
Report to the Home Office by Stephen Shaw*, London: TSO.

63 See Martinsson, L and Reimers, E (2019) 'Civil Servants Talk Back – Political Subjectivity and (Re)constructions of the Nation', *Critical Sociology*, Online First 5 April, https://doi.org/10.1177/0896920519839768, p.1, discussed below.

64 Ibid., p.1.

65 Jones, H (2013) *Negotiating Cohesion, Inequality and Change: Uncomfortable Positions in Local Government*, Bristol: Policy Press; Mountz, A (2010) *Seeking Asylum: Human Smuggling and Bureaucracy at the Border*, Minneapolis: University of Minnesota Press.

66 Martinsson, L and Reimers, E (2019) 'Civil Servants Talk Back – Political Subjectivity and (Re)constructions of the Nation', *Critical Sociology*, Online First 5 April, https://doi.org/10.1177/0896920519839768, p.10.

67 Jolly, A (2018) '"You Just Have to Work with What You've Got": Practitioner Research with Precarious Migrant Families', *Practice*, 30(2):99–116, p.112.

68 House of Commons and House of Lords (2007) *Joint Committee on Human Rights – Tenth Report*, Session 2006–7. London: Houses of Parliament, https://publications.parliament.uk/pa/jt200607/jtselect/jtrights/81/8102.htm, paragraph 93.

69 Ibid., paragraph 94.

70 Britton, P (2005) 'Do Your Own Dirty Work', *Manchester Evening News*, 24 August, https://www.manchestereveningnews.co.uk/news/greater-manchester-news/do-your-own-dirty-work-1081336.amp

71 Jolly, A (2018) '"You Just Have to Work with What You've Got": Practitioner Research with Precarious Migrant Families', *Practice*, 30(2):99–116, p.112.

72 Lyons, K (2017) 'Destitute Immigrants in UK Are Threatened with Having Children Removed', *The Guardian*, 13 June, https://www.theguardian.com/uk-news/2017/jun/13/destitute-immigrants-uk-threatened-with-having-children-removed

73 Back, L (2002) 'Guess Who's Coming to Dinner? The Political Morality of Investigating Whiteness in the Gray Zone', in Ware, V and Back, L (eds) *Out of Whiteness: Color, Politics and Culture*, Chicago: University of Chicago Press, pp.33–59.

74 Ibid., p.35.

75 Ibid., p.36.

76 Ibid., p.34.

77 Haylett, C (2001) 'Illegitimate Subjects?: Abject Whites, Neoliberal Modernisation, and Middle-Class Multiculturalism', *Environment and Planning D: Society and Space*, 19(3):351–70.

78 Hewitt, R (2005) *White Backlash and the Politics of Multiculturalism*, Cambridge: Cambridge University Press, p.53.

79 Benson, M (2019) 'Focus: Class, Race, Brexit', *Discover Society*, 2 October, https://discoversociety.org/2019/10/02/focus-class-race-brexit/

80 Emejulu, A (2016) 'On the Hideous Whiteness of Brexit: "Let Us Be Honest about Our Past and Our Present if We Truly Seek to Dismantle White Supremacy"', *Verso Blog*, 28 June, https://www.versobooks.com/blogs/2733-on-the-hideous-whiteness-of-brexit-let-us-be-honest-about-our-past-and-our-present-if-we-truly-seek-to-dismantle-white-supremacy

81 In Britain, Nick Griffin in the 2000s, Nigel Farage in the 2010s; in France, Jean-Marie and Marine Le Pen; in the United States, Donald Trump, etc.

Chapter 7

1   Extract from Lorde, A (1997 [1978]) 'But What Can You Teach My Daughter', in *The Collected Poems of Audre Lorde*, New York: W W Norton, p.309.

2   McGoey, L (2019) *The Unknowers: How Strategic Ignorance Rules the World*, London: Zed.

3   Mills, C W (1997) *The Racial Contract*, Ithaca: Cornell University Press; Mills, C W (2007) 'White Ignorance', in Sullivan, S and Tuana, N (eds) *Race and Epistemologies of Ignorance*, Albany: State University of New York Press, pp.11–38.

4   Lorde, A (1997 [1981]) 'The Uses of Anger', *Women's Studies Quarterly*, 25(1/2):278–85.

5   Booth, R (2019) 'How Grenfell Survivors Came Together – and How Britain Failed Them', *The Guardian*, 11 June, https://www.theguardian.com/uk-news/2019/jun/11/how-grenfell-survivors-came-together-to-change-britain

6   Sirriyeh, A (2018) *The Politics of Compassion: Immigration and Asylum Policy*, Bristol: Bristol University Press.

7   See Chapter 4.

8   Trouillot, M-R (1995) *Silencing the Past: Power and the Production of History*, Boston: Beacon Press; and see Chapter 4.

9   Buller, E A (2017 [1943]) *Darkness over Germany: A Warning from History*, London: Arcadia Books, p.9.

10 Though it may also have bought additional time for individual potential deportees to mount appeals.

Bibliography

Abbott, T (2015) 'Transcript: Tony Abbott's Controversial Speech at the Margaret Thatcher Lecture', *The Sydney Morning Herald*, 28 October, https://www.smh.com.au/politics/federal/transcript-tony-abbotts-controversial-speech-at-the-margaret-thatcher-lecture-20151028-gkkg6p.html

Addley, E, Elgot, J and Perraudin, F (2016) 'Jo Cox: Thousands Pay Tribute on What Should Have Been MP's Birthday', *The Guardian*, 22 June, https://www.theguardian.com/uk-news/2016/jun/22/jo-cox-murder-inspired-more-love-than-hatred-says-husband-brendan

Affleck, B (2015), Facebook Post, 22 April, https://www.facebook.com/benaffleck/posts/849207928486969

Ahmed, S (2008) 'Liberal Multiculturalism Is the Hegemony – It's an Empirical Fact – A Response to Slavoj Žižek', *Dark Matter*, 19 February, http://www.darkmatter101.org/site/2008/02/19/%E2%80%98liberal-multiculturalism-is-the-hegemony-%E2%80%93-its-an-empirical-fact%E2%80%99-a-response-to-slavoj-zizek/

Al Jazeera (2016) 'Church Collapses in Uyo, Killing Dozens of Nigerians', 11 December, https://www.aljazeera.com/news/2016/12/church-collapses-nigeria-uyo-killing-scores-161211041437146.html

Allison, E and Hattenstone, S (2017) 'G4S May Make More Profit than Allowed from Removal Centres, Figures Suggest', *The Guardian*, 13 September, https://www.theguardian.com/business/2017/sep/13/g4s-may-make-more-profit-than-allowed-from-removal-centres-figures-suggest

Amnesty International (2015) *By Hook or by Crook: Australia's Abuse of Asylum Seekers at Sea*, London: Amnesty International.

Anderson, B (2013) *Us and Them? The Dangerous Politics of Migration Control*, Oxford: Oxford University Press.

Anderson, B (2017) 'The Politics of Pests: Immigration and the Invasive Other', *Social Research*, 84(1):7–28.

Anderson, D (2005) *Histories of the Hanged: Britain's Dirty War in Kenya and the End of Empire: Testimonies from the Mau Mau Rebellion in Kenya*, London: Wiedenfeld and Nicolson.

Anderson, D (2011) 'Mau Mau in the High Court and the "Lost" British Empire Archives: Colonial Conspiracy or Bureaucratic Bungle?' *The Journal of Imperial and Commonwealth History*, 39(5):699–716, p.710.

Anthony, A (2016) 'Is Free Speech in British Universities under Threat?' *The Guardian*, 24 January, https://www.theguardian.com/world/2016/jan/24/safe-spaces-universities-no-platform-free-speech-rhodes

Apps, P (2019) 'PM's Chief of Staff Did Not Act on Multiple Warnings about Fire Safety in Months before Grenfell, New Letters Show', *Inside Housing*, 13 June, https://www.insidehousing.co.uk/news/news/pms-chief-of-staff-did-not-act-on-multiple-warnings-about-fire-safety-in-months-before-grenfell-new-letters-show-61883

Arendt, H (1968 [2006]) *Eichmann in Jerusalem: A Report on the Banality of Evil*, London: Penguin Classics.

Ashe, S (2015) 'The Rise of UKIP: Challenges for Anti-Racism', in Khan, O and Sveinsson, K (eds) *Race and Elections*, London: Runnymede, pp.15–17.

Associated Press in Savannah, Georgia (2015) 'Ben Affleck's Slave-Owning Family: Records Sketch a Conflicted Past', *The Guardian*, 17 May, https://www.theguardian.com/film/2015/may/17/ben-affleck-slave-owning-family-tree-records

Attar, S (2010) *Debunking the Myths of Colonization: The Arabs and Europe*, Maryland: University Press of America.

Back, L (2002) 'Guess Who's Coming to Dinner? The Political Morality of Investigating Whiteness in the Gray Zone', in Ware, V and Back, L (eds) *Out of Whiteness: Color, Politics and Culture*, Chicago: University of Chicago Press, pp.33–59.

Back, L (2018) 'Silent Steps', *Streetsigns*, 26 January, https://cucrblog.wordpress.com/2018/01/26/silent-steps/

Back, L, Keith, M, Khan, A, Shukra, K and Solomos, J (2002) 'New Labour's White Heart: Politics, Multiculturalism and the Return of Assimilation', *The Political Quarterly*, 73(4):445–54.

Badger, A (2012) 'Historians, a Legacy of Suspicion and the "Migrated Archives"', *Small Wars & Insurgencies*, 23(4–5):799–807.

Barling, K (2017) 'Foreword', in Buller, E A (ed.) (2017 [1943]) *Darkness over Germany: A Warning from History*, London: Arcadia Books. vii–xxxiv.

Barthes, R (1981) *Camera Lucida*, trans. Howard, R, New York: Hill and Wang.

BBC (2015) 'Ben Affleck Slavery Row Leads to TV Show Suspension', *BBC News*, 25 June, https://www.bbc.co.uk/news/entertainment-arts-33267697

BBC1 (2017) *British Jews, German Passports*, 2 May, https://www.bbc.co.uk/programmes/b08mfgsj

BBC News (2013) 'Bangladesh Factory Collapse Toll Passes 1,000', 10 May, https://www.bbc.co.uk/news/world-asia-22476774

BBC News (2015) 'UKIP's Nigel Farage Calls for Immigration Visa Points System', 4 March, https://www.bbc.co.uk/news/av/uk-politics-31724979/ukip-s-nigel-farage-calls-for-immigration-visa-points-system

BBC News (2016) 'Jo Cox Murder: Judge's Sentencing Remarks to Thomas Mair', *www.bbcnews.co.uk*, 23 June, https://www.bbc.co.uk/news/uk-38076755

BBC News (2017) 'Jewish and Muslim Women MPs "Face Most Abuse"', *BBC News*, 21 March, http://www.bbc.co.uk/news/uk-politics-39339487

BBC News (2018a) 'Darren Osborne Guilty of Finsbury Park Mosque Murder', *BBC News*, 1 February, http://www.bbc.co.uk/news/uk-42910051

BBC News (2018b) 'National Action: Men Jailed for Being Members of Banned Neo-Nazi Group', *BBC News*, 18 July, https://www.bbc.co.uk/news/uk-politics-44873178

BBC News (2018c) 'US Senator Elizabeth Warren Faces Backlash after Indigenous DNA Claim', *BBC News*, 16 October, https://www.bbc.co.uk/news/world-us-canada-45869804

BBC News (2019) 'Grenfell Tower Fire: "Agonising Memories" of Families and Friends', 14 June, https://www.bbc.co.uk/news/uk-england-london-48634630

BBC Trending (2014) '#BBCTrending: The Two Faces of Michael Brown', 11 August, https://www.bbc.co.uk/news/blogs-trending-28742301

Beaumont-Thomas, B (2018) 'Stormzy Asks "Theresa May, Where's the Money for Grenfell?" at Brit Awards', *The Guardian*, 21 February, https://www.theguardian.com/music/2018/feb/21/stormzy-asks-may-wheres-the-money-for-grenfell-at-brit-awards

Benson, M (2019) 'Focus: Class, Race, Brexit', *Discover Society*, 2 October, https://discoversociety.org/2019/10/02/focus-class-race-brexit/

Berger, J and Mohr, J (1975) *A Seventh Man: The Story of a Migrant Worker in Europe*, Harmondsworth: Penguin.

Berglund, O (2017) 'Using Empty Luxury Homes to House Grenfell Tower Victims Is a No Brainer', *The Conversation*, 26 June, https://theconversation.com/using-empty-luxury-homes-to-house-grenfell-tower-victims-is-a-no-brainer-80025

Bhambra, G K (2016) 'Undoing the Epistemic Disavowal of the Haitian Revolution: A Contribution to Global Social Thought', *Journal of Intercultural Studies*, 37(1):1–16.

Birnberg Peirce & Partners, Medical Justice and the National Coalition of Anti-Deportation Campaigns (2008) *Outsourcing Abuse: The Use and Misuse of State-Sanctioned Force during the Detention and Removal of Asylum Seekers*, London: Medical Justice.

Bolt, D (2018) *An Inspection of the Vulnerable Persons Resettlement Scheme August 2017–January 2018*, London: Independent Chief Inspector of Borders and Immigration.

Boltanski, L (1999) *Distant Suffering: Morality, Media and Politics*, trans. Burchell, G, Cambridge: Cambridge University Press.

Booth, R (2019) 'How Grenfell Survivors Came Together – and How Britain Failed Them', *The Guardian*, 11 June, https://www.theguardian.com/uk-news/2019/jun/11/how-grenfell-survivors-came-together-to-change-britain

Brennan, D (2016) *Femicide Census: Profiles of Women Killed by Men, Redefining an Isolated Incident*, London: Women's Aid and nia.

Britton, P (2005) 'Do Your Own Dirty Work', *Manchester Evening News*, 24 August, https://www.manchestereveningnews.co.uk/news/greater-manchester-news/do-your-own-dirty-work-1081336.amp

Buller, E A (2017 [1943]) *Darkness over Germany: A Warning from History*, London: Arcadia Books.

Bulley, D, Edkins, J and El-Enany, N (2019) *After Grenfell: Violence, Resistance and Response*, London: Pluto Press.

Butler, J (2020) *The Force of Non-Violence*, London: Verso.

Byrne, B (2015) 'Rethinking Intersectionality and Whiteness at the Borders of Citizenship', *Sociological Research Online*, 20(3):16.

Césaire, A (1972 [1955]) *Discourse on Colonialism*, trans. Pinkham, J, New York: Monthly Review Press.

Cobain, I (2013) 'Revealed: The Bonfire of Papers at the End of Empire', *The Guardian*, 29 November, http://www.theguardian.com/uk-news/2013/nov/29/revealed-bonfire-papers-empire

Cobain, I, Parveen, N and Taylor, M (2016) 'The Slow-Burning Hatred that Led Thomas Mair to Murder Jo Cox', *The Guardian*, 23 November, https://www.theguardian.com/uk-news/2016/nov/23/thomas-mair-slow-burning-hatred-led-to-jo-cox-murder

Collins, L (2012) 'Mail Supremacy', *The New Yorker*, 26 March, https://www.newyorker.com/magazine/2012/04/02/mail-supremacy

Collinson, P (2019) 'UK Applicants for Irish Passports "Face Excessive Delays and Costs"', *The Guardian*, 7 September, https://www.theguardian.com/politics/2019/sep/07/please-ireland-help-sort-out-my-eu-membership

Connolly, K (2019) 'Germany Citizenship Rules for Descendants of Nazi Victims Eased', *The Guardian*, 29 August, https://www.theguardian.com/world/2019/aug/29/germany-to-ease-citizenship-law-for-descendants-of-nazi-victims

Cooper, Y (2013) 'Yvette Cooper's Immigration Speech in Full', *politics.co.uk*, 7 March, https://www.politics.co.uk/comment-analysis/2013/03/07/yvette-cooper-s-immigration-speech-in-full

Corporatewatch2 (2018) 'Immigration Detention Centres Factsheet: New Edition May 2018', https://corporatewatch.org/immigration-detention-centres-factsheet-new-edition-updated-may-2018/

Cox, B (2017) *Jo Cox: More in Common*, London: Two Roads.

Cumberland Lodge (n.d.) 'Darkness over Germany', https://www.cumberlandlodge.ac.uk/about-us/history-and-heritage/darkness-over-germany

D'Ancona, M (2017) *Post-Truth: The New War on Truth and How to Fight Back*, London: Penguin.

Davies, W (2019) *Nervous States: How Feeling Took over the World*, London: Penguin.

Davis, A (1998) 'Masked Racism: Reflections on the Prison-industrial Complex', *ColorLines*, 10 September, https://www.colorlines.com/articles/masked-racism-reflections-prison-industrial-complex

Dearden, L (2015) 'Katie Hopkins "Claims Aylan Kurdi's Drowned Body Was Staged on Turkish Beach"', *The Independent*, 25 September, https://www.independent.co.uk/news/people/katie-hopkins-claims-aylan-kurdis-drowned-body-was-staged-on-turkish-beach-10516423.html

DeCarlo, S (2014) 'The World's 10 Largest Employers', *Fortune*, 12 November, http://fortune.com/2014/11/12/worlds-largest-employers/

Demianyk, G (2017a) 'Centrist Campaign Group "More United" Crowdfunds £370,000 to Donate to "Progressive" Election Candidates', *Huffington Post*, 2 May, https://www.huffingtonpost.co.uk/entry/more-united-progressive-centrist-election-candidates_uk_5907940ce4b0bb2d08705a2a?393i; https://www.moreunited.co.uk

Demianyk, G (2017b) 'Daily Telegraph Admits "Decolonise" Cambridge Curriculum Story Was Wrong as Student Lola Olufemi Condemns Newspaper', *Huffington Post*, 26 October, https://www.huffingtonpost.co.uk/entry/telegraph-lola-olufemi_uk_59f1fe0fe4b077d8dfc7eaf9

De Noronha, L (2016) 'The Deportation Charter Flight – What's All the Fuss About?' *The Gleaner*, 11 September, http://jamaica-gleaner.com/article/focus/20160911/luke-de-noronha-deportation-charter-flight-whats-all-fuss-about

Detained Voices (n.d.) Detained Voices Twitter Account, https://twitter.com/detainedvoices

Dhaliwal, S and Forkert, K (2016) 'Deserving and Undeserving Migrants', *Soundings*, 61:49–61.

Dhrodia, A (2017) 'We Tracked 25,688 Abusive Tweets Sent to Women MPs – Half Were Directed at Diane Abbott', *New Statesman*, 5 September, https://www.newstatesman.com/2017/09/we-tracked-25688-abusive-tweets-sent-women-mps-half-were-directed-diane-abbott

Direct.gov (2007) 'New Points Based Migration System to Start in the New Year', *Direct.gov*, 18 April, archived at https://webarchive.nationalarchives.

gov.uk/20100104234058/http://www.direct.gov.uk/en/Nl1/Newsroom/DG_067655

Du Bois, W E B (1903 [2007]) *The Souls of Black Folk*, Oxford: Oxford University Press.

Du Bois, W E B (1940 [1984]) *Dusk of Dawn: An Essay towards an Autobiography of a Race Concept*, London: Transaction.

Earle, W (2019) 'Barca Nostra: Is This Art?' *Spiked*, 23 May, https://www.spiked-online.com/2019/05/23/barca-nostra-is-this-art/

Economist, The (2003) 'The Albanian Solution', *The Economist*, 13 March, http://www.economist.com/node/1632873

Edwards-Jones, I (2017) 'Grenfell Tower Has United London's "Have and Have Yachts" Like I've Never Seen Before', *The Telegraph*, 15 June, https://www.telegraph.co.uk/women/life/grenfell-tower-has-united-londons-have-have-yachts-like-never/

Elkins, C (2011) 'Alchemy of Evidence: Mau Mau, the British Empire, and the High Court of Justice', *The Journal of Imperial and Commonwealth History*, 39(5):731–48.

Elkins, C (2014) 'Review: Huw Bennett. Fighting the Mau Mau: The British Army and Counter-Insurgency in the Kenya Emergency. (Cambridge Military Histories.) New York: Cambridge University Press. 2013. Pp. xii, 307. $29.99', *American Historical Review*, April 2014, pp.653–4.

Elliott, M (2017) 'The Inconvenient Ancestor: Slavery and Selective Remembrance on Genealogy Television', *Studies in Popular Culture*, 39(2):73–90.

El-Tayeb, F (2011) *European Others: Queering Ethnicity in Postnational Europe*, Minneapolis: University of Minnesota Press.

Emejulu, A (2016) 'On the Hideous Whiteness of Brexit: "Let Us Be Honest about Our Past and Our Present If We Truly Seek to Dismantle White Supremacy"', *Verso Blog*, 28 June https://www.versobooks.com/blogs/2733-on-the-hideous-whiteness-of-brexit-let-us-be-honest-about-our-past-and-our-present-if-we-truly-seek-to-dismantle-white-supremacy

Espinoza, J (2015) 'Politically Correct Universities "Are Killing Free Speech"', *The Telegraph*, 18 December, https://www.telegraph.co.uk/education/educationnews/12059161/Politically-correct-universities-are-killing-free-speech.html

European Commission (2017) 'EU Trust Fund for Africa Adopts €46 Million Programme to Support Integrated Migration and Border Management in Libya', Press Release, 28 July, https://ec.europa.eu/commission/presscorner/detail/en/IP_17_2187

European Parliament (2019) 'Legislative Train 12.2019, 8 towards a New Policy on Migration, EU Statement and Action Plan', 20 September, http://www.

europarl.europa.eu/legislative-train/api/stages/report/current/theme/
towards-a-new-policy-on-migration/file/european-border-and-coast-guard

Eurostat (2016) 'Asylum in the EU Member States Record Number of over 1.2
Million First Time Asylum Seekers Registered in 2015 Syrians, Afghans
and Iraqis: Top Citizenships', 4 March, https://ec.europa.eu/eurostat/
documents/2995521/7203832/3-04032016-AP-EN.pdf/790eba01-381c-4163-
bcd2-a54959b99ed6

Ezra, M (2007) 'The Eichmann Polemics: Hannah Arendt and Her Critics',
Democratiya, 9:141–65.

Falvey, D (2018) 'Theresa May Delivers Emotional Heartfelt Message to Jo Cox's
Children about "Mummy"', *Sunday Express*, 18 January, https://www.express.
co.uk/news/uk/906339/jo-cox-minister-for-loneliness-theresa-may-tracey-
crouch-labour-mp-murder

Farrell, P and Doherty, B (2016) 'Nauru Files Show Wilson Security Staff
Regularly Downgraded Reports of Abuse', *The Guardian*, 11 August, https://
www.theguardian.com/australia-news/2016/aug/12/nauru-files-show-
wilson-security-staff-regularly-downgraded-reports-of-abuse

Ferguson, K (2012) *All in the Family: On Community and Incommensurability*,
Durham and London: Duke University Press, p.81.

Fisk, R (2016) 'Alan Kurdi Symbolised an Army of Dead Children. We Ignore
Them at Our Peril', *The Independent*, 1 September, https://www.independent.
co.uk/voices/a-year-on-from-alan-kurdi-we-continue-to-ignore-the-facts-
in-front-of-us-and-we-ignore-them-at-our-a7220111.html

Fletcher, M (2018) 'The Polite Extremist: Jacob Rees-Mogg's Seemingly
Unstoppable Rise', *New Statesman*, 20 February, https://www.newstatesman.
com/politics/uk/2018/02/polite-extremist-jacob-rees-mogg-s-seemingly-
unstoppable-rise

Frank, N (1991) *In the Shadow of the Reich*, trans. Wensinger, A, New York:
Alfred A Knopf.

Frank, N (2019) 'Sohn eines NS-Verbrechers über AfD-Rhetorik: Da spricht
ja mein Vater!', *Der Spiegel*, 6 September, https://www.spiegel.de/plus/
sohn-eines-ns-verbrechers-ueber-afd-rhetorik-da-spricht-ja-mein-vater
-a-00000000-0002-0001-0000-000165813287

Freire, P (2000 [1970]) *Pedagogy of the Oppressed*, trans. Bergman Ramos, M,
New York: Continuum.

Frickel, S, Gibbon, S, Howard, J, Kempner, J, Ottinger, G and Hess, D J (2010)
'Undone Science: Charting Social Movement and Civil Society Challenges to
Research Agenda Setting', *Science, Technology and Human Values*, 35(4):444–
73.

Friedersdorf, C (2015) 'The New Intolerance of Student Activism', *The Atlantic*, 9 November, https://www.theatlantic.com/politics/archive/2015/11/the-new-intolerance-of-student-activism-at-yale/414810/

Fryer, P (1984) *Staying Power: The History of Black People in Britain*, London: Pluto.

G4S (2017) 'Detainee Custody Officer, Job Reference 5437, Closing Date Dec 11 2017', http://careers.g4s.com/jobs/job/Detainee-Custody-Officer/89863

Gebrial, D (2015) 'We Don't Want to Erase Cecil Rhodes from History. We Want Everyone to Know His Crimes', *The Telegraph*, 22 December, https://www.telegraph.co.uk/education/universityeducation/12064939/We-dont-want-to-erase-Cecil-Rhodes-from-history.-We-want-everyone-to-know-his-crimes.html

Gebrial, D (2018) 'Rhodes Must Fall: Oxford and Movements for Change', in Bhambra, G K, Gebrial, D and Nişancıoğlu, K (eds) *Decolonising the University*, London: Pluto Press, pp.19–36.

Gentleman, A (2019a) *The Windrush Betrayal*, London: Guardian Faber.

Gentleman, A (2019b) 'Windrush Victim Dies without Compensation or Apology', *The Guardian*, 12 November, https://www.theguardian.com/uk-news/2019/nov/12/windrush-victim-dies-without-compensation-or-apology

German Missions in the United Kingdom (n.d.) 'Restoration of German Citizenship (Article 116 II Basic Law)', https://uk.diplo.de/uk-en/02/citizenship/restoration-of-citizenship

Giddens, A (1999) *The Third Way: The Renewal of Social Democracy*, London: Polity Press.

Gilmore, R W (2007) *Golden Gulag: Prisons, Surplus, Crisis, and Opposition in Globalizing California*, Berkeley: University of California Press.

Gleeson, M (2016) *Offshore: Behind the Wire on Manus and Nauru*, Sydney: NewSouth.

Gordon, A F (2008) *Ghostly Matters: Haunting and the Sociological Imagination*, Minneapolis: University of Minnesota Press.

Great Get Together (2017) 'The Great Get Together Aims to Unite Britain for Jo Cox', Video, https://www.youtube.com/watch?v=pgQf8JMX3_0

Greenwood, C, Brooke, C and Dolan, A (2016) 'What a Tragic Waste', *The Daily Mail*, 17 June, p.1.

Grenfell Action Group (2016) 'KCTMO – Playing with Fire!', 20 November, https://grenfellactiongroup.wordpress.com/2016/11/20/kctmo-playing-with-fire/

Grenfell Action Group (2017) 'Grenfell Tower Fire', 14 June, https://grenfellactiongroup.wordpress.com/2017/06/14/grenfell-tower-fire/

Grenfell Tower Inquiry (2019a) *Independent Grenfell Tower Inquiry Financial Report to 31 March 2019*, https://assets.grenfelltowerinquiry.org.uk/inline-

files/Grenfell%20Tower%20Inquiry%20financial%20report%20to%2031%20
March%202019.pdf

Grenfell Tower Inquiry (2019b) *Path to Phase 2 Hearings*, https://assets.
grenfelltowerinquiry.org.uk/inline-files/Path%20to%20P2%20hearings%20
English.pdf

Grenfell Tower Inquiry (2019c) *Updated List of Issues*, September, https://assets.
grenfelltowerinquiry.org.uk/inline-files/List%20of%20Issues%2025%20
September%202019%20%281%29.pdf

Grierson, J (2018) 'Immigration Detention: How the UK Compares with
Other Countries', *The Guardian*, 10 October, https://www.theguardian.com/
uk-news/2018/oct/10/immigration-detention-how-the-uk-compares-with-
other-countries

Griffiths, B (2017) 'WIDOWER TELLS ALL Jo Cox's Husband Brendan Reveals
Taking Kids to See Murdered Wife's Body "Was the Hardest Decision of His
Life"', *The Sun*, 4 June.

Griggs, B (2015) 'Photographer Describes "Scream" of Migrant Boy's "Silent
Body"', *CNN World*, 3 September, https://edition.cnn.com/2015/09/03/
world/dead-migrant-boy-beach-photographer-nilufer-demir/index.html

Gross, M and McGoey, L (eds) (2015) *Routledge International Handbook of
Ignorance Studies*, 1st Edition, London: Routledge.

Grzymski, J (2019) 'Seeing Like a EUropean Border: Limits of the European
Borders and Space', *Global Discourse*, 9(1):135–51.

Guardian, The, 6 December 2017, https://www.theguardian.com/society/
video/2017/dec/06/heidi-allen-mp-tears-frank-field-impact-of-universal-
credit-video

Gurner, J (2015) 'Alan Kurdi: Why One Picture Cut Through', *BBC News*, 4
September, https://www.bbc.co.uk/news/world-europe-34150419

Hage, G (2017) *Is Racism an Environmental Threat?* London: Polity.

Hague, W (2013) 'Statement to Parliament on Settlement of Mau Mau Claims',
6 June, https://www.gov.uk/government/news/statement-to-parliament-on-
settlement-of-mau-mau-claims

Hall, A (2010) '"These People Could Be Anyone": Fear, Contempt (and
Empathy) in a British Immigration Removal Centre', *Journal of Ethnic and
Migration Studies*, 36(6):881–98, p.891.

Hall, S (1998) 'The Great Moving Nowhere Show', *Marxism Today*, November/
December, 9–14, p.10.

Hall, S (1999) 'From Scarman to Stephen Lawrence', *History Workshop Journal*,
48:187–97.

Haoussou, K (n.d.) 'Survivors Speak OUT', https://www.freedomfromtorture.
org/survivor_activism/survivors_speak_out

Haraway, D (1988) 'Situated Knowledges: The Science Question in Feminism and the Privilege of Partial Perspective', *Feminist Studies*, 14(3):575–99.

Harpin, L (2018) 'Surge in British Jews Applying for German Citizenship since Brexit', *The Jewish Chronicle*, 21 October, https://www.thejc.com/news/uk-news/surge-in-british-jews-applying-for-german-citizenship-since-brexit-1.471269

Harris, C I (1993) 'Whiteness as Property', *Harvard Law Review*, 106(8):1707–91.

Harris, T (2018) 'Metropolitans Tipped to Lead a "Centrist Party" Are Undermining the Project before It Has Begun', *The Telegraph*, 23 October, https://www.telegraph.co.uk/politics/2018/10/23/metropolitans-tipped-lead-centrist-party-undermining-project/

Hartman, S (2002) 'The Time of Slavery', *South Atlantic Quarterly*, 101(4):757–77, pp.759–60.

Hattenstone, S and Allison, E (2014) 'G4S, the Company with No Convictions – but Does It Have Blood on Its Hands?' *The Guardian*, 22 December, https://www.theguardian.com/commentisfree/2014/dec/22/g4s-convictions-deaths-employees-racial-overtones

Hawken, A (2018) 'Oxford Suggests Creating a Second Cecil Rhodes Statue for Students to Write Explicit Graffiti on as University Makes Plans to Broaden Its Appeal to Minorities', *MailOnline*, 15 April, https://www.dailymail.co.uk/news/article-5618131/Oxford-University-suggests-creating-second-Cecil-Rhodes-statue.html

Haylett, C (2001) 'Illegitimate Subjects?: Abject Whites, Neoliberal Modernisation, and Middle-Class Multiculturalism', *Environment and Planning D: Society and Space*, 19(3):351–70.

Heller, C and Pezzani, L (2017) *Blaming the Rescuers*, https://blamingtherescuers.org/report/

Helm, T, Graham-Harrison, E and McKie, R (2020) 'How Did Britain Het Its Coronavirus Response So Wrong?' *The Guardian*, 19 April, https://www.theguardian.com/world/2020/apr/18/how-did-britain-get-its-response-to-coronavirus-so-wrong

Helman, S and Rapoport, T (1997) 'Women in Black: Challenging Israel's Gender and Socio-Political Orders', *British Journal of Sociology*, 48(4):681–700.

Hewitt, R (2005) *White Backlash and the Politics of Multiculturalism*, Cambridge: Cambridge University Press.

Heyden, T (2015) 'The 10 Greatest Controversies of Winston Churchill's Career', *BBC News Magazine*, 26 January, https://www.bbc.co.uk/news/magazine-29701767

Hirsch, M (2008) 'The Generation of Postmemory', *Poetics Today*, 29(1):103–28.

Hirsch, M (2012) *The Generation of Postmemory: Writing and Visual Culture after the Holocaust*, New York: Columbia University Press.

Holdsworth, A (2011) *Television, Memory and Nostalgia*, Basingstoke: Palgrave.

Home Office (2001) *The Detention Centre Rules*, https://www.legislation.gov.uk/uksi/2001/238/article/3/made?view=plain

Home Office (2016) 'National Statistics: Asylum, Updated 2 March 2016', https://www.gov.uk/government/publications/immigration-statistics-october-to-december-2015/asylum#nationalities-applying-for-asylum

House of Commons and House of Lords (2007) *Joint Committee on Human Rights – Tenth Report*, Session 2006–7. London: Houses of Parliament, https://publications.parliament.uk/pa/jt200607/jtselect/jtrights/81/8102.htm

Hutton, M (2014) 'Drownings on the Public Record of People Attempting to Enter Australia Irregularly by Boat since 1998', 2 February, http://sievx.com/articles/background/DrowningsTable.pdf

IOM [International Organisation for Migration] (2017) 'Migration Data Portal: Migrant Deaths and Disappearances', https://migrationdataportal.org/themes/migrant-deaths-and-disappearances, last accessed 2 June 2019.

Iqbal, N (2018) 'Stansted 15: "We Are Not Terrorists, No Lives Were at Risk. We Have No Regrets"', *The Guardian*, 16 December, https://www.theguardian.com/world/2018/dec/16/migrants-deportation-stansted-actvists

Itabaaza, S (2019) 'Remove *Barca Nostra* from Venice Biennale', *Change.org*, https://www.change.org/p/ralph-rugoff-remove-barca-nostra-from-venice-biennale

ITV (2017) 'Jo Cox's Children Set to Unveil Coat of Arms Dedicated to Mum', *ITV News*, 24 June, http://www.itv.com/news/2017-06-24/jo-coxs-children-unveil-coat-of-arms-dedicated-to-mum/

Jenne, A (2015) 'Mary Beard Says Drive to Remove Cecil Rhodes Statue from Oxford University Is a "Dangerous Attempt to Erase the Past"', *The Independent*, 22 December, https://www.independent.co.uk/news/education/education-news/mary-beard-says-drive-to-remove-cecil-rhodes-statue-from-oxford-university-is-a-dangerous-attempt-to-a6783306.html

Johnston, C (2018) 'Sadiq Khan Speech Disrupted by Brexit and Trump Supporters', *The Guardian*, 13 January, https://www.theguardian.com/politics/2018/jan/13/sadiq-khan-speech-disrupted-by-protesters-backing-brexit-and-trump-white-pendragons

Jolly, A (2018) '"You Just Have to Work with What You've Got": Practitioner Research with Precarious Migrant Families', *Practice*, 30(2):99–116.

Jones, H (2013) *Negotiating Cohesion, Inequality and Change: Uncomfortable Positions in Local Government*, Bristol: Policy Press.

Jones, H (2015) 'Public Opinion on the Refugee Crisis Is Changing Fast – and for the Better', *The Conversation*, 4 September, https://theconversation.com

com/public-opinion-on-the-refugee-crisis-is-changing-fast-and-for-the-better-47064

Jones, H (2019) 'More in Common: The Domestication of Misogynist White Supremacy and the Assassination of Jo Cox', *Ethnic and Racial Studies*, 42(14):2431–49.

Jones, H (2020) '"We Are the European Family": Unsettling the Role of Family in Belonging, Race, Nation and the European Project', *Open Arts Journal*, (8) Summer 2020:15–27, https://openartsjournal.org/issue-8/article-1/

Jones, H, Gunaratnam, Y, Bhattacharyya, G, Davies, W, Dhaliwal, S, Forkert, K, Jackson, E and Saltus, R (2017) *Go Home? The Politics of Immigration Controversies*, Manchester: Manchester University Press.

Kapoor, N and Narkowicz, K (2019) 'Unmaking Citizens: Passport Removals, Pre-emptive Policing and the Reimagining of Colonial Governmentalities', *Ethnic and Racial Studies*, 42(16):45–62, pp.48–9.

Kessler, M (2002) *'Ich muss doch meinen Vater lieben, oder?': Die Lebensgeschichte der Monika Göth, der Tochter des KZ-Kommandanten aus Schindlers Liste*, Cologne: Bastei Entertainment.

Kingsley, P and Rankin, J (2016) 'EU-Turkey Refugee Deal – Q&A', *The Guardian*, 8 March, https://www.theguardian.com/world/2016/mar/08/eu-turkey-refugee-deal-qa

Kramer, A-M (2011a) 'Kinship, Affinity and Connectedness: Exploring the Role of Genealogy in Personal Lives', *Sociology*, 45(3):379–95.

Kramer, A-M (2011b) 'Mediatizing Memory: History, Affect and Identity in *Who Do You Think You Are?*' *European Journal of Cultural Studies*, 14(4):428–44.

Lambert, C (2020) 'The Ambivalence of Adoption: Adoptive Families' Stories', *Sociology*, 54(2):363–79, https://doi.org/10.1177/0038038519880107.

Lawrence, D (2018) 'Grenfell Inquiry Brings Painful Memories of the Fight for Justice for My Son, Stephen Lawrence', *The Guardian*, 2 June, https://www.theguardian.com/commentisfree/2018/jun/02/grenfell-inquiry-brings-painful-memories-of-fight-for-justice-for-my-son-stephen-lawrence

LBC (2018) 'Jacob Rees-Mogg Lays into "Disgraceful" Home Office over Windrush Row', 16 April, https://www.lbc.co.uk/radio/special-shows/ring-rees-mogg/jacob-rees-mogg-disgraceful-home-office-windrush/

Levitas, R (1998) *The Inclusive Society? Social Exclusion and New Labour*, London: Palgrave.

Levy, C (2010) 'Refugees, Europe, Camps/State of Exception: "Into the Zone", the European Union and Extraterritorial Processing of Migrants, Refugees, and Asylum-Seekers (Theories and Practice)', *Refugee Survey Quarterly*, 29(1):92–119.

Lister, R (2001) 'New Labour: A Study in Ambiguity from a Position of Ambivalence', *Critical Social Policy*, 21(4):425–47.

Lister, R (2018) 'From Windrush to Universal Credit – the Art of "Institutional Indifference"', *Open Democracy*, 10 October, https://www.opendemocracy. net/en/opendemocracyuk/from-windrush-to-universal-credit-art-of-institutional-indifference/

Local News: What Are We Missing? (2017) BBC Radio 4, 22 November, https:// www.bbc.co.uk/programmes/b09fy6g9

Lorde, A (1997 [1978]) 'But What Can You Teach My Daughter', in *The Collected Poems of Audre Lorde*, New York: W W Norton, p.309.

Lorde, A (1997 [1981]) 'The Uses of Anger', *Women's Studies Quarterly*, 25(1/2):278–85.

Lowkey ft. KAIA (2018) *Ghosts of Grenfell 2*, https://youtu.be/SQplVg9vE0I

Lowkey ft. Mai Khalil (2017) *Ghosts of Grenfell*, https://www.youtube.com/watc h?v=ztUamrChczQ&feature=youtu.be

Luhmann, S (2009) 'Gender and the Generations of Difficult Knowledge: Recent Responses to Familial Legacies of Nazi Perpetration', *Women in German Yearbook*, 25:174–98.

Lyons, K (2017) 'Destitute Immigrants in UK are Threatened with Having Children Removed', *The Guardian*, 13 June, https://www.theguardian.com/ uk-news/2017/jun/13/destitute-immigrants-uk-threatened-with-having-children-removed

Maclean, R and Marks, S (2020) '10 African Countries Have No Ventilators. That's Only Part of the Problem', *The New York Times*, 18 April, https://www. nytimes.com/2020/04/18/world/africa/africa-coronavirus-ventilators.html

Mail Online Reporter (2015) 'How Many More Can Kos Take? Thousands of Boat People from Syria and Afghanistan Set up Migrant Camp in Popular Greek Island – With Holidaymakers Branding the Situation "Disgusting"', *MailOnline*, 27 May, https://www.dailymail.co.uk/news/article-3099736/ Holidaymakers-misery-boat-people-Syria-Afghanistan-seeking-asylum-set-migrant-camp-turn-popular-Greek-island-Kos-disgusting-hellhole.html

Mair, E (2018) *The Grenfell Tower Inquiry Podcast with Eddie Mair: Episode 7: Commemoration: Day 2*, BBC, 22 May, https://www.bbc.co.uk/programmes/ p067y12v

Mako, S (2012) 'Cultural Genocide and Key International Instruments: Framing the Indigenous Experience', *International Journal on Minority and Group Rights*, 19:175–94.

Malik, K (2017) 'Kenan Malik on Cultural Appropriation', *Art Review*, December, https://artreview.com/features/ar_december_2017_feature_cultural_appropriation_kenan_malik/

Marks, K (2002) 'Refugee Camp Children Sew Their Lips in Protest', *Independent*, 22 January, https://www.independent.co.uk/news/world/australasia/refugee-camp-children-sew-their-lips-in-protest-5362577.html

Marr, D (2016) 'The Nauru Files Are Raw Evidence of Torture. Can We Look Away?' *The Guardian*, 10 August, https://www.theguardian.com/australia-news/2016/aug/10/the-nauru-files-are-raw-evidence-of-torture-can-we-look-away

Marr, D and Laughland, O (2014) 'Australia's Detention Regime Sets Out to Make Asylum Seekers Suffer, Says Chief Immigration Psychiatrist', *The Guardian*, 4 August, https://www.theguardian.com/world/2014/aug/05/-sp-australias-detention-regime-sets-out-to-make-asylum-seekers-suffer-says-chief-immigration-psychiatrist

Marsh, S, Rawlinson, K and Agencies (2017) 'Hundreds Evacuated from London Tower Blocks over Fears of Grenfell Repeat', *The Guardian*, 24 June, https://www.theguardian.com/uk-news/2017/jun/23/camden-to-evacuate-taplow-tower-over-fire-safety-fears-after-grenfell-disaster

Martin, G (2015) 'Stop the Boats! Moral Panic in Australia over Asylum Seekers', *Continuum: Journal of Cultural and Media Studies*, 29(3):304–22.

Martinsson, L and Reimers, E (2019) 'Civil Servants Talk Back – Political Subjectivity and (Re) Constructions of the Nation', *Critical Sociology*, Online First 5 April, https://doi.org/10.1177/0896920519839768.

Maylam, P (2005) *The Cult of Rhodes: Remembering an Imperialist in Africa*, Cape Town: David Philip.

McAdam, J and Chong, F (2014) *Refugees: Why Seeking Asylum Is Legal and Australia's Policies Are Not*, Sydney: NewSouth.

McGoey, L (2016) *No Such Thing as a Free Gift: The Gates Foundation and the Price of Philanthropy*, London: Verso.

McGoey, L (2019) *The Unknowers: How Strategic Ignorance Rules the World*, London: Zed.

Médecins Sans Frontières (2017) 'Issue Brief: Humanitarian NGOs Conducting Search and Rescue Operations at Sea: A "Pull Factor"?' August, http://searchandrescue.msf.org/assets/uploads/files/170831_Analysis_SAR_Issue_Brief_Final.pdf

Medical Justice (2015) 'Mental Health in Detention: Written Evidence Submitted by Medical Justice to the Shaw Review', http://www.medicaljustice.org.uk/wp-content/uploads/2016/04/alHealthinDetention-SummarybyMedicalJusticeforShawReview.pdf

Migration Observatory (2019) 'Immigration Detention in the UK', 29 May, https://migrationobservatory.ox.ac.uk/resources/briefings/immigration-detention-in-the-uk/

Mills, C W (1997) *The Racial Contract*, Ithaca: Cornell University Press.

Mills, C W (2007) 'White Ignorance', in Sullivan, S and Tuana, N (eds) *Race and Epistemologies of Ignorance*, Albany: State University of New York Press, pp.13–38.

Moore, N, Salter, A, Stanley, S and Tamboukou, M (2017) *The Archive Project: Archival Research in the Social Sciences*, London: Routledge.

Moore-Bick, M (2019) *Grenfell Tower Inquiry: Phase 1 Report Overview*, London: APS Group, https://assets.grenfelltowerinquiry.org.uk/GTI%20-%20Phase%201%20report%20Executive%20Summary.pdf

Moreton-Robinson, A (2015) *The White Possessive: Property, Power and Indigenous Sovereignty*, Minneapolis: University of Minnesota Press.

Morning, A (2014) 'Does Genomics Challenge the Social Construction of Race?' *Sociological Theory*, 32(3):189–207.

Mountz, A (2010) *Seeking Asylum: Human Smuggling and Bureaucracy at the Border*, Minneapolis: University of Minnesota Press.

Mukerjee, M (2010) *Churchill's Secret War: The British Empire and the Ravaging of India during World War II*, New York: Basic Books.

Mulgan, G (2006) 'Thinking in Tanks: The Changing Ecology of Political Ideas', *The Political Quarterly*, 77(2):147–55.

Mydans, S (2001) 'Which Australian Candidate Has the Harder Heart?' *The New York Times*, 9 November, https://www.nytimes.com/2001/11/09/world/which-australian-candidate-has-the-harder-heart.html

National Museum of Australia (n.d.) 'Defining Moments: "Tampa Affair"', https://www.nma.gov.au/defining-moments/resources/tampa-affair

Neshat, S (2018) 'When Does Political Art Cross the Line?', *The New York Times*, 5 December, https://www.nytimes.com/2018/12/05/opinion/shirin-neshat-political-art.html

Newbold, A (2017) 'Grenfell Tower Fire Inspires Generosity', *Vogue.co.uk*, 15 June, https://www.vogue.co.uk/article/grenfell-tower-fire-celebrity-reaction

Newby, G (2017) 'Why No-One Heard the Grenfell Blogger's Warnings', *BBC News*, 24 November, https://www.bbc.co.uk/news/stories-42072477

Newman, J (2001) *Modernizing Governance: New Labour, Policy and Society*, London: Sage.

Nolan, D and Graham-Harrison, E (2015) 'Hungarian Police Order Refugees Off Train Heading to Austrian Border', *The Guardian*, 3 September, https://www.theguardian.com/world/2015/sep/03/budapest-station-reopens-no-trains-running-western-europe-migration-crisis-europe

Oakley, A (1974) *Housewife*, London: Allen Lane.

OCR [Oxford, Cambridge and RSA Examinations] (2017) *GCSE (9–1) Candidate Style Answers History B (Schools History Project)*, Cambridge: OCR, p.5, https://www.ocr.org.uk/Images/369892-migrants-to-britain-c.1250-to-present-candidate-style-answers.pdf

Okri, B (2017) 'Grenfell Tower, June 2017: A Poem by Ben Okri', *Financial Times*, 23 June, https://www.ft.com/content/39022f72-5742-11e7-80b6-9bfa4c1f83d2

Okri, B (2018) 'The Tower and the Poem', *Financial Times*, 9 June, Life and Arts Section p2, https://www.ft.com/content/44484824-6a44-11e8-b6eb-4acfcfb08c11

Oldham, S (2015) 'Ben Affleck Apologizes for PBS Slavery Censorship: "I Was Embarrassed"', *Variety*, 21 April, https://variety.com/2015/biz/news/ben-affleck-slavery-pbs-censor-ancestors-1201477075/

O'Neill, B (2015) 'Never Mind Rhodes – It's the Cult of the Victim That Must Fall', *Spiked*, 28 December, https://www.spiked-online.com/2015/12/28/never-mind-rhodes-its-the-cult-of-the-victim-that-must-fall/

Orwell, G (1946) 'Politics and the English Language', *Horizon*, 13(76):252–65.

Palm, A (2017) 'The Italy-Libya Memorandum of Understanding: The Baseline of a Policy Approach Aimed at Closing All Doors to Europe?' *EU Migration Law Blog*, 2 October, https://eumigrationlawblog.eu/the-italy-libya-memorandum-of-understanding-the-baseline-of-a-policy-approach-aimed-at-closing-all-doors-to-europe/

Panorama (2017) *Undercover: Britain's Immigration Secrets*, TV, BBC1. 4 September. 2100 hrs.

Papailias, P (2019) 'Memeifying the Corpse: The Photograph and the Dead Body between Evidence and Bereavement', in Kohn, T, Gibbs, M, Nansen, B and van Ryn, L (eds) *Residues of Death: Disposal Reconfigured*, London: Routledge, pp.169–83.

Passport Index (2019) 'Global Passport Power Rank 2019', https://www.passportindex.org/byRank.php

Payne, A (2018) 'Anti-Brexit Politicians from All the Main Parties Are in Secret Talks about Forming a New "Centrist" Movement', *Business Insider*, 8 August, http://uk.businessinsider.com/politicians-britain-political-parties-are-in-secret-talks-about-forming-a-new-centrist-movement-brexit-2018-8

Pell, S (2015) 'Radicalizing the Politics of the Archive: An Ethnographic Reading of an Activist Archive', *Archivaria*, 80:33–57.

Perera, S (2009) *Australia and the Insular Imagination: Beaches, Borders, Boats, and Bodies*, New York: Palgrave Macmillan.

Phillips, J and Spinks, H (2013) 'Boat Arrivals in Australia since 1976', Canberra: Parliament of Australia, https://www.aph.gov.au/about_parliament/parliamentary_departments/parliamentary_library/pubs/rp/rp1314/boatarrivals

Philo, G, Briant, E and Donald, P (2013) *Bad News for Refugees*, London: Pluto Press.

Poole, L and Mooney, G (2006) 'Privatizing Education in Scotland? New Labour, Modernization and "Public" Services', *Critical Social Policy*, 26(3):562–86.

Pritchard, S (2019) '"Our Boat": Zombie Art Biennale Turns Venice into the Island of the Living Dead', 10 May, http://colouringinculture.org/blog/ourboat

Proctor, R N (1996) *Cancer Wars: How Politics Shapes What We Know and Don't Know about Cancer*, New York: Basic Books.

Proctor, R N and Schiebinger, N (eds) (2008) *Agnotology: The Making and Unmaking of Ignorance*, Stanford: Stanford University Press.

Ration Challenge (n.d.) 'Ration Challenge', https://www.rationchallenge.org.uk/

Ration Challenge (n.d.) 'The Rations Explained', https://actforpeace. rationchallenge.org.au/the-challenge/the-rations-explained/

Rawlinson, K (2017) 'There Are 1,399 Homes a Stone's Throw from Grenfell Tower Left Empty by Millionaires. Time to Move in the Victims', *The Independent*, 15 June, https://www.independent.co.uk/voices/grenfell-tower-fire-deaths-homeless-kensington-and-chelsea-luxury-properties-empty-a7791671.html

Rawlinson, K (2018) '100 Households around Grenfell Still in Temporary Accommodation', *The Guardian*, 29 March, https://www.theguardian.com/uk-news/2018/mar/29/100-households-around-grenfell-still-in-temporary-accommodation

Reynolds, H (2000) *Why Weren't We Told? A Personal Search for the Truth about Our History*, Sydney: Penguin.

Reynolds, H (2013) *Forgotten War*, Sydney: NewSouth.

Rhodes Must Fall Movement (2018) *Rhodes Must Fall: The Struggle for Justice at the Heart of Empire*, London: Zed.

Roth, W D and Ivemark, B (2018) 'Genetic Options: The Impact of Genetic Ancestry Testing on Consumers' Racial and Ethnic Identities', *American Journal of Sociology*, 124(1):150–84.

Rothberg, M (2009) *Multidirectional Memory: Remembering the Holocaust in the Age of Decolonization*, Stanford: Stanford University Press.

Rowbotham, S (1973) *Hidden from History: 300 Years of Women's Oppression and the Fight against It*, London: Pluto Press.

Roy, A (2020) 'Arundhati Roy: "The Pandemic Is a Portal"', *Financial Times*, 3 April, https://www.ft.com/content/10d8f5e8-74eb-11ea-95fe-fcd274e920ca

Sands, P (2016) *East West Street*, London: Wiedenfel and Nicolson.

Santos, B d S (2007) 'Beyond Abyssal Thinking: From Global Lines to Ecologies of Knowledges', *Review (Fernand Braudel Center)*, 30(1):45–89.

Sato, S (2017) '"Operation Legacy": Britain's Destruction and Concealment of Colonial Records Worldwide', *The Journal of Imperial and Commonwealth History*, 45(4):697–719.

Savage, M (2018) 'New Centrist Party Gets £50m Backing to 'Break Mould' of UK Politics', *The Guardian*, 8 April, https://www.theguardian.com/politics/2018/apr/07/new-political-party-break-mould-westminster-uk-brexit

Searle, A (2018) 'Tania Bruguera at Turbine Hall Review – "It Didn't Make Me Cry but It Cleared the Tubes"', *The Guardian*, 1 October, https://www.theguardian.com/artanddesign/2018/oct/01/tania-bruguera-turbine-hall-review-tate-modern

Sedgwick, E K (1990) *Epistemology of the Closet*, Berkeley: University of California Press.

Sharman, J (2018) 'G4S Can Keep Running Brook House Immigration Removal Centre Following Detainee Abuse Scandal, Home Office Quietly Announces', *The Independent*, 4 May, https://www.independent.co.uk/news/uk/home-news/g4s-brook-house-choke-detainees-undercover-tinsley-home-office-contract-a8337051.html

Shaw, S (2016) *Review into the Welfare in Detention of Vulnerable Persons: A Report to the Home Office by Stephen Shaw*, London: TSO.

Shaw, S (2018) *Assessment of Government Progress in Implementing the Report on the Welfare in Detention of Vulnerable Persons: A Follow-Up Report to the Home Office*, Cm 9661, London: TSO.

Shire, W (n.d.) *Home*, https://www.care.org/sites/default/files/lesson_1_-_home-poem-by-warsan-shire.pdf

Shropshire Star (2018) 'Grenfell Tower Painting Given to PM by Survivors "Will Hang in Downing Street"', 11 May, https://www.shropshirestar.com/news/uk-news/2018/05/11/grenfell-tower-painting-given-to-pm-by-survivors-will-hang-in-downing-street/

Silverman, S J (2017) *Briefing: Immigration Detention in the UK*, Oxford: The Migration Observatory, http://www.migrationobservatory.ox.ac.uk/wp-content/uploads/2016/04/Briefing-Immigration_Detention-2.pdf

Simpson, J (2019) 'Bolton Fire: Combustible Membrane Pictured behind Cladding on Student Halls', *Inside Housing*, 22 November, https://www.insidehousing.co.uk/news/news/bolton-fire-combustible-membrane-pictured-behind-cladding-on-student-halls-64247

Sims, P (2016) 'Murdered in Cold Blood', *The Sun*, 17 June, p.1.

Sirriyeh, A (2018) *The Politics of Compassion: Immigration and Asylum Policy*, Bristol: Bristol University Press.

Sky News (2017) 'Gavin Barwell, Ex-housing Minister, Refuses to Answer Questions about Grenfell Tower – Video', *The Guardian*, 16 June, https://www.theguardian.com/uk-news/video/2017/jun/16/gavin-barwell-ex-housing-minister-refuses-to-answer-questions-about-grenfell-tower-video

Sloan, A (2013) 'Sleeping Rough for Charity Hides the Real Homelessness Crisis', *The Guardian*, 29 October, https://www.theguardian.com/housing-network/2013/oct/29/homeless-sleep-out-charity

Smart, C (2011) 'Families, Secrets and Memories', *Sociology*, 45(4):539–55.

Smith, P (2016) 'Jewish MP Feared for Her Safety after Receiving 2,500 Abusive Messages a Day', *BuzzFeed News*, 5 December, https://www.buzzfeed.com/patricksmith/jewish-mp-feared-for-her-safety-after-receiving-2500-abusive?utm_term=.moxBv57P7#.clxvn6qwq

Sontag, S (1967) 'Aesthetics of Silence', in Sontag, S (ed.) (2009) *Styles of Radical Will*, London: Penguin Classics, pp. 3–34.

Sontag, S (2003) *Regarding the Pain of Others*, London: Penguin.

Sperling, D (2017) 'In 1825, Haiti Paid France $21 Billion to Preserve Its Independence – Time for France to Pay It Back', *Forbes*, 6 December, https://www.forbes.com/sites/realspin/2017/12/06/in-1825-haiti-gained-independence-from-france-for-21-billion-its-time-for-france-to-pay-it-back/

Spiegelman, A (1987) *Maus: My Father Bleeds History*, New York: Pantheon.

Srivastava, S (2005) '"You're Calling Me a Racist?" The Moral and Emotional Regulation of Antiracism and Feminism', *Signs: Journal of Women in Culture and Society*, 31(1):29–62.

Staton, B and Wright, R (2019) 'Boris Johnson Eyes Australia-Style Immigration System', *Financial Times*, 25 July, https://www.ft.com/content/6afee982-af03-11e9-8030-530adfa879c2

Sullivan, S and Tuana, N (eds) (2007) *Race and Epistemologies of Ignorance*, Albany: State University of New York Press.

Tallbear, K (2018) 'Statement on Elizabeth Warren's DNA Test', 15 October, https://twitter.com/kimtallbear/status/1051906470923493377?lang=en

Tanner, B (2019a) 'Former Housing Ministers Could "Potentially Be in the Dock for Corporate Manslaughter"', *24 Housing*, 28 January, https://www.24housing.co.uk/news/former-housing-ministers-could-potentially-be-in-the-dock-for-corporate-manslaughter/

Tanner, B (2019b) '"Grenfell" Housing Minister Joins Clarion Board', *24 Housing*, 17 December, https://www.24housing.co.uk/news/grenfell-housing-minister-joins-clarion-board/

Tate (2019) 'Hyundai Commission, Tania Bruguera: 10,148,451', https://www.tate.org.uk/whats-on/tate-modern/exhibition/hyundai-commission-tania-bruguera

Tavan, G (2005) *The Long, Slow Death of White Australia*, Carlton North: Scribe.

Taylor, D (2017) 'Brook House Asylum Seekers in Legal Fight over Lock-in Procedures', *The Guardian*, 16 November, https://www.theguardian.com/

uk-news/2017/nov/16/brook-house-asylum-seekers-in-legal-challenge-over-lock-in-procedures

Taylor, D (2019) 'Grenfell Survivor in Legal Fight with Council to Get Home without a Lift', *The Guardian*, 25 February, https://www.theguardian.com/uk-news/2019/feb/25/grenfell-survivor-legal-fight-council-flat-without-lift

Teege, J and Sellmair, N (2015) *My Grandfather Would Have Shot Me: A Black Woman Discovers Her Family's Nazi Past …*, trans. Sommer, C, London: Hodder and Stoughton.

TellMAMA (2018) 'Who Are the White Pendragons?' 15 January, http://tellmamauk.org/who-are-the-white-pendragons/

Thompson, E P (1963) *The Making of the English Working Class*, London: Gollancz.

Tondo, L (2019) 'I Have Seen the Tragedy of Mediterranean Migrants. This 'Art' Makes Me Feel Uneasy', *The Guardian*, 12 May, https://www.theguardian.com/world/2019/may/12/venice-biennale-migrant-tragedy-art-makes-me-uneasy

Triggle, N (2020) 'Coronavirus: Testing, PPE and Ventilators – How Has the Government Done?' *BBC News*, 3 April, https://www.bbc.co.uk/news/health-52142083

Trouillot, M-R (1997) *Silencing the Past: Power and the Production of History*, Boston: Beacon Press.

Tyler, I (2013) *Revolting Subjects: Social Abjection and Resistance in Neoliberal Britain*, London: Zed.

UNHCR (2018) 'Figures at a Glance: Statistical Yearbooks', 19 June 2018, https://www.unhcr.org/uk/figures-at-a-glance.html

UNHCR (2019a) 'Six People Died Each Day Attempting to Cross Mediterranean in 2018 – UNHCR Report', 30 January, https://www.unhcr.org/uk/news/press/2019/1/5c500c504/six-people-died-day-attempting-cross-mediterranean-2018-unhcr-report.html

UNHCR (2019b) 'Syria Refugee Crisis', https://www.unrefugees.org/emergencies/syria/

Vidler, E and Clarke, J (2005) 'Creating Citizen-Consumers: New Labour and the Remaking of Public Services', *Public Policy and Administration*, 20(2):19–37.

Vine, S (2018) 'The Windrush Scandal Is yet Another Example of How Poorly Britain Treats Those to Whom It Owes a Great Debt and How Twisted Our Bureaucratic Morals Are, Says Sarah Vine', *Daily Mail*, 18 April, https://www.dailymail.co.uk/debate/article-5627811/Windrush-scandal-example-poorly-Britain-treats-owes-says-SARAH-VINE.html

Viner, K (2019) 'Foreword', in Gentleman, A (ed.) *The Windrush Betrayal*, London: Guardian Faber, pp.1–4.

Wallace, M (2017) 'Spring, Renew, Advance, Forward Together … What Is behind the Flurry of Wannabe British Macrons?' *Conservative Home*, 8 November, https://www.conservativehome.com/leftwatch/2017/11/spring-renew-advance-forward-together-what-is-behind-the-flurry-of-wannabe-british-macrons.html

Ware, V (2010) 'Whiteness in the Glare of War: Soldiers, Migrants and Citizenship', *Ethnicities*, 10(3):313–30.

Wekker, G (2016) *White Innocence: Paradoxes of Colonialism and Race*, Durham, NC: Duke University Press.

Wheeler, B and Carter, A (2017) 'MPs Tell of Death Threats and Abuse at 2017 Election', *BBC News*, 18 September, http://www.bbc.co.uk/news/uk-politics-41237836

Wheeler, C (2018) 'David Miliband Eyes UK Return as Rumours of New Centrist Party Grow', *The Sunday Times*, 11 November, https://www.thetimes.co.uk/article/david-miliband-eyes-uk-return-as-rumours-of-new-centrist-party-grow-8fh7vrsxc

Williams, C (2015) 'Patriality, Work Permits and the European Economic Community: The Introduction of the 1971 Immigration Act', *Contemporary British History*, 29(4):508–38.

Wintour, P (2015) 'UK to Take Up to 20,000 Refugees over Five Years, David Cameron Confirms', *The Guardian*, 7 September, https://www.theguardian.com/world/2015/sep/07/uk-will-accept-up-to-20000-syrian-refugees-david-cameron-confirms

Younge, G (2018) 'Ambalavaner Sivanandan Obituary', *The Guardian*, 7 February, https://www.theguardian.com/world/2018/feb/07/ambalavaner-sivanandan

Yuval-Davis, N, Wemyss, G and Cassidy, K (2018) 'Everyday Bordering, Belonging and the Reorientation of British Immigration Legislation', *Sociology*, 52(2):228–44.

Index

Affleck, Ben 109–14, 121, 123, 132, 135–6, 168, 172
agnotology. *See* ignorance studies
anger 9, 19, 22, 26, 28–9, 34, 50, 52, 146–7, 171, 178, 182, 184
archives 84–8, 90, 97, 100–11, 107, 112, 116, 124, 126, 172–3, 180–2
asylum seekers. *See* refugees
Australia 70–5, 77, 82, 90, 199 n.26, 200 n.30

Barca Nostra 31, 62–4, 81, 176–7
Barthes, Roland 40–1
Berger, John 61, 68–70
Blair, Tony 27–8, 75
blame 32, 110–11, 114–5, 126, 135–7, 141–2, 149, 151–2, 162–4, 171, 174, 182
border control x, xii, 2–4, 30–2, 45–6, 49–50, 67, 71–2, 74–81, 97–102, 105, 135, 139–42, 158–61, 168–70, 174, 182–3, 199 n.26, 200 n.30, 207 n.47. *See also* border crisis; detention; deportation; EU (European Union) border control; Home Office; hostile environment
border crisis 30–1, 49–51, 61–9, 72–3, 81, 119, 133, 159, 171; 175–7. *See also* border control; EU (European Union) border

control; hostile environment; Kurdi, Alan; Lampedusa disaster; refugees
Brexit x, xii, 1–2, 15, 19, 25–6, 119, 134–5, 163
Brook House Immigration Removal Centre 139–41, 153–7, 159, 170. *See also* detention; detention outsourcing; G4S
Bruguera, Tania 31, 80–2
Buller, Amy 142–52, 178–9
bystanders 14, 32, 82, 115, 127, 139–41, 152–3, 164

Cameron, David 49–50
Carayol, Damel 51–3
centrism 24–9, 32, 189 n.53, 199 n.26
colonialism x, 8–9, 31, 71–2, 83–7, 92, 96, 98–100, 107, 114, 118, 137, 150, 172, 181. *See also* decolonise the curriculum
Commonwealth 88, 98–101, 103–7, 168, 207 n.47. *See also* Windrush Scandal
Corbyn, Jeremy 20, 26, 33
Covid-19 xi–xiii, 54, 196 n.61
Cox, Jo 1–4, 15–26, 29–30, 40–2, 132, 168, 170–1, 174–5, 187 n.28, 188 n.36, 199 n.26, 202 n.50
husband 15–19, 21, 25–6
Cumberland Lodge 142–3, 150

decolonise the curriculum 88, 92, 94–6, 136

Demir, Nilüfer 47–8, 60

deportation 79, 102, 104–5, 126, 133, 139–41, 152, 155–6, 161, 179–80, 208 n.63

detention 32, 66, 72, 74–8, 86, 97, 141, 153–9, 164, 170, 200 n.34, 216 n.58. *See also* Brook House Immigration Removal Centre

outsourcing 74, 154, *see also* G4S

DNA 112, 116–18, 130, 136

Du Bois, W E B 9–12, 87

education xi, 9–10, 28, 32, 65, 88, 92–5, 122, 133, 142–9, 152–3, 159–60, 178–9. *See also* decolonise the curriculum

Eichmann, Adolf 1, 5–7, 12, 23, 162

EU (European Union) border control 2, 30–1, 45–6, 50, 63, 75, 119, 133. *See also* border control; border crisis; Brexit; Kurdi, Alan; Lampedusa disaster

families x, 4, 16–19, 29, 33, 41, 45–7, 51, 67, 79, 95, 107, 109–31, 133–7, 151, 161–2, 172, 174

family history 31, 109–29, 133, 135–7

far right 16–21, 162–3, 171, 175, 187 n.26, 208 n.63. *See also* Nazism and the European Holocaust

feeling and emotion 1–4, 7, 9, 15, 28–31, 40, 44, 48, 66–7, 76, 80, 82, 149–50, 155, 171, 175–7, 182. *See also* anger; blame; punctures

focus on the present, the 12–14, 180

Frank, Niklas 125, 127

G4S 74, 76, 153–6, 158, 164. *See also* outsourcing

genes, genetics. *See* DNA

Gentleman, Amelia 102–3, 208 n.53, 208–9 n.64, 209 n.67

German citizenship 119, 134–5

Germany 68–9, 72, 119, 143–4, 148–50, 198 n.11, 211 n.21. *See also* German citizenship; Nazism and the European Holocaust

Gordon, Avery 109, 113

Great Get Together, The 3, 19, 22–4, 25, 28, 42, 202 n.50

Grenfell Tower
construction 36–7, 54–5, 178
fire 23–4, 30, 33–9, 41, 44, 51–7, 59, 169–71, 175, 178, 182
Grenfell Silent Walk 57–9, 177–8, 196 n.61
public inquiry 35, 51, 53–5, 57
residents' activism 36, 51, 53, 55–60, 168, 172, 177–8

Hartman, Saidiya 83, 87, 107, 121–2

haunting 31, 41, 44, 78, 109, 111–14, 118–20, 135, 168, 211 n.21. *See also* and memory; memory; post-memory

history x, 32, 85–8, 90–5, 99, 101, 107, 111–13, 118, 128, 131–3, 137, 177, 181
and colonialism xi, 29, 31, 88–9, 92, 94–7, 100
and family. *See* family history
and memory xi, 16, 122, 181, *see also* memory

Holocaust. *See* Nazism and the European Holocaust

Home Office 2, 77, 97–8, 100–4, 106, 153–4, 158, 160–1, 199 n.26, 216 n.58

hope 14, 19, 87, 148–51, 165, 184

hostile environment 3, 98, 101–6,
    175, 209 n.67. *See also*
    border control; border crisis;
    deportation; detention; EU
    (European Union) border
    control

ignorance studies 5, 10–11, 166–7
immigration. *See* border control
indigenous people 8, 90–1, 110, 114,
    117–18
institutional indifference 33, 38,
    55–6, 96, 170, 177, 182

Kenya 83–7, 100, 107, 114, 137,
    172, 181
Kurdi, Alan 30, 35, 39, 41, 45–50, 60,
    67, 169–71, 175, 182, 193–4
    n.33

Lampedusa disaster 62–4, 81, 176–7
Lorde, Audre 147, 165, 171
Luhmann, Susanne 123–4, 212 n.45

May, Theresa 2, 33, 35, 52–5, 100,
    103, 188 n.36
McGoey, Linsey 10, 25, 167
media 15, 46–7, 95, 163
    ancestry tracing shows 109–13,
        123
    and democracy 28, 34, 37
    distancing effect of reporting 33,
        42, 46–7
    news values 17–19, 34, 40, 77,
        79–80, 106, 163, 179–80
    Panorama documentary 139–40,
        153–8
    xenophobic reporting 46–7, 61–2,
        79–80, 179–80
memory 3, 15–16, 19, 31, 42, 44, 52,
    69, 84–8, 92–3, 101, 107, 116,
    122, 125, 127, 172–3, 214 n.33.

See also and memory
    post-memory 119–20, 131, 136
Mills, Charles W 8, 11, 167
misogyny xii, 4, 15–18, 20–1, 29–30,
    91, 147, 170–1, 174, 187 n.26
Mohr, Jean 61, 68–9, 81

Nazism and the European Holocaust
    5–7, 31–2, 69, 81, 93, 119–36,
    142–51, 152–3, 163–4, 168,
    172–4, 178–9, 187 n.26, 214
    n.33. *See also* Eichmann, Adolf;
    Frank, Niklas; Nissen, Margaret;
    Schindler, Oskar; Teege,
    Jennifer; von Wächter, Horst
Nissen, Margaret 123–4, 126–7, 136
numbers 65–71, 73, 78, 80–2, 171, 181

Okri, Ben 33, 37–9, 51–2

photography 40–8, 53, 60, 68–9, 82,
    118–19, 124, 136, 173, 175,
    182–3, 211 n.21
punctures 14, 39, 40–4, 47–8, 59, 66,
    68–9, 79–80, 98, 118, 136

refugees 4, 15, 30, 45–6, 49–50, 61–3,
    66–7, 75–9, 119, 133, 159–60,
    171, 174, 200 n.34
resistance ix, 31–2, 59, 76–80, 85–6,
    91–2, 103–5, 114, 117, 141,
    143–8, 152, 159, 161, 165,
    172–84. *See also* decolonise
    the curriculum; Grenfell
    Tower – residents' activism;
    Grenfell Tower – Silent Walk
responsibility 32, 44, 115, 141–2, 146,
    152–3
Rhodes, Cecil 92–5

scabs 42, 59, 169–70
Schindler, Oskar 129, 173

silence 15, 28, 47, 57–60, 70, 87,
    89–90, 99–101, 105, 118,
    156, 166, 169, 172, 177–8,
    180, 183. *See also* Grenfell
    Silent Walk
slavery 8, 87, 89, 93, 107, 109–11,
    113–14, 121–2, 132, 136–7, 143,
    168, 172, 199 n.22, 205 n.21
Sontag, Susan ix–x, 42–4, 48, 52,
    57–8, 122, 173

Teege, Jennifer 128–31, 136–7,
    172–3
torture 31, 64, 74, 77, 84, 86, 95, 107,
    127–9, 151
Trouillot, Michel-Rolph xi, 11, 89–90,
    98–9, 101, 104, 177
Tulley, Callum 139–41, 153–8

USA 9–11, 66, 87, 90, 107, 110,
    117–18, 144–5, 199 n.22, 205
    n.21, 218 n.81

veil xii, 41, 65, 80, 84, 169. *See also*
    Du Bois, W E B
violent ignorance (definition) ix–xi,
    4, 8, 10, 12–14, 29–30, 36,
    42, 63–8, 79, 91, 107, 124–5,
    131–3, 136, 165–73
von Wächter, Horst 125–9, 136, 147

Warren, Elizabeth 117–18
Wekker, Gloria 8–9, 43–4
White Ignorance 8, 167
White Innocence 7–9, 43–4
white supremacy 8, 16–17, 20, 30, 92,
    94, 171, 174, 200 n.30, 208 n.63
whiteness 8–12, 15–16, 20–1, 23, 40,
    44, 47, 67, 71–2, 79–80, 92–5,
    99, 106, 110, 118, 120–1, 130,
    132–3, 142, 163, 200 n.30. *See
    also* White Ignorance; White
    Innocence; white supremacy
Windrush Scandal 31, 88, 98–106,
    168, 175, 181, 208 n.58

www.ingramcontent.com/pod-product-compliance
Lightning Source LLC
Chambersburg PA
CBHW070357270326
41926CB00014B/2598